2005

The SMALL BUSINESS ECONOMY

A REPORT TO THE PRESIDENT

United States Government Printing Office

Washington: 2005

U.S. Government Printing Office
Washington, D.C. 20402

For sale by the Superintendent of Documents, U.S. Government Printing Office
Internet: bookstore.gpo.gov Phone: toll free (866) 512-1800; DC area (202) 512-1800
Fax: (202) 512-2250 Mail: Stop SSOP, Washington, DC 20402-0001

ISBN 0-16-075114-4

Dear Mr. President:

The Office of Advocacy of the U.S. Small Business Administration is pleased to present *The Small Business Economy: A Report to the President*. In 2004, the overall economic indicators improved as the recovery gained momentum, and small businesses led the way. Continued strong growth requires an environment that fosters ongoing small business activity.

Small businesses were active in the economy of 2004, which was characterized by stable prices and healthy increases in output, productivity, and private sector employment. Financial market conditions favored continued growth, and small business borrowing increased. Small businesses also continued to benefit from federal government acquisition of goods and services in 2004.

In March 2005, Economic Development Administration Assistant Secretary David A. Sampson talked about the importance of small business at the Office of Advocacy's conference on Putting it Together: The Role of Entrepreneurship in Economic Development. He said, "Entrepreneurs are the engines of economic vitality and job creation because they are committed to tapping in and leveraging the power and the opportunities that private markets provide. We need to increase the number of entrepreneurs and spread the spirit of innovation and enterprise all across our country—even to regions that are less vibrant than the rest of the country."

This year's report focuses a spotlight on the contributions and challenges of entrepreneurs in several demographic groups, namely minorities and veterans. A review of literature by Robert Fairlie pulls together the findings of a number of studies on minorities, including African Americans, Asians, and Hispanics—their involvement in entrepreneurship, including current trends, and the challenges that stand in the way of even more impressive achievements.

A report on veteran business ownership draws together a wealth of information from various studies on veteran business ownership published by the Office of Advocacy. It also reports on the results of a survey administered to a residential population of post-Korean conflict veterans and to a population of veteran business owners from all conflicts and peacetime periods.

Also featured is a report on federal and state agencies' efforts to make regulations less burdensome for small businesses. This year is the 25th anniversary of the enactment of the federal Regulatory Flexibility Act of 1980 (RFA), and over its history, the Office of Advocacy has worked diligently to monitor federal agency compliance with the law. The Small Business Regulatory Enforcement Fairness Act, passed in 1996, strengthened its provisions, and your Executive Order 13272 of August 2002 was crucial in fostering an environment in which agencies take small firms into account when drafting new federal rules. We continue to work to ensure that small business owners have a say in the regulatory process. In fiscal year 2004, Advocacy's involvement resulted in more than $17 billion in regulatory cost savings and more than $2 billion in recurring annual savings.

Small firms also face regulatory burdens at the state level. The Office of Advocacy's model legislation, developed in 2002, is designed to encourage states to adopt regulatory flexibility laws. The initiative has received a great deal of support from governors and state legislators, resulting in the adoption of similar legislation or executive orders that attempt to minimize regulatory burden on small business.

As the economy continues to improve, with an active and innovative small business sector leading the way, we will continue to focus on issues designed to create an environment where entrepreneurship can flourish. Your administration's leadership and support for America's dynamic small business sector continues to be critical.

Thomas M. Sullivan
Chief Counsel for Advocacy

Chad Moutray
Chief Economist

Acknowledgments

The Small Business Economy: A Report to the President was prepared by the U.S. Small Business Administration, Office of Advocacy. The Chief Counsel for Advocacy is Thomas M. Sullivan; the Deputy Chief Counsel is Shawne McGibbon. The Chief Economist is Chad Moutray, the Director of Interagency Affairs is Charles Maresca, the Director of the Office of Information is Jody Wharton, the Director of Administrative Support is Luckie Wren, and the Director of Regional Affairs is Viktoria Ziebarth. The project was managed by Kathryn J. Tobias, senior editor. Thanks to Rebecca Krafft for editorial assistance. Specific chapters were written or prepared by the following staff and outside contributors:

Chapter 1	Brian Headd
Chapter 2	Charles Ou
Chapter 3	Major Clark
Chapter 4	Robert W. Fairlie, University of California, Santa Cruz, with review by Ying Lowrey
Chapter 5	Waldman Associates and REDA International with review by Joseph Sobota
Chapter 6	Radwan Saade and Joseph Johnson
Chapter 7	Carrol Barnes, with contributions by Claudia Rogers and Sarah Wickham
Chapter 8	William J. Baumol
Appendix A	Brian Headd and Victoria Williams
Appendix B	Regulatory flexibility law and executive order

The Office of Advocacy appreciates the interest of all who helped prepare the report. Thanks also to the U.S. Government Printing Office and designfarm for their assistance.

Contents

Executive Summary

In this fourth edition of *The Small Business Economy*, the Office of Advocacy reviews the economic environment for small businesses in the year 2004, as well as the financial and federal procurement marketplaces. New research on minority and veteran entrepreneurship are the subjects of Chapters 4 and 5. Chapter 6 takes a new look at tax issues affecting small firms. In 2005, the Office of Advocacy marks 25 years of working to improve the regulatory environment for small businesses through the Regulatory Flexibility Act of 1980 and its subsequent improvements. Chapter 7 summarizes recent developments in that arena, including Advocacy's initiative to carry regulatory flexibility successes to the state level. Chapter 8 examines the critical role of small businesses in market-driven innovation. Appendices provide additional data on small businesses and background information on the Regulatory Flexibility Act.

The Small Business Economy in 2004

The economic recovery that began to emerge in 2003 continued apace in 2004. Real gross domestic product increased at annual rates of 3.75 percent over the course of the year. The labor market experienced moderate growth, as the economy added 1.3 million net new nonfarm private jobs. The estimated number of new employer firms increased more rapidly than terminations, and the number of self-employed also increased. Five quarters of available data, including data for the first three quarters of 2004, indicated increases in establishments and employment from firm turnover, in contrast to the negative figures from the beginning of 2001 to mid-2003.

Small Business Financing

Growth continued in the financial markets in 2004, as the economy continued to expand. Spending by the household and business sectors increased, and the core inflation rate remained moderate. Rates paid by small firms moved with overall movements in interest rates, and net borrowing continued to increase significantly. Federal borrowing declined slightly from the high of 2003, and state and local governments returned to healthy budgetary conditions in 2004. Most of the business borrowing was in the nonfinancial corporate business sector; noncorporate businesses increased borrowing, but at a moderate pace. The number and value of the smallest loans under $100,000 declined, but at lower rates than in the previous year. In the face of large banks' increasing share of total bank assets, their declining share of medium-sized loans warrants continued attention from small business policymakers. Total business receivables by finance companies increased moderately. The U.S. stock markets finished up slightly for the year in a trend that was adequate to stimulate a very healthy market for initial public offerings (IPOs). The overall IPO market was very active, with new 2004 issues valued at more than double the average levels of 2002–2003.

Federal Procurement from Small Firms

Small businesses benefited not only from federal acquisition of goods and services from small firms in 2004, but also from changes that helped clarify the federal procurement environment for small businesses. New subcontracting regulations provided more and better guidance to large business subcontracting with small businesses. Small business stakeholders were invited to participate in the process of redesigning small business size standards. New regulations governing the counting of procurement awards to small firms acquired by large firms were issued. As part of an effort to provide greater transparency in federal procurement, the fourth generation of the Federal Procurement Data System was introduced. The Office of Advocacy also released a number of studies related to the federal procurement marketplace in 2004.

Minority Entrepreneurship

Of the various ethnic and racial groups in the United States, White non-Latinos and Asians have the highest self-employment rates. The likelihood of business ownership among Latinos is roughly 60 percent of that for White non-Latinos, and the African-American self-employment rate is roughly 40 percent of the White non-Latino rate. Business ownership rates among women, which track somewhat differently from those of men by ethnicity or race, show that self-employment for African-American women and Latinas, while relatively low, increased steadily over the 1979–2003 period. Self-employment rates for Asian women remained roughly constant.

The research looks at causes for lower rates of minority business ownership, as well as the literature on racial differences in business outcomes, and at contracting set-asides. Overall, research finds that, among other things, low levels of assets limit entry into business ownership and increase business exit among minorities. Also, lower levels of family, business, and human capital limit opportunities for African Americans and Latinos to start businesses. The study finds that barriers to business entry and success for minority-owned business may impose a large efficiency loss in the overall U.S. economy.

Entrepreneurship among Veterans and Service-Disabled Veterans

New data on veteran business ownership should help policymakers more accurately respond to veterans' concerns and needs. A residential survey conducted during the summer of 2003 revealed that a significant 22.1 percent of veterans in the household population were either purchasing or starting a new business or considering doing so.

Tax Complexity and Uncertainty and Their Effects on Small Business

The effects of complexity and of uncertainty in complying with the tax code have been examined extensively in the literature, usually separately. The researchers here develop an argument that supports complexity having an impact on uncertainty. The study reinforces the conclusion that policies that promote ease of compliance while reducing uncertainty are more conducive to economic growth and further supports the notion that a well understood and predictable environment in which simple, stable rules are the norm is optimal for small business success.

Implementing the Regulatory Flexibility Act in Fiscal Year 2004

The Regulatory Flexibility Act (RFA), enacted in 1980, requires federal agencies to determine the impact of their rules on small entities, consider alternatives that minimize small entity impacts, and make their analyses available for public comment. President Bush's Executive Order 13272, signed in August 2002, gave agencies new incentives to improve their compliance with the RFA.

Throughout 2004, the Office of Advocacy continued efforts to represent small businesses before regulatory agencies, lawmakers, and policymakers. The office worked closely with small entities and their representatives to identify and comment on agency rules that would affect their interests. In fiscal year 2004, the Office of Advocacy helped small businesses achieve more than $17 billion in regulatory cost savings and more than $2 billion in recurring annual savings.

Moreover, the Office of Advocacy continued to pursue its initiative to work with states to enact and implement similar state legislation for the benefit of small businesses and other small entities struggling to keep up with the cumulative burden of regulation at all levels of government.

Why Market-Driven Innovation Can't Get Along without Small Firms

Economist William Baumol explores why small businesses continue to make a critical contribution to market economies' growth and innovative accomplishments. There are important reasons for the basic division of labor between the entrepreneurial search for radical innovations performed by small firms, and the development and marketing of those innovations by larger firms. The market prevents either group from a massive invasion of the other's innovative terrain, Baumol maintains.

1 *The* SMALL BUSINESS ECONOMY

Synopsis

At the heart of the vital small business sector in the United States are the self-employed and nonemployer businesses. Both segments remained strong as the U.S. economy emerged from the downturn that marked the opening of the 21st century. By the end of 2004, the recovering equity and labor markets moved toward more stable footing.

The year 2004 saw stable prices and healthy increases in output, productivity, commercial and industrial lending, and private sector employment. Small businesses also fared well, with declines in business bankruptcies and growth in sole proprietorship income, and increases in the numbers of self-employed and employer firms.

Introduction

Entrepreneurship has long been implicit in the American Dream—the belief that, given constitutional freedom, it is possible through hard work, courage, and imagination to achieve financial security. The federal government too has underscored the fundamental importance of entrepreneurship and small business to a vibrant, growing, sustainable economy. The most recent edition of The *Economic Report of the President*, for example, listed 12 variations on the term "entrepreneur."[1]

On the economic side, small businesses employ about half of the private sector work force, produce about half of private sector output, fill niche markets, innovate, and contribute to the competition in free markets. On the human side, small businesses give individuals the chance to achieve their own versions of the American Dream, and allow entry into employment by individuals and demographic groups who might otherwise be shut out of the labor market.

---

1 *Economic Report of the President, 2005*, http://www.gpoaccess.gov/eop/.

Although the small business role in the economy tends to remain constant over time, the status of various small business sectors and how they affect the economy are subject to change, particularly around business cycles. Small businesses had large impacts on the economy as it continued to emerge from the downturn in 2004.[2]

The complex task of gathering and analyzing statistics that accurately portray the ever-changing small business sector has generated two important small business data stories, covered here:

1. The distinctions between noncmployers and self-employment, and

2. The evolution in the data about jobs away from static counts to a more nuanced documentation of the labor market's dynamic churn.

Small Business in 2004

The economy in 2004 continued the momentum of the trends in 2003 toward solid growth in gross domestic product and productivity, a declining unemployment rate, and restrained inflation *(Table 1.1)*. The recent positive economic developments were in stark contrast to the negative economic trends surrounding the 2001 downturn.

The two areas of the economy most acutely affected by the downturn, equity markets and labor markets, turned the corner in 2004. The first signs of a return to slow and steady increases in the equity markets appeared as the S&P 500 Index experienced a steady 4 percent climb. The NASDAQ had a slightly bouncy ride to 6 percent growth in 2004.

The labor market also experienced moderate growth, as the economy added 1.3 million net new nonfarm private jobs in 2004.[3] Meanwhile, the unemployment rate continued to fall, hitting 5.4 percent by the end of the year.

---

2 While data showing the "silver bullet" of small business contributions to current economic conditions do not exist, current information allows researchers to develop a picture of current small business conditions.

3 This figure is based on the monthly average in 2003 versus 2004. Comparing December 2003 to December 2004 results in an increase of 2.2 million.

Table 1.1 Quarterly Economic Measures, 2003–2004 (percent)

	2003				2004			
	Q 1	Q 2	Q 3	Q 4	Q 1	Q 2	Q 3	Q 4
Real GDP change (annual rates)	1.9	4.1	7.4	4.2	4.5	3.3	4.0	3.8
Unemployment rate	5.8	6.1	6.1	5.9	5.7	5.6	5.4	5.4
GDP price deflator (annual rates)	2.9	1.1	1.3	1.4	2.7	3.2	1.4	2.1
Productivity change (annual rates)	4.1	7.6	8.1	2.1	4.0	2.9	2.0	3.7
Establishment births	-4.9	-0.3	-0.9	6.1	0.3	-1.7	3.2	NA
Establishment closures	1.5	-1.8	-3.0	1.3	1.9	0.6	4.5	NA

Source: U.S Small Business Administration, Office of Advocacy, from figures provided in *Economic Indicators* by the U.S. Department of Commerce, Bureau of Economic Analysis, and the U.S. Department of Labor, Bureau of Labor Statistics.

Although productivity was lower in 2004 than 2003, quarterly productivity figures fluctuated within a comparatively smaller range in 2004. Productivity is notoriously unpredictable in the business cycle, so its stability is another sign of slow, steady growth in the economy.

Small businesses also fared well in 2004. It is estimated that employer firm births outpaced employer terminations, and the number of the self-employed increased. Small business finances also improved *(Table 1.2)*. Nonfarm proprietors' income rose 6.9 percent in 2004, while costs were contained. Inflation was up 2.7 percent; interest rates remained historically low; and wage costs, as indicated by the wage and salary index, gained 2.4 percent.

Small businesses are overrepresented in business turnover; that is, they have relatively high rates of establishment (business location) births and closures.[4]

---

4   Note that establishment births can be new firms, new locations for existing small businesses, or new locations for existing large businesses. Establishment closures can be closed firms, closed locations of existing small businesses, or closed locations of existing large businesses. A separate issue is data on bankruptcies: Robert M. Lawless and Elizabeth Warren ("The Myth of the Disappearing Business Bankruptcy," *California Law Review*, June 2005) found data collection issues with the reported business bankruptcies over time, but taking this into account should still result in a representative one-year change.

Table 1.2 Business Measures, 2003–2004

	2003	2004	Percent change
Employer firms (nonfarm)	e 5,679,000	e 5,683,700	0.1
Employer firm births	e 553,500	e 580,900	5.0
Employer firm terminations	e 572,300	e 576,200	0.7
Self-employment, nonincorporated	10,295,000	10,431,000	1.3
Self-employment, incorporated	5,000,000	5,200,000	4.0
Business bankruptcies	35,037	34,317	(2.1)

e estimate

Sources: U.S. Small Business Administration, Office of Advocacy, from data provided by the U.S. Department of Commerce, Bureau of the Census; the U.S. Department of Labor; and Administrative Office of the U.S. Courts.

For this reason, statistics on business turnover are an indicator of small business contributions to the economy, and high levels of turnover are often correlated with high levels of overall economic growth. Five quarters of available data, including data for the first three quarters of 2004, indicated net increases in establishments and employment resulting from turnover, in contrast to the negative figures seen for 2001 to mid-2003. Still, as of 2004, there was room for expansion: the economy had not yet returned to the level of turnover seen in the late 1990s. The peak quarterly level of establishment births and employment from births was in 1999.

Although data on business openings and closings provided by the U.S. Department of Commerce, Bureau of the Census (U.S. Census Bureau) *(Appendix Table A.8)*, are not strictly comparable with data provided by the U.S. Department of Labor, Bureau of Labor Statistics (BLS) *(Table A.9)*, both reflect considerable turnover in the course of a year. Many businesses seem to have a seasonal component, closing and then reopening within the same year.

Demographics

Because demographic characteristics are descriptions of an owner in an occupation rather descriptions of the business, the appropriate data for tracking current demographic levels and trends are statistics on self-employment.[5] Self-employment data are available from the joint U.S. Census Bureau and BLS Current Population Survey (CPS). BLS publishes information on individuals whose primary occupation is unincorporated self-employment, but makes microdata available for other definitions. The tax status chosen by the owner is not relevant for this analysis, so the incorporated self-employed are included; the combined figures are in Table A.10.[6]

From 1995 to 2003, self-employment increased by 8.2 percent, or 1.1 million, to a total of 15 million self-employed people. Women represented half of the increase; their share of self-employment was up from 33.1 to 34.2 percent.

Following population trends, Hispanic individuals and Asians / American Indians had significant increases in self-employment from 1995 to 2003: 65.8 percent and 38.4 percent, respectively. African American self-employment also rose, by 20.3 percent over the period. These gains were significantly higher than the 4.8 percent increase in White self-employment.

The rate of self-employment among White Americans remained the highest among all the race and ethnic categories, and they constituted 54 percent of the 1.1 million increase.

Other demographic characteristics of the self-employed tracked the demographic shifts of recent years. Self-employment was up in the suburbs, among older individuals, and the college-educated. Also following population trends, the number of veterans whose occupation was self-employment fell sharply from 1995 to 2003.

---

5 The U.S. Census Bureau conducts an Economic Census in years ending in 2 and 7, which is useful in matching up owner demographics with business characteristics (for example, size of business). However, the delay in the availability of Economic Census data, and its continually changing data specifications, make trend analysis difficult. Fortunately, the 2002 Economic Census, unlike the 1997 Economic Census, will include business characteristics under the Survey of Business Owners program.

6 Appendix Table A.10 relies upon the longest occupation over the year from the CPS Annual Demographic Supplement, while Table A.1 relies upon BLS unincorporated self-employment data for the primary occupation.

Although the increases in self-employment overall were higher around the downturn of the early 2000s, self-employment in demographic categories other than Whites and males grew more steadily over the 1995–2003 time frame.

Self-employment rates were higher than average among veterans, the disabled, older individuals, those with higher formal education, and residents of rural areas.

Overall, the relatively level aggregate self-employment rate trends in recent years hide the interesting trends among different demographic groups.

Measuring Microenterprise: Data on Self-employment and Nonemployers

What statistics are best used to measure the small business universe and what exactly do these statistics describe? Two measures commonly used—and confused—are self-employment and businesses without employees, or nonemployers. Data on self-employment and nonemployer businesses are similar, but different in important ways.

Self-employment data track an occupation and an owner. The tax status of the venture can be unincorporated (generally sole proprietors filing Schedule Cs with their personal tax returns) or incorporated.

Nonemployers are business ventures without employees and payroll. They can also be unincorporated or incorporated, although incorporated nonemployers are rare, as the owner is considered an employee of the venture and would have to avoid payroll to be considered a nonemployer.

Self-employment data are generally available from the U.S. Census Bureau's Current Population Survey (CPS), prepared with funding from BLS.[7] The data are available monthly with a time lag of only a few months and annually via the CPS Annual Demographic Survey. Individuals are asked to self-identify their employment status as out of the labor force, unemployed, wage work, or self-employment.

---

7 Limited self-employment data are also available through the U.S. Social Security Administration. See http://www.ssa.gov/policy/data_sub125.html.

BLS publishes figures on agriculture and nonagricultural businesses, men and women whose primary occupation is self-employment, and unincorporated businesses. Figures in tables are generally listed under the classification of "class of worker." Microdata from the CPS containing many variables are made available by the Census Bureau so researchers can produce customized cross-tabulations or use the data for economic models.[8]

The CPS and BLS published figures are most likely underrepresenting the number of self-employed.[9] The CPS question on which the data are based does not ask whether the respondent plans to file Internal Revenue Service personal tax forms using a Schedule C to declare sole proprietorship income, or corporate business forms. Individuals may not recognize having business income as self-employment activity. This may be particularly true of individuals in specific occupations such as sales and real estate agents, who often work for one organization, but are paid as sole proprietors.[10] And BLS published figures underrepresent the number of self-employed, as they tend to exclude individuals whose secondary occupation is self-employment. For 2004, the CPS showed 486,500 individuals with a secondary occupation as self-employment whose primary occupation was not self-employment.

Considering that the labor force has been growing over time, that self-employment peaks in the summer months, and that data have limitations, researchers tend to use seasonally adjusted self-employment rates as measures of entrepreneurial activity. Self-employment rates could definitely be considered a weak entrepreneurial indicator, as they do not capture overall entrepreneurial intensity; for example, fewer self-employed individuals could have higher sales than more self-employed individuals.

The nonemployer database is the universe of businesses without employees composed primarily of sole proprietors (about 87 percent). Aggregate tables

---

8   See http://dataferrett.census.gov/TheDataWeb/index.html. Examples of using the CPS to create self-employment data that include incorporated self-employment can be found in Table A.10 of the Appendix and in the Office of Advocacy-funded, *Self-Employed Business Ownership: 1979–2003*, by Robert Fairlie (http://www.sba.gov/advo/research/rs243tot.pdf).

9   However, there is no reason to believe that this underrepresentation changes over time, allowing an accurate capturing of trends using historical figures.

10 For example, while primary occupation self-employment rates of 41 percent for real estate agents and 27 percent for insurance sales agents are higher than average, they are most likely understated.

are available from the U.S. Census Bureau.[11] The nonemployer database has been published annually and has about six years of data available with a time lag of about 2.5 years. Available cross tabulations exist by location, and industry and receipts data are also available.[12] The Census Bureau restricts the nonemployer universe with some basic editing, and, with a few exceptions, limits the universe to businesses with no payroll but with annual receipts between $1,000 and $1 million.[13]

Because most business ventures are unincorporated one-person operations, data on self-employment and nonemployers overlap significantly. But owners can have more than one business, a business can have more than one owner and owners can have payroll. BLS, which generally focuses on unincorporated self-employment as a primary occupation, reports about 10 million in the self-employment database, while the nonemployer database has a level of about 17 million.[14]

Overall, nonemployer figures are very useful for determining the number of businesses in an industry or area, while self-employment data are very useful for describing owner demographics and current and historical trends for very small ventures. It is interesting to note that in recent years, nonemployer counts have been rising above self-employment counts, implying that more individuals are involved in personal business activity, while fewer view the activity as self-employment.

---

11 See http://www.census.gov/epcd/nonemployer/index.html.

12 Note that preliminary work at the U.S. Census Bureau is under way to link the annual nonemployer files to create longitudinal data, so that entry, exit, age, and growth can be tracked. Individuals associated with the work include Richard Boden, Alfred Nucci, Steven Davis, John Haltiwanger, Ron Jarmin, C.J. Krizan, and Javier Miranda. The Office of Advocacy contribution was to support Richard Boden, on sabbatical from the University of Toledo, in his preliminary work at the Census Bureau.

13 See http://www.census.gov/epcd/nonemployer/view/covmeth.htm.

14 Possible reasons for the large discrepancy in the figures include the self-employed excluding incorporated ventures, some self-employed having employees, a large number of self-employed ventures as a secondary occupation, and some unique occupations such as sales and real estate agents that file as sole proprietors, but when asked their occupation in the CPS, respond yes to wage work and no to self-employment. Also, the turnover of ventures is captured differently; self-employment figures tend to be monthly averages, while nonemployer figures are the number that existed at any point over the year. Self-employment and nonemployers measure different concepts, so reconciliation of the databases may not be a realistic endeavor.

Availability of Data on Jobs and Job Change

Data on job creation, retention, and loss help define small businesses' role and status in the economy and are therefore important to those trying to analyze the small business market. Data from the U.S. Census Bureau's Statistics of U.S. Business (SUSB) show firm size employment levels. Tracking establishments of firms over time with the SUSB data shows the dynamic nature of job turnover (creation and destruction) with respect to firm size. Over the years, statistics have shown that small businesses play an important role in business starts and stops and in job creation and destruction, but the data often lack the timeliness that would make them useful for policy analysis. More current data for the entire economy showing both business and job turnover are needed for an understanding of the small business market. These data are just becoming available.

A true understanding of the labor market involves the art of evaluating many indicators. Researchers are moving beyond earlier controversies about which federal government data set—the household survey or the payroll survey—best describes the economy.[15] Relying upon just the payroll or household survey can give a less than balanced view of the labor market. Moreover, both the household and payroll surveys offer static views of the economy—snapshots of a point in time, rather than the moving picture of ongoing dynamic change associated with employment gains and losses.

The Bureau of Labor Statistics has two relatively new data sources that show job turnover and are relevant to an understanding of the small business job market. They are the Job Openings and Labor Turnover Survey (JOLTS) and Business Employment Dynamics (BED).

Since 2001, JOLTS has provided monthly figures on job openings, hires and separations (quits and layoffs) by industry. These data allow analysts to better understand where aggregate job gains or losses come from. But with only a few years of data available, comparing the downturn of 2001 with previous downturns is still not possible.

---

15 To determine the ranks of the employed and other information, BLS surveys businesses with payrolls (the payroll survey) and as part of the Current Population Survey, a joint BLS and Census venture, Census surveys individuals (the household survey).

BED has also been available only in the last few years, but BLS did create quarterly estimates going back to mid-1992. The data have so far shown that the domain of small businesses—establishment births and closures—is consistently at a high level. The high numbers of both business starts and closures means that net gains or losses in the numbers of both firms and jobs tend to be relatively small.

It is interesting to note that the downturn in 2001 was associated more with a decline in business births than with an increase in closures. Thus, the net increase in establishments and employment from establishment turnover was more related to the decline in establishment closures than to the small increase in business starts.

Continued Growth?

Signs of positive developments in 2004 point to positive future trends. Continued expansion is in the sights of an increasing number of small business owners. By the end of 2004, the National Federation of Independent Business' small business survey found a growing percentage of owners felt that the next three months would be a good time to expand.[16]

---

16 See NFIB's *Small Business Economic Trends* at http://www.nfib.com/page/researchFoundation.

2 SMALL BUSINESS FINANCING *in* 2004

Synopsis

Entrepreneurs looking for financing for their businesses generally benefited from the continued recovery in the economy and the relatively abundant supply of credit in 2004. Borrowing in the financial markets continued to show significant increases in 2004, dominated by household, government, and corporate borrowing. Small business borrowing also increased moderately.

Equity capital markets also benefited from the recovery, especially in larger later-stage financing; small initial public offerings remained limited. Equity funding was difficult to find for early-stage companies. Angel investors continued to be important in providing funding for early-stage entrepreneurs in 2004.

Economic and Credit Conditions in 2004

The pace of economic expansion continued in 2004 as real gross domestic product (GDP) grew 3.75 percent after strong growth of 4.5 percent in the previous year. Continued robust spending by the household sector was accompanied by notable increases in capital spending by businesses. While a substantial rise in oil prices caused a drag on overall economic activity, economic growth remained solid, and the core inflation rate remained moderate. Moreover, a relatively stimulative fiscal policy accompanied by an accommodative monetary policy, at least during the first quarter of 2004, provided a favorable environment for steady growth in 2004.

Financial market conditions continued to favor stable growth in economic activity in 2004. Long-term rates remained stable even as the Federal Reserve Board (FRB) removed "accommodation" from its policy instructions in January, prompting overall rate increases, especially in short-term rates. In fact, long-term rates ended the year not much higher than at the year's beginning. Short-term rates continued to edge up throughout the year, especially after the FRB initiated steps to raise the federal fund targets after the June meeting of the Federal Open Market Committee (FOMC).

Interest Rate Movements

After a year of robust recovery in economic activity, with more than 4 percent growth in GDP, the FRB decided to move away from the "accommodating" stance in monetary policy in January 2004. However, steps to raise the target rates for federal funds, the policy variable in the conduct of monetary policy, were not undertaken until the June FOMC meeting. The target rates have been raised steadily at every FOMC meeting since, and by the end of 2004 reached 2.25 percent, up from 1 percent at the beginning of the year. Prime rates, the index rates for most variable-rate loans, moved up from 4 percent during the first half of 2004 to end the year at 5.25 percent. The movement in long-term rates, determined primarily by the supply of and demand for loanable funds in the financial markets, remained nearly unchanged through the year. AAA corporate bond rates moved to above 6 percent during spring 2004 in response to strong demand and in anticipation of rising federal funds rates. However, as the strength of economic growth slowed and remained moderate, corporate rates declined to 5.4 percent.

Overall, interest rates paid by small firms moved, with a time lag, with the overall movements in interest rates in the capital and credit markets. The prime rate is the "base" rate for most small business loans, serving either as the index for rate adjustments in existing loans or as the "base" for a premium add-on on fixed-rate loans. As the prime rate rose from 4.0 percent to 5.14 percent by the end of 2004,[1] rates for adjustable-rate loans paid by small business owners also grew steadily over the last two quarters of 2004. For example, the rates for 2- to 30-day adjustable-rate loans of $100,000 to under $500,000 rose from 3.79 percent in the fourth quarter of 2003 to 4.69 percent in the fourth quarter of 2004. Fixed-rate term loans (one year or longer in maturity), however, were a mixed bag: rates for medium-sized small business loans of

---

1 The role the prime rate plays in the interest costs paid by small firms is rather complex. Since most business loans are made as variable-rate loans and the spreads (over the index rate) charged by the lenders vary widely, changes in the prime rates become more of an indicator of the change in the interest costs of "existing" loans rather than an indication of costs of borrowing to existing borrowers. In fact, with average margins (over prime) of 2 to 3 percent for most loans to small firms, the rates they paid during 2003 would be 6 to 7 percent.

$100,000 to $500,000 remained unchanged, while those for larger small business loans of $500,000 to under $1 million moved up *(Table 2.1)*. Overall, rates for the smallest loans under $100,000 saw the least upward movement, partly because they reflect two different types of loans: very small loans for smaller businesses and "loans" related to small business credit cards. Rates for small business credit card account balances are more difficult to interpret.[2]

Uses of Funds by Major Nonfinancial Sectors in the Capital Markets

Net borrowing in the financial markets by the nonfinancial sectors continued to increase significantly—by 15 percent, from $1,662 billion in 2003 to $1,916 billion in 2004—only slightly less than the 22 percent increase from 2002 to 2003. The increased borrowing can be attributed to continued strong borrowing by the federal government, further increases in borrowing by the heavily indebted household sector, and a further recovery in borrowing by the business sector, especially by corporate businesses *(Table 2.2)*.

Borrowing by the Federal Government and by State and Local Governments

Borrowing by the federal government totaled $363 billion in 2004, slightly less than the historic high of $396 billion in 2003, and contributed to the ongoing high budget deficit *(Table 2.2)*.

Fiscal restraint in 2002 and 2003, accompanied by continued recovery in the U.S. economy, enabled state and local governments to return to healthy budgetary conditions in 2004. Increases in receipts and expenditures kept pace with each other, resulting in an overall state budgetary balance that began after the second half of 2003. To take advantage of low interest rates, state and local governments continued borrowing in the financial markets for capital construction projects. The 2004 level of borrowing by state and local governments—at $115 billion—remained at about the 2003 level ($118 billion) *(Table 2.2)*.[3]

---

2 Several rates are involved—the promotion rates, rates for account transfers, rate adjustments that may or may not be linked to an index rate after the promotion period, and "penalty" rates when an account is found to be in less than top credit status.

3 See Federal Reserve Bank of St. Louis, "Government revenues, spending, and debt," *National Economic Trends*, August 2003, 16.

Table. 2.1 Loan Rates Charged by Banks by Loan Size, February 2003–November 2004

	Loan size (thousands of dollars)	Fixed-rate term loans	Variable-rate loans (2–30 days)	Variable-rate loans (31–365 days)
November 2004	1–99	6.76	4.52	6.53
	100–499	6.21	4.69	5.75
	500–999	4.80	4.41	5.08
	Minimum-risk loans	4.42	2.62	2.96
August 2004	1–99	6.71	4.59	6.25
	100–499	5.81	4.06	5.06
	500–999	4.54	3.99	4.45
	Minimum-risk loans	5.52	2.07	3.33
May 2004	1–99	6.49	4.21	6.05
	100–499	5.77	3.73	4.90
	500–999	5.24	3.50	3.62
	Minimum-risk loans	5.42	1.67	2.54
February 2004	1–99	6.80	4.29	6.05
	100–499	5.31	3.76	4.58
	500–999	3.73	3.41	4.81
	Minimum-risk loans	5.50	1.59	1.81
November 2003	1–99	6.53	4.27	6.11
	100–499	5.68	3.79	5.03
	500–999	4.99	3.22	3.94
	Minimum-risk loans	5.50	1.59	1.81
August 2003	1–99	6.68	4.15	6.34
	100–499	6.01	3.49	4.74
	500–999	5.67	3.69	3.97
	Minimum-risk loans	4.85	1.58	2.33
May 2003	1–99	6.84	4.78	6.49
	100–499	6.13	3.92	5.56
	500–999	5.83	3.34	4.21
	Minimum-risk loans	5.62	1.87	2.41
February 2003	1–99	6.8	4.29	6.05
	100–499	5.31	3.76	4.58
	500–999	3.73	3.41	4.81
	Minimum-risk loans	4.08	2.64	2.40

Note: Small loans refer to loans under $100,000.

Source: Board of Governors of the Federal Reserve System, *Survey of Terms of Lending*, Statistical Release E.2, various issues, and special tabulations prepared by the Federal Reserve Board for the U.S. Small Business Administration, Office of Advocacy.

Table 2.2 Credit Market Borrowing by the Nonfinancial Sector, 1989–2004 (billions of dollars)

	1989	1990	1991	1992	1993	1994	1995	1996	1997	1998	1999	2000	2001	2002	2003	2004
Total domestic borrowing	720.3	669.4	480.6	544.5	589.4	575.2	712.0	731.4	804.7	1,041.9	1,026.6	836.60	1,115.3	1,315.6	1,661.7	1,916.4
Government																
Federal	146.4	278.2	304	256.1	155.9	155.9	144.4	145.0	23.1	-52.6	-71.2	-295.9	-5.6	257.6	396.0	362.6
State and local	246.9	46.6	81.6	31	74.7	-46.2	-51.5	-6.8	56.1	67.7	38.5	15.5	105.8	143.9	117.8	115.4
Business																
Farm	0.6	1.0	2.1	1.3	2.6	4.4	2.9	4.8	6.2	8.0	5.5	10.9	10.5	7.8	7.7	12.3
Nonfarm noncorporate	69.6	1.1	-11.0	-16	3.2	3.3	30.6	81.4	94.7	159.7	189.4	197.1	162.7	148.5	156.1	168.2
Nonfinancial corporate	183.2	110.0	-53.0	42.7	45.5	142.3	243.7	148.8	291.1	408.4	371.6	350.5	221.2	27.7	144.7	240.1
Total	253.4	112.1	-61.9	28.0	51.3	150.0	277.2	235.0	392.0	576.1	566.5	558.5	394.4	184	308.6	420.5
Households	269.5	263.7	182.7	160.7	205.9	316.3	350.3	358.1	332.7	450.8	492.8	558.6	620.7	730.2	839.4	1,017.9
Foreign borrowing in the United States	10.2	23.9	14.8	23.7	69.8	-13.9	71.1	88.4	71.8	31.2	13.0	57	-49.7	5.6	-15.7	64.7

Source: Board of Governors of the Federal Reserve System, *Flow of Funds Accounts, Second Quarter 2003: Flows and Outstandings,* May 2004.

Borrowing by the Household Sector

Among nonfinancial sectors, households remained the dominant borrowers, accounting for more than 50 percent of total net borrowing in the U.S. financial markets. Total 2004 household borrowing grew by 21 percent, to $1,018 billion from $839 billion in 2003 *(Table 2.2)*. A booming housing market was sustained by continued low mortgage rates. Increased household wealth tied to rising housing prices encouraged household borrowing to finance spending, and resulted in very low personal savings rates.

Business Borrowing

Borrowing by nonfinancial businesses increased from $309 billion in 2003 to $421 billion in 2004. Most of the increase is a result of increased borrowing by nonfinancial corporate businesses, whose borrowing had grown from the depressed 2002 level, an annual rate of $28 billion, to $145 billions in 2003. With growing optimism in the U.S. economy in 2004, evidenced by continued healthy growth in the economy and substantially improved corporate earnings and cash flow, borrowing by this sector increased further in 2004, to $240 billion. The increases were moderate compared with corporate borrowing in the 1998 to 2000 period, when the annual rate of net borrowing averaged about $377 billion *(Table 2.2)*. Most of the growth came from borrowing in the public corporate bond and commercial paper markets *(Tables 2.2 and 2.3)*. Borrowing from banks resumed to finance increased merger and acquisition activity and inventory financing.

Net borrowing by nonfarm, noncorporate businesses also increased, although only moderately—from $156 billion in 2003 to $168 billion in 2004, a 7.7 percent increase. Net income for the nonfarm, noncorporate sector increased by 8.7 percent, from $871 billion to $947 billion. Increased cash flow complemented the borrowing to finance increases in capital expenditures and inventory accumulation *(Tables 2.2 and 2.4)*.

Table 2.3 Major Sources and Uses of Funds by Nonfarm, Nonfinancial Corporate Businesses, 1989–2004 (billions of dollars)

	1989	1990	1991	1992	1993	1994	1995	1996	1997	1998	1999	2000	2001	2002	2003	2004
Before-tax profit	236.5	236.5	217.1	256.7	307.4	391.9	437.7	458.8	494.5	460.1	456.7	422	309.8	323.3	396.9	488.4
Domestic undistributed profit	32.2	20.5	8.3	33.7	55.9	106.0	111.7	108.3	120.2	65.1	63.2	2.6	-45.1	-18.2	-6.1	26.9
Depreciation with inventory valuation adjustment	349.3	354.3	364.3	373.7	384.4	418.6	430.7	504.2	548.2	570.6	598.1	615.2	688.9	745.2	787.3	845.9
Total internal funds, on book basis	384.8	377.9	372.6	407.3	440.3	524.5	542.4	612.5	659.9	635.7	660.4	631.8	632.4	728.2	798.1	911.1
Net increase in liability	347.4	183.5	67.1	161.3	217.9	241.6	390.8	398.5	283.5	616.0	987.6	1237.4	95.2	111.1	273.3	351.8
Funds raised in credit markets	183.2	110	-55.1	42.7	45.5	134.1	218.6	148.8	291.9	408.4	371.6	350.5	221.2	27.7	144.7	240.1
Net new equity issues	-124.2	-63	18.3	27	21.3	-44.9	-58.3	-69.5	-114.4	-215.5	-110.4	-118.2	-47.4	-41.6	-57.8	-210
Capital expenditures	399.4	394.5	371.9	382	445.2	511.1	567.7	684.7	760.2	826.5	866.7	928.6	802.5	762.6	769.6	900.4
Net financial investment	-113.9	-68.3	62.7	-8.9	124.1	41.7	42.7	4.8	-11.1	-46.1	-17.7	-28.2	82.4	39.4	214.3	172.1

Source: Board of Governors of the Federal Reserve System, *Flow of Funds Accounts.*

Table 2.4 Major Sources and Uses of Funds by Nonfarm, Noncorporate Businesses, 1989–2004 (billions of dollars)

	1989	1990	1991	1992	1993	1994	1995	1996	1997	1998	1999	2000	2001	2002	2003	2004
Net income	407.0	434.9	464.1	441	473.9	495.3	534.2	569.7	609.9	656.5	710.6	767.3	819.9	824.1	870.9	947.4
Gross investment	77.0	80.6	67.5	82.9	84.4	64.7	56.4	110.8	118.5	125.0	148.7	168.7	149.3	151.3	159.3	166.8
Fixed capital expenditures	118.0	106.4	91.1	96.8	93.5	94.6	99.2	109.6	118.8	123.9	185.8	215.3	195.5	163.6	175.5	201.0
Changes in inventories	1.6	0.3	-0.1	0.1	1.3	2.5	1.9	1.1	3.0	3.6	3.5	2.9	-1.8	0.6	-0.1	2.3
Net financial investments	-42.6	-26.1	-23.5	-14.1	-10.5	-32.5	-44.7	0	-3.3	-2.5	-40.6	-49.5	-44.6	-12.9	-15.9	-36.4
Net increase in credit market debt	61.1	13.8	-15.0	-16.4	3.2	3.3	23.9	81.4	94.7	159.7	189.4	197.1	162.7	148.5	156.1	168.2
Mortgages	56.1	4.1	-9.9	-15.1	-1.5	-13.8	-2.2	50.9	47.7	117.7	135.1	137.5	121.2	121.0	160.8	146.8
Net investment by proprietors	-28.1	20.3	18.5	28.6	26.9	61.8	51.9	-18.1	-55.1	-64.8	-82.3	-47.2	-17.2	-102.3	-96.3	-55.9

Source: Board of Governors of the Federal Reserve System, *Flow of Funds Accounts, Flows and Outstandings.*

Bank Loans to Small Businesses

Because data on bank lending to small businesses are available only for the period ending in June 2004, the discussion of small business lending activities by commercial banks will cover the June 2003 to June 2004 period, with flow data from available Community Reinvestment Act (CRA) statistics covering the year 2003.

Borrowing from banks continued to recover, increasing moderately. This trend was confirmed in the February 2005 edition of the Federal Reserve Board's Senior Loan Officer Survey. The February edition covers the three months before the survey, which is conducted in January. The report noted that most banks continued to ease or maintain easy lending terms and reduced rate margins. It also reported rising demand for commercial and industrial (C&I) and real estate loans in 2004.[4] With continued improvement in loan quality and still favorable, although slightly narrower, interest margins, net operating income for domestic chartered banks reached a high of $104.7 billion, compared with $102.6 billion in 2003.[5]

Lending to Small Businesses by Commercial Banks

Overall, small business lending by commercial banks showed moderate increases in the June 2003 to June 2004 period compared with the June 2002 to June 2003 period. The rate of growth in the dollar amounts of loans outstanding for all small business loans (defined here as loans under $1 million) increased 5.5 percent, from $495 billion in June 2003 to $522 billion in June 2004, compared with 2.3 percent from June 2002 to June 2003 *(Tables 2.5 and 2.6)*. The increase was comparable to the annual increases in borrowing between June 2000 and June 2002. The increases were primarily in the larger small business loans of $100,000 to $1 million. Medium-sized loans between $100,000 and $250,000 and large small business loans between $250,000 and $1 million increased 4.9 percent and 8.4 percent, respectively *(Table 2.7)*. The number of these loans also increased 4.9 and 8.5 percent, respectively, during

---

4   Federal Reserve Board, "Senior Loan Officer Opinion Survey on Bank Lending Practices," February 2005, 1.

5   Federal Deposit Insurance Corporation, "Quarterly Banking Profile," Table III-A, on the agency's website at www2.fdic.gov/qbp/2004dec/qbp.pdf.

Table 2.5 Dollar Amount and Number of Small Business Loans Outstanding, June 2000 to June 2004 (dollars in billions, numbers in millions)

Loan Size		2000	2001	2002	2003	2004	Percent change 2003–2004
Under $100,000	Dollars	121.4	126.8	128.9	125.7	125.3	-0.31
	Number	9.80	10.79	15.65	14.09	13.58	-3.64
Under $250,000	Dollars	209.4	218.4	225.0	224.0	228.4	1.96
	Number	10.54	11.57	16.50	14.92	14.45	-3.16
Under $1 million	Dollars	437.0	460.4	484.0	495.1	522.3	2.30
	Number	11.17	12.25	17.24	15.67	15.26	-9.10
Total business loans	Dollars	1,300.3	1,324.5	1,307.0	1,318.1	1,373.3	0.85

Source: U.S. Small Business Administration, Office of Advocacy, *Small Business Lending in the United States*, various issues, and special tabulations of the June 2004 call reports (*Consolidated Reports of Condition and Income for U.S. Banks* prepared for the Office of Advocacy by James Kolari, A&M University, College Station, Texas).

this period *(Table 2.8)*. The value of total business loans also increased more than in the previous year, from $1,318 billion to $1,373 billion, up 4.2 percent. Corporate borrowing in loan sizes over $1 million resumed, but increased only at lower rates than in the late 1990s because of competition from alternatives available to corporate borrowers in the public credit markets, such as corporate bonds and commercial paper.

Table 2.6 Number and Amount of Business Loans Outstanding by Loan Size and Bank Size, June 2004

Bank Size	Under $100,000		$100,000–<$250,000		$250,000–<$1 million		Under $1 million		Over $1 Million	All
	Number of loans	Amount (billions of dollars)	Number of loans	Amount (billions of dollars)	Number of loans	Amount (billions of dollars)	Number of loans	Amount (billions of dollars)	Amount (billions of dollars)	Amount (billions of dollars)
All banks	13,579,962	125.28	869,241	103.08	814,795	293.97	15,263,998	522.33	850.94	1,373.27
Under $100 million	495,335	14.61	60,122	7.43	46,286	16.21	601,743	38.26	5.09	43.34
$100 million–$500 million	1,649,534	29.72	237,119	28.50	197,586	73.39	2,084,239	131.62	62.47	194.09
$500 million–$1 billion	1,258,844	7.96	74,331	8.95	69,784	25.60	1,402,959	42.51	40.47	82.98
$1 billion–$10 billion	4,353,012	19.42	165,550	19.16	166,707	58.39	4,685,269	96.98	147.63	244.61
Over $10 billion	5,823,237	53.57	332,119	39.03	334,432	120.37	6,489,788	212.97	595.27	808.24
Share by bank size (percentage)										
All banks	100.0	100.0	100.0	100.0	100.0	100.0	100.0	100.0	100.0	100.0
Under $100 million	3.6	11.7	6.9	7.2	5.7	5.5	3.9	7.3	0.6	3.2
$100 million–$500 million	12.1	23.7	27.3	27.7	24.2	25.0	13.7	25.2	7.3	14.1
$500 million–$1 billion	9.3	6.4	8.6	8.7	8.6	8.7	9.2	8.1	4.8	6.0
$1 billion–$10 billion	32.1	15.5	19.0	18.6	20.5	19.9	30.7	18.6	17.3	17.8
Over $10 billion	42.9	42.8	38.2	37.9	41.0	40.9	42.5	40.8	70.0	58.9

Source: U.S. Small Business Administration, Office of Advocacy, *Small Business Lending in the United States,* various issues, and special tabulations of the June 2004 call reports (*Consolidated Reports of Condition and Income for U.S. Banks* prepared for the Office of Advocacy by James Kolari, A&M University, College Station, Texas).

Table 2.7 Change in the Dollar Amount of Business Loans by Loan Size, June 1996–June 2004 (percent)

Loan size	1997–1998[1]	1998–1999[2]	1999–2000[2]	2000–2001	2001–2002	2002–2003	2003–2004
<$100,000	3.0	2.5	6.7	4.4	1.7	-2.49	-0.31
$100,000–250,000	8.1	6.3	8.5	4.1	4.9	2.26	4.87
$250,000–$1 million	7.7	11.2	11.8	6.4	7.0	4.72	8.42
>$1 million	13.0	14.6	16.1	0.9	-4.8	0	3.40

1 Changes for 1997–1998 were estimated based on revised estimates for Keycorp in 1997.

2 So that 1998–1999 trends could be shown, 1998 figures were revised to exclude the credit card operation of Mountain West Financial, which was purchased by a nonbank financial intermediary and thus excluded from 1999 data.

Source: U.S. Small Business Administration, Office of Advocacy, *Small Business Lending in the United States*, various issues, and special tabulations of the June 2004 call reports (*Consolidated Reports of Condition and Income for U.S. Banks* prepared for the Office of Advocacy by James Kolari, A&M University, College Station, Texas).

Table 2.8. Change in the Number of Small Business Loans by Loan Size, June 1996–June 2004 (percent)

Loan size	1997–1998[1]	1998–1999[2]	1999–2000[2]	2000–2001	2001–2002	2002–2003	2003–2004
<$100,000	19.3	10.1	26.9	10.1	45.0	-9.96	-3.64
$100,000–$250,000	1.8	5.4	7.0	5.9	8.8	-2.12	4.93
$250,000–$1 million	1.4	7.6	8.4	7.0	9.8	0.92	8.52

1 Changes for 1997–1998 were estimated based on revised estimates for Keycorp in 1997.

2 So that 1998–1999 trends could be shown, 1998 figures were revised to exclude the credit card operation of Mountain West Financial, which was purchased by a nonbank financial intermediary and thus excluded from 1999 data.

Source: U.S. Small Business Administration, Office of Advocacy, *Small Business Lending in the United States*, various issues, and special tabulations of the June 2004 call reports (*Consolidated Reports of Condition and Income for U.S. Banks* prepared for the Office of Advocacy by James Kolari, A&M University, College Station, Texas).

In the smallest loans under $100,000, statistics are difficult to interpret because of continued efforts by major small business credit card issuers to consolidate their data reporting.[6] The number and the dollar amounts of loans under $100,000 declined further, although at lower rates—by 0.31 percent in the value of the loans and 3.6 percent in the number (*Tables 2.7 and 2.8*). While the number of these smallest business loans outstanding declined from 14.1 million to 13.6 million and the value declined from $125.7 billion to $125.3 billion in June 2004, indications are that the declines are, again, an accounting phenomenon.[7] Moreover, it appears that most major small business credit card lenders continued to promote small business credit cards and reported continued increases in the number and dollar amounts of the smallest loans in the CRA report for loan activities in 2003.[8] Statistics from the 2003 CRA study indicated that the rates of increase in the number and dollar amounts of loans made in 2003 were comparable for the smallest loans under $100,000 and medium-sized loans of $100,000 to under $1 million.[9]

Bank consolidations continued to affect the relative importance of banks of different sizes in the small business loan markets. The number of commercial

---

6 Small business credit cards accounted for an increasingly important part of the category of the smallest loans under $100,000, especially the number of these loans. See U.S. Small Business Administration, Office of Advocacy, *Small Business and Micro Business Lending in the United States, 2002 Edition* at www.sba.gov/advo/research/2002.html#sbl.

7 The numbers used in the analysis include adjustment in the statistics reported by American Express Centurion Bank, one of the largest business card issuers, because American Express has transferred most small business lending activities to a new federal savings bank since the beginning of 2004, not reported in the call report database utilized in this study. Without adjustment, statistics from the June 2004 call report showed an even larger decline. Continued efforts by banks such as BB&T to consolidate credit card accounts held by employees under the same employer also contributed to adjustments.

8 Moreover, one major credit card bank, Capital One, reported in the CRA report (under the Federal Savings Bank file) large increases in the number and dollar amounts of loans made that are not captured in the call report data for commercial banks in this study.

9 The numbers and dollar amounts of loans for the BHCs/ banks with assets identified in the call reports were $80.3 billion in 5,711,993 loans from 998 banks in 2003 and $72.3 billion in 5,293,178 loans from 905 banks in 2002.

banks filing call reports declined by 137 between June 2003 and June 2004. Again, all of the decline came from the smallest banks with assets of less than $100 million (*Table 2.9*).[10]

To provide a better picture of the changing banking structure and the changing share of small business loans by banks and bank holding companies (BHCs) of different sizes, call report data are consolidated to produce Table 2.10.

Of a total of 6,423 U.S. BHCs and banks, the 72 largest (with assets over $10 billion) accounted for three-quarters of total domestic assets and about two-thirds of total business loans in the United States. Because of their promotion of small business credit cards, these very large BHCs/banks accounted for two-thirds of the total number of accounts for the smallest loans (under $100,000) and about 50 percent of the total amount of these loans outstanding.

These largest banks' small share of medium-sized loans between $100,000 and $1 million nevertheless indicates a potential problem in the small business loan markets. While the share of total domestic assets held by giant BHCs/banks increased from 69.7 percent to 75.3 percent between June 1999 and June 2004, their share of the medium-sized small business markets declined from 46.8 percent to 45 percent of the dollar amount and from 46.5 percent to 44.6 percent of the number (*Table 2.11*). Their share of total business loans has also declined, from 69.5 percent to 63.3 percent during this period. The developments observed over the past five years warrant continued attention by small business policy makers.[11]

---

10 Changes in the number of reporting banks could also be caused by the financial reporting consolidation of several BHCs. While the number of banks declined, the number of banking offices, including both offices and branches, continued to increase. See FDIC, Statistics on Banking, on the FDIC website, www2.fdic.gov/SDI/SOB/.

11 See also studies conducted for the Office of Advocacy: P.M Keypoint, *The Effects of Mergers and Acquisitions on Small Business Lending by Large Banks*, A report submitted to the U.S. Small Business Administration, Office of Advocacy, contract no. SBAHQ-02-Q-0024.; Craig, S and P. Hardee, *The Impact of Bank Consolidation on Small Business Credit Availability*, a report submitted to the U.S. Small Business Administration, contract.no. SBA HQ-01-R-0005; and Charles Ou, *Banking Consolidation and Small Business Lending—A Review of Recent Research* OER working paper, Office of Advocacy, 2005.

Table 2.9 Number of Reporting Banks by Asset Size, 1997–2004

Bank asset size	1997	1998	1999	2000	2001	2002	2003	2004
<$100 million	6,047	5,644	5,302	5,034	4,674	4,369	4,022	3,815
$100 million–$500 million	2,590	2,656	2,683	2,751	2,777	2,839	2,990	3,059
$500 million–$1 billion	292	303	290	302	320	353	393	386
$1 billion–$10 billion	300	302	309	293	306	311	331	336
>$10 billion	64	61	75	79	76	77	79	82
Total	9,293	8,966	8,659	8,459	8,158	7,949	7,815	7,678

Source: U.S. Small Business Administration, Office of Advocacy, *Small Business Lending in the United States*, various issues, and special tabulations of the June 2004 call reports (*Consolidated Reports of Condition and Income for U.S. Banks* prepared for the Office of Advocacy by James Kolari, A&M University, College Station, Texas).

Table 2.10 Shares of Assets and Business Loans Outstanding by Size for All BHCs and Banks in the United States, by BHC/Bank Size, June 2004 (percent except first row)

	Asset size of bank or BHC (as of June 30, 2004)						
	More than $50 billion	$10 billion to $50 billion	More than $10 billion	$1 billion to $10 billion	$500 million to $1 billion	Less than $500 million	All banks and BHCs
Number of banks/BHCs	22	50	72	300	345	5,706	6,423
Small business loans (less than $100,000)							
Amount	34.27	15.45	49.72	13.08	6.12	31.08	100
Number	53.44	14.04	67.48	14.81	6.74	10.98	100
Small business loans ($100,000–$1 million)							
Amount	28.83	16.16	45.00	19.96	8.24	26.80	100
Number	28.58	16.02	44.59	20.02	8.24	27.15	100
Total business loans							
Amount	46.64	16.62	63.26	16.83	5.40	14.52	100
Total domestic assets							
Amount	59.36	15.96	75.32	11.19	3.33	10.17	100

Source: U.S. Small Business Administration, Office of Advocacy, *Small Business Lending in the United States*, various issues, and special tabulations of the June 2004 call reports (*Consolidated Reports of Condition and Income for U.S. Banks* prepared for the Office of Advocacy by James Kolari, A&M University, College Station, Texas).

Table 2.11 Shares of Assets and Business Loans by Size for All BHCs and Banks in the United States, 1999–2004 (percent, except first row for each year)

	Asset size of bank/BHC						All banks and BHCs
	Over $50 billion	$10 billion to $50 billion	Over $10 billion	$1 billion to $10 billion	$500 million to $1 billion	Under $500 million	
June 30, 1999							
Number of banks/BHCs	15	44	59	224	234	6,384	6,901
Small business loans (under $100,000)							
Amount	20.66	15.61	36.27	15.46	6.09	42.18	100
Number	25.89	24.98	50.87	18.04	3.59	27.49	100
Small business loans ($100,000–$1 million)							
Amount	25.74	21.06	46.80	20.39	7.04	25.78	100
Number	24.91	21.61	46.52	19.82	7.05	26.61	100
Total business loans (amount)	45.83	23.65	69.48	13.97	3.65	12.89	100
Total domestic assets (amount)	46.68	23.01	69.69	13.50	3.39	13.42	100
June 30, 2002							
Number of banks/BHCs	19	45	64	233	321	5,954	6,572
Small business loans (under $100,000)							
Amount	31.01	15.36	46.36	12.96	6.38	34.30	100
Number	38.27	21.69	59.96	21.04	6.42	12.58	100
Small business loans ($100,000–$1 million)							
Amount	29.58	16.51	46.08	18.69	8.86	26.37	100
Number	32.01	16.18	48.18	18.05	8.37	25.40	100
Total business loans (amount)	49.33	17.49	66.82	14.40	5.21	13.56	100
Total domestic assets (amount)	55.53	17.78	73.31	11.55	3.69	11.45	100

June 30, 2003

Number of banks/BHCs	22	45	67	272	357	5,798	6,494
Small business loans (under $100,000)							
Amount	33.61	14.01	47.62	12.99	6.84	32.55	100
Number	51.10	13.18	64.28	18.19	6.65	10.88	100
Small business loans ($100,000–$1 million)							
Amount	29.62	14.99	44.60	19.14	8.96	27.29	100
Number	29.43	15.05	44.48	19.46	8.91	27.15	100
Total business loans (amount)	49.30	15.54	64.84	15.39	5.65	14.12	100
Total domestic assets (amount)	58.48	15.84	74.32	11.36	3.72	10.61	100

June 30, 2004

Number of banks/BHCs	22	50	72	300	345	5,706	6,423
Small business loans (under $100,000)							
Amount	34.27	15.45	49.72	13.08	6.12	31.08	100
Number	53.44	14.04	67.48	14.81	6.74	10.98	100
Small business loans ($100,000–$1 million)							
Amount	28.83	16.16	45.00	19.96	8.24	26.80	100
Number	28.58	16.02	44.59	20.02	8.24	27.15	100
Total business loans (amount)	46.64	16.62	63.26	16.83	5.40	14.52	100
Total domestic assets (amount)	59.36	15.96	75.32	11.19	3.33	10.17	100

Source: U.S. Small Business Administration, Office of Advocacy, *Small Business Lending in the United States,* various issues, and special tabulations of the June 2004 call reports (*Consolidated Reports of Condition and Income for U.S. Banks* prepared for the Office of Advocacy by James Kolari, A&M University, College Station, Texas).

Lending by Finance Companies

The market for business receivables served by finance companies recovered slightly.[12] Total business receivables outstanding for finance companies rose moderately, by 3.1 percent. Large increases in receivables for vehicles offset a small decline in receivables for equipment lending. The total asset value for business receivables grew from $457.4 billion in 2003 to $471.9 billion by the end of 2004 *(Table 2.12)*.

Equity Borrowing

After a significant rebound in 2003 from more than three years of major declines, the U.S. stock markets consolidated and drifted downward for the first nine months of 2004, surging to finish up slightly for the year as a result of resumed optimism during the last three months. A consolidated market with a slight upward trend was adequate to stimulate a very healthy market for initial public offerings (IPOs), especially for larger public offerings. The overall IPO market was very active, with 251 new issues valued at $48 billion for 2004, compared with an average of $22 billion in 2002–2003. However, investors' enthusiasm for smaller companies, (those with assets before issuance of $25 million or less) remained limited. While the number and dollar amounts of IPOs for small companies rose, they remained below the levels of 2000 and 2001, and considerably below the levels reached during the small issue market peak of 1996–1999. (The overall IPO market peaked in 2000). Seven of the smallest IPOs (for companies with initial assets below $10 million) were issued; the amount for these IPOs totaled $335 million. There were 14 IPOs valued at $598 million for companies with assets under $25 million *(Table 2.13)*.

---

12 Statistics for the small business share of business receivables provided by finance companies are not available. A recent study of the 1998 National Survey of Small Business Finances found that finance companies accounted for 31 percent of total equipment and vehicle loans to small businesses in 1998. Their share of other markets—credit lines and commercial mortgages—was much smaller, about 10 percent. See George Haynes, *Finance Companies and Small Business Borrowers: Evidence from the 1993 and 1998 Surveys of Small Business Finances*, a report submitted to U.S. Small Business Administration, Office of Advocacy, April 2005.

Table 2.12 Business Loans Outstanding from Finance Companies, December 31, 1980–December 31, 2004

	Total receivables outstanding		Annual change in chain-type* price index for GDP (percent)
	Billions of dollars	Change	
December 31, 2004	471.9	3.2	2.1
December 31, 2003	457.4	0.5	1.8
December 31, 2002	455.3	1.9	2.0
December 31, 2001	447.0	-2.5	2.4
December 31, 2000	458.4	16.3	2.1
December 31, 1999	405.2	16.6	1.4
December 31, 1998	347.5	9.1	1.2
December 31, 1997	318.5	2.9	2.0
December 31, 1996	309.5	2.6	1.8
December 31, 1995	301.6	9.7	2.4
December 31, 1994	274.9	NA	2.5
December 31, 1993	294.6	-2.3	2.3
December 31, 1992	301.3	1.9	2.5
December 31, 1991	295.8	0.9	2.6
December 31, 1990	293.6	14.6	3.4
December 31, 1989	256.0	9.1	4.6
December 31, 1988	234.6	13.9	3.9
December 31, 1987	206.0	19.7	4.0
December 31, 1986	172.1	9.3	3.2
December 31, 1985	157.5	14.3	2.5
December 31, 1984	137.8	21.9	3.5
December 31, 1983	113.4	12.9	3.8
December 31, 1982	100.4	0	5.3
December 31, 1981	100.3	11.1	8.5
December 31, 1980	90.3		

* Changes from the fourth quarter of the year before.

Source: Board of Governors of the Federal Reserve System, *Federal Reserve Bulletin*, Table 1.52 (or 1.51), various issues; U.S. Department of Commerce, Bureau of Economic Analysis, *Business Conditions Digest*, various issues; and idem., *Survey of Current Business*, various issues.

Table 2.13 Common Stock Initial Public Offerings by All and Small Issuers, 1995–2004

	Common stock		
	Number	Amount (millions of dollars)	Average size (millions of dollars)
Offerings by all issuers			
2004	251	48,382.4	192.8
2003	86	16,116.6	187.4
2002	95	28,126.3	296.1
2001	99	37,526.0	379.1
2000	387	60,871.0	157.3
1999	512	63,017.4	123.1
1998	366	38,075.3	104.0
1997	623	45,785.0	73.5
1996	850	52,190.3	61.4
1995	570	32,786.1	57.5
Offerings by issuers with assets of $25 million or less			
2004	14	598.4	42.7
2003	6	511.9	85.3
2002	10	410.4	41.0
2001	14	477.2	34.1
2000	56	3,323.9	59.4
1999	207	10,531.0	50.9
1998	128	4,513.7	35.3
1997	241	5,746.1	23.8
1996	422	10,642.0	25.2
1995	248	5,603.1	22.6

(continued, next page)

Table 2.13 (continued)

	Common stock		
	Number	Amount (millions of dollars)	Average size (millions of dollars)
Offerings by issuers with assets of $10 million or less			
2004	7	335.0	47.9
2003	2	16.9	8.5
2002	4	150.9	37.7
2001	5	54.9	11.0
2000	13	407.2	31.3
1999	87	3,556.9	40.9
1998	62	2,208.0	35.6
1997	132	2,538.6	19.2
1996	268	5,474.4	20.4
1995	159	2,545.2	16.0

Note: Excludes closed end funds. Registered offerings data from the Securities and Exchange Commission are no longer available; data provided by Securities Data Company are not as inclusive as those registered with the SEC.

Source: Special tabulations prepared for the U.S. Small Business Administration, Office of Advocacy, by Thomson Financial Securities Data, May 2005.

IPO offerings by venture-backed companies improved significantly in 2004—the number of venture-backed IPOs increased from 27 in 2003 to 83 in 2004 and the total amount increased from $1.9 billion to $8.4 billion.[13] The average size of venture-backed IPOs was $102 million, the largest ever.[14] Venture-backed IPOs accounted for a significant share of total IPOs in 2004.[15]

13 Total 2004 exits, including both venture-capital-backed initial public offerings (IPOs) and merger and acquisition (M&A) activities totaled 416, 83 for IPOs and 333 for M&A deals. See National Venture Capital Association, *NVCA Yearbook 2005*, 73 and 78.

14 National Venture Capital Association, *NVCA Yearbook 2004*, Arlington, Va., June 2004, 75–76. A similar picture was observed for the alternative exit—private mergers and acquisitions, as was discussed in the yearbook.

15 See *NVCA Yearbook 2004*, 73, Figure 6.02. However, the total number of all IPOs in the report, 191, is much smaller than the number provided by Thomson Financial to the Office of Advocacy. See Table 2.13 of this report.

Venture Capital Funds

While investment in venture capital companies mirrored the recovery experienced in the IPO markets, investment by venture capital companies showed a more modest recovery. Total funds raised by venture capital firms increased from $11.5 billion to $18.2 billion in 2004, while total disbursements increased from $18.9 billion to $21.0 billion for 2,399 companies, 46 companies more than in the previous year. First-round investment, however, remained low— with an average amount of $4 billion in 2002–2004, compared with $5 billion in 1996–1998. The number of invested companies averaged 800, compared with 1,300 in the previous period. Again, while low in comparison with the peaks of 1999–2001, the amounts of fund commitment and investment in portfolio companies are comparable to the levels for 1998, when venture capital activities surged ahead after more than 10 years of activity at about $3 billion to $5 billion. Total capital under management increased slightly to $267 billion by the end of 2004 *(Table 2.14)*. Investment in small business portfolio companies by small business investment companies (SBICs) increased in FY 2004, again only modestly *(Table 2.15)*. Total financing provided by SBICs amounted to $2.84 billion, a moderate increase from $2.47 billion in FY 2003. The number of financings decreased from 4,833, an extremely high level, in FY 2003 to 4,462 in FY 2004. The amount of first-round or initial investment, again, was larger than the amount of follow-on investment, $1,706 million compared with $1,131 million.[16] Investment by specialized SBICs (301d companies or SSBICs) remained very small.

---

16 In contrast to investment by venture capital companies, the dollar amount of first-round investment by SBICs has been greater than the follow-on investment—follow-on investments by venture capital companies usually are three to four times the size of first-round investments.

Table 2.14 New Commitments, Disbursements, and Total Capital Pool of the Venture Capital Industry, 1982–2004 (billions of dollars)

	Commitments	Disbursements	Initial-round	Follow-on	Capital under management
2004	18.2	21.0	4.40	16.60	266.7
2003	11.5	18.9	3.60	15.30	256.7
2002	9.0	21.6	4.50	17.20	255.0
2001	38.0	40.9	7.50	33.40	251.6
2000	106.0	105.9	29.00	76.90	223.1
1999	58.2	54.4	16.08	38.36	145.9
1998	30.4	21.2	7.30	13.94	91.4
1997	18.2	14.8	4.72	10.06	63.2
1996	11.6	11.5	4.29	7.26	49.3
1995	10.0	7.7	3.65	4.10	40.7
1994	7.8	4.2	1.73	2.47	36.1
1993	3.8	3.9	1.43	2.41	32.2
1992	5.1	3.6	1.27	2.11	30.2
1991	1.9	2.2	0.56	1.67	29.3
1990	3.3	2.8	0.84	1.97	31.4
1989	5.4	3.3	0.98	2.32	30.4
1988	4.4	3.3	1.03	2.23	27.0
1987	4.8	4.5	0.94	2.23	24.6
1986	3.7	4.1	0.89	2.09	20.3
1985	3.1	3.4	0.71	2.01	17.2
1984	3.2	3.3	0.86	2.09	13.9
1983	4.2	3.1	0.90	1.97	10.6
1982	2.0	1.8	0.59	1.00	6.7

Source: Venture Capital Journal (various Issues) and National Venture Capital Association Yearbook 2004, prepared by Venture Economics.

Table 2.15 Disbursements to Small Businesses by Small Business Investment Companies, Initial and Follow-on Financing, FY 1992–FY 2004 (amounts in millions of dollars)

Fiscal year	Initial financing		Follow-on financing		Total	
	Number	Amount	Number	Amount	Number	Amount
2004	1,307	1,706	3,155	1,131	4,462	2,837
2003	1,624	1,456	3,209	1,015	4,833	2,471
2002	1,060	1,274	2,944	1,386	4,004	2,660
2001	1,477	2,497	2,800	1,958	4,277	4,455
2000	2,251	3,860	2,388	1,606	4,639	5,466
1999	1,379	2,926	1,717	1,295	3,096	4,221
1998	1,721	2,037	1,725	1,202	3,446	3,239
1997	1,360	1,658	1,371	711	2,731	2,369
1996	1,081	1,022	1,026	594	2,107	1,616
1995	1,322	725	899	524	2,221	1,249
1994	1,241	517	1,107	484	2,348	1,001
1993	1,086	443	906	364	1,992	807
1992	1,056	322	943	222	1,999	544

Source: U.S. Small Business Administration, Investment Division.

Angel Investment

The national angel investor market continued to recover in 2004.[17] Total investment by angel investors rose 24 percent to $22.5 billion in 2004 compared with $18.1 billion in the previous year. About 48,000 entrepreneurial ventures received angel funding in 2004, up 24 percent from 2003. Active investors in 2004 totaled 225,000 individuals, up 2.5 percent from 2003. On average, 4 to 5 investors joined forces to fund an entrepreneurial start-up.[18]

---

17   According to a new report about the 2004 national angel investor market. The report was released by the Center for Venture Research at the University of New Hampshire Whittemore School of Business and Economics.

18   See the press release concerning the Center for Venture Research report about the 2004 angel investor market from Jeff Sohl, titled "Angel Investor Market Sustains Modest Recovery in 2004" at www. imakenews.com/innovationphiladelphia/e_article000376110.cfm?x=b4RdQR3,b2fwVfrT,w

Conclusion

Overall borrowing in the financial markets continued to show significant increases in 2004, again dominated by household borrowing for housing investment, by the government sector, and by a resumption in corporate borrowing. Small business borrowing also increased, although only moderately. Increased earnings and cash flow were adequate to meet the increased demand for funding. There was no indication that small business borrowing was constrained by an inadequate supply of funding.

The equity capital market also recovered, especially for larger later-stage financing—as indicated by large increases in venture-backed IPOs and mergers and acquisitions. Small IPOs remained very limited. While investment by venture capital companies continued to recover, equity funding was difficult to find for early-stage companies, and first-round startup financing remained at low levels. Angel investors continued to be important in providing funding for early-stage entrepreneurs in 2004.

3 FEDERAL PROCUREMENT *from* SMALL FIRMS

Synopsis

President Bush's 2002 Small Business Agenda called for a number of steps that would create an environment in which small firms could flourish, among them ensuring that U.S. government contracts are open to all small businesses that can supply the government's needs.

A number of steps taken in 2004 have helped move the federal procurement markets further along that path, including improvements in guidance for large businesses subcontracting to small firms, efforts to improve the small business size standards, clarification of the "novation" regulations that apply to small businesses acquired by larger ones, moves toward greater transparency in federal procurement data, and initiatives to reduce the bundling of contracts that can leave small firms out of the competition.

As a result of these and other efforts in federal contracting, small businesses were awarded $69.23 billion or 23.09 percent of the $299.9 billion in federal prime contracts in FY 2004.

The SBA's Office of Advocacy publishes various research studies in an effort to improve the climate for, among other things, small business contracting. Advocacy procurement studies published in 2004 looked at electronic procurement, contracting with veteran-owned businesses, and the coding of businesses for procurement purposes.

Federal Procurement Policy Initiatives in 2004

Small businesses continued to be the backbone of the nation in 2004. In his 2002 Small Business Agenda, President Bush called for improving small business access to government contracts, specifically for efforts to:

- Ensure that government contracts are open to all small businesses that can supply the government's needs,

- Avoid unnecessary contract bundling, and
- Streamline the appeals process for small businesses that contract with the federal government.

In the federal procurement arena, small businesses made significant gains toward a more level playing field, as efforts were under way to reduce contract bundling and improve small business access to federal procurement opportunities.

Subcontracting

With small business support, regulations were promulgated in 2004 that provided guidance to "other than small" contractors (large businesses) subcontracting with small businesses.[1] The final rule also authorized the evaluation of past performance in meeting subcontracting goals as a source selection factor for use by federal agencies in placing orders through the Federal Supply Schedules, governmentwide agency schedules, and multiple-agency contracts. These changes were in line with the President's Small Business Agenda.

Small Business Size Standards

An effort was made in 2004 to revamp the entire small business size standard program. In the Small Business Act, the Congress authorized the U.S. Small Business Administration (SBA) to establish guidelines for determining the sizes of businesses that should be eligible for federally funded program assistance. The SBA subsequently established size standards for small businesses, based on a company's annual revenue over a three-year period or on its number of employees. Over the years, concerns have been expressed that the size of businesses were defined as either too large or too small. The SBA attempted to address some of these concerns in a draft size standard rulemaking in June 2004. Through the direct involvement of the Office of Advocacy, the Small Business Administration, and stakeholders across the country, the proposed regulations were withdrawn in favor of issuing an advance notice of proposed rulemaking. This process has allowed small business stakeholders to attend field hearings across the country to discuss how best to redesign the existing size standard program.

---

1   See Small Business Government Contracting Programs; Subcontracting (RIN: 3245-AF12) published in the *Federal Register*, December 20, 2004, 69 Fed. Reg. 75820.

Size Determinations: Contract Novation

The debate on the appropriate size of a small business extended to a debate on the status of a small business after it has been acquired by another company. To answer at least one element of this debate, the SBA issued final "novation" regulations in 2004.[2] Novation is the process whereby one company is acquired by another and its contracts are changed over to the name of the acquiring company. In the past, some small business contracts not novated to the large business continued to be counted as small business awards. In the new novation process, once a small business has been acquired by means of a purchase or merger, the contract is written to reflect the transfer of ownership and the small business owner must reaffirm its small business status by submitting a written self-certification statement to the contracting officer of the procuring agency.

Small Business Procurement Data

Efforts have been initiated to provide greater transparency in federal procurement data. In 2004, the General Services Administration and the Office of Federal Procurement Policy (OMB/OFPP) introduced the fourth generation of the Federal Procurement Data System (FPDS). The new system is referred to as FPDS-NG. There have been problems with the quality, timeliness, and accuracy of the data under the new system. When the system is fully operational, small business stakeholders will be able to retrieve federal small business procurement numbers in real time and thus should be able to make policy and marketing decisions more quickly and accurately.[3]

Contract Bundling

Contract bundling is the practice of combining two or more contracts into a large single agreement, a practice that most of the time pushes small firms out of the competition. A study by the Office of Advocacy revealed that in 2001, contract bundling was at a ten-year high. President Bush in his 2002 Small Business Agenda requested agencies to stop the unnecessary bundling of contracts. The agenda also required the OMB/OFPP to develop a detailed

---

2 See the proposed regulation at 67 *Federal Register* 70339, November 22, 2002; final, 69 *Federal Register* 29192, May 21, 2004; final rule correction, 69 *Federal Register* 45551, July 30, 2004.

3 See Amendment 2004–04, General Services Acquisition Regulations (GSAR) Case 2004-G509, Access to the Federal Procurement Data System, December 28, 2004.

plan to implement this objective.[4] The SBA and OMB/OFPP initiated regulatory action. The proposed regulation was published in the *Federal Register* on January 31, 2003; the final regulation on October 20, 2003.[5] In May 2004 the Government Accountability Office (GAO) published a report, *Contract Management: Impact of Strategy to Mitigate Effects of Contract Bundling*, which found that agency bundling data in the Federal Procurement Data System were miscoded because of confusion about the statutory definition of contract bundling, inadequate verification of information, and ineffective controls in the FPDS reporting process.

Advocacy Procurement Studies

The Office of Advocacy is charged in its authorizing statute to "examine the role of small business in the American economy and the contribution which small business can make in improving competition…" In line with its research mandate, the Office of Advocacy in 2004 published three reports on federal government purchasing from small firms.

Trends in Electronic Procurement and Electronic Commerce and Their Impact on Small Business, prepared by Innovation and Information Consultants, Inc., was published in June 2004.[6] The report examined the extent to which businesses are using Internet and electronic information technologies in government procurement. The report found small businesses increasing their use of the Internet for e-procurement. In FY 2000, only 2 percent of all small business procurement dollars were obtained through e-procurement; by FY 2002, the share had risen to 6.5 percent.

Characteristics of Federal Government Procurement Spending with Veteran-Owned Businesses: FY 2000–FY 2003 (3Q), published in June 2004, was prepared under contract with Eagle Eye Publishers, Inc.[7] The study found that federal agencies were actually providing more contracts and dollars to veteran-owned firms

---

4   The OMB/OFPP report is available at *www.acqnet.gov*.

5   67 *Federal Register* 47244, January 31, 2003, and 68 *Federal Register* 60015, October 20, 2003.

6   The report is available at *http://www.sba.gov/advo/research/rs240tot.pdf*

7   The report may be found at *http://www.sba.gov/advo/research/rs239tot.pdf*

than they were reporting. Some of the findings in the study supported a subsequent legislative initiative designed to increase federal procurement dollar awards to small businesses owned by service-disabled veterans.

Published in December 2004, *Analysis of Type of Business Coding for the Top 1,000 Contractors Receiving Small Business Awards in FY 2002* found coding problems with small business contracts.[8]

The change in the novation policy and several other regulatory changes in proposal stages are significant initiatives to improve the process of providing more transparency in counting small business contract awards. The new FPDS-NG is also designed to reduce the potential for human error in transferring data from the contractor to the contracting agency to the FPDS. These achievements are among the highlights of the FY 2004 small business contracting activities.

Federal Contracting with Small Firms in FY 2004

Small businesses are eager to pursue government contracts. In fiscal year 2004, the federal government awarded more procurement dollars to small firms than in the past. The federal government awarded a total of $299.9 billion in contracts for the purchase of goods that were available for small business participation *(Table 3.1)*.

Small businesses were awarded $69.23 billion in direct prime contracts in 2004 or 23.09 percent of the total. In FY 2003, small businesses were awarded approximately $45.5 billion in subcontracts from prime contractors. The FY 2004 subcontracting numbers are not available but it is estimated based on the FY 2003 level of subcontracting that small businesses were awarded nearly $50 billion. The total procurement amount for small businesses in FY 2004, including both prime contracts and subcontracts, is estimated at $119.2 billion.

Sources of Small Business Awards by Department/Agency

The largest share of all federal purchases in contracts has historically come from the Department of Defense (DOD) *(Tables 3.2–3.4)*. The DOD share of

---

8   The report is available at *http://www.sba.gov/advo/research/rs246tot.pdf*

Table 3.1 Total Federal Prime Contract Actions, FY 2002, FY 2003, and FY 2004

	Numbers as Produced by Eagle Eye			Numbers as Produced by SBA[1]		
	Thousands of dollars			Thousands of dollars		
	Total	Small business share (percent)	Small business	Total	Small business share (percent)	Small business
Total, FY 2002	**259,084,850**	**54,080,122**	**20.9**	**235,417,413**	**53,250,281**	**22.6**
Actions under $25,000	14,506,369	6,854,072	47.2			
Actions over $25,000[2]	244,578,481	47,226,050	19.3			
Total, FY 2003	**307,459,171**	**65,752,994**	**21.4**	**277,477,716**	**65,505,924**	**23.6**
Actions under $25,000	15,140.026	5,939,664	39.2			
Actions over $25,000[2]	292,319,145	59,813,330	20.5			
Total, FY 2004[3]				**299,886,097**	**69,228,771**	**23.09**

1 The U.S. Small Business Administration's Office of Government Contracting (OGC) calculated the share of federal dollars going to small businesses as part of its goaling process with other agencies. The OGC excluded certain categories of contract awards from the base or denominator of percentages awarded to small businesses because SBA officials believe that small businesses do not have a reasonable opportunity to compete for them. In the FPDC figures no contracts are excluded from the analysis.

2 Reported individually.

3 In 2004, the General Services Administration and the Office of Federal Procurement Policy (OMB/OFPP) introduced the fourth generation of the FPDS. The new FPDS-NG data shown here, unless otherwise noted, reflect all contract actions available for small business competition, not just those over $25,000. The figures are not strictly comparable with those shown for previous years.

Source: General Services Administration, Federal Procurement Data Center.

Table 3.2 Procurement Dollars in Contract Actions over $25,000 by Major Agency Source, FY 1984–FY 2003, and in Total, FY 2004

Fiscal year	Total (thousands of dollars)	Percent of total			
		DOD	DOE	NASA	Other
2004*	299,886,098	67.8	1.3	2.6	28.3
2003	292,319,145	67.9	7.2	4.0	20.9
2002	258,125,273	65.1	7.4	4.5	23.1
2001	248,985,613	58.2	7.5	4.5	29.8
2000	207,401,363	64.4	8.2	5.3	22.2
1999	188,846,760	66.4	8.4	5.8	19.4
1998	184,178,721	64.1	8.2	5.9	21.8
1997	179,227,203	65.4	8.8	6.2	19.5
1996	183,489,567	66.5	8.7	6.2	18.7
1995	185,119,992	64.3	9.1	6.3	20.2
1994	181,500,339	65.4	9.9	6.3	18.4
1993	184,426,948	66.7	10.0	6.4	16.8
1992	183,081,207	66.3	10.1	6.6	16.9
1991	193,550,425	70.2	9.5	6.1	14.2
1990	179,286,902	72.0	9.7	6.4	11.9
1989	172,612,189	75.0	8.8	5.7	10.6
1988	176,544,042	76.9	8.2	4.9	10.0
1987	181,750,326	78.6	7.7	4.2	9.5
1986	183,681,389	79.6	7.3	4.0	9.0
1985	188,186,597	80.0	7.7	4.0	8.3
1984	168,100,611	79.3	7.9	4	9.0

DOD = Department of Defense; DOE = Department of Energy; NASA = National Aeronautics and Space Administration.

* For FY 2004, the new FPDS-NG data shown here reflect all contract actions available for small business competition (excluding some categories), not just those over $25,000. The figures are not strictly comparable with those shown for previous years.

Note: For FY 1983 through FY 2003, the dollar threshold for reporting detailed information on DOD procurement actions was $25,000. For civilian agencies, the figure increased from $10,000 to $25,000 starting in FY 1986 and continuing in the data shown here through FY 2003.

Source: General Services Administration, Federal Procurement Data Center, Eagle Eye Publishers, and Special Report 87458A, prepared for the U.S. Small Business Administration, Office of Advocacy (Washington, D.C.: U.S. Government Printing Office, May 19, 1988).

Table 3.3 Distribution of Small Business Share of Dollars in Contract Actions by Procuring Agency Source, FY 2003 and FY 2004*

	Total small business		Small business distribution (percent)		Rank	
	FY 2004*	FY 2003	FY 2004*	FY 2003	FY 2004*	FY 2003
Total, all agencies	**69,228,771,571**	**59,813,315,875**	100.00	100.00	100.00	100.00
Agency for International Development (1152, 7200)	51,944,280	286,346,162	0.08	0.48	18	18
Commission on National and Community Service	—	5,414,167	—	0.01	—	34
Commodity Futures Trading Commission	3,537,943	2,596,098	0.01	0.00	34	38
Consumer Product Safety Commission	5,253,688	3,903,553	0.01	0.01	32	36
Department of Agriculture	1,957,587,894	2,102,422,715	2.83	3.51	5	3
Department of Commerce	794,439,680	686,886,946	1.15	1.15	12	13
Department of Defense	46,928,476,346	36,912,997,871	67.79	61.71	1	1
Department of Education	102,648,093	162,806,134	0.15	0..27	20	20
Department of Energy	918,251,981	844,270,905	1.32	1.41	11	12
Department of Health and Human Services	2,339,000,990	1,732,359,097	3.38	2.90	3	4
Department of Homeland Security	1,706,076,224	969,767,603	2.46	1.62	7	9
Department of Housing and Urban Development	686,939,213	528,899,557	0.99	0.88	14	15
Department of the Interior	1,240,593,866	1,584,251,672	1.79	2.65	9	6

(continued, next page)

* Through FY 2003, the contract dollars reflected in the data were in contracts over $25,000. For FY 2004, the new FPDS-NG data shown here reflect all contract actions available for small business competition (excluding some categories), not just those over $25,000. The figures are not strictly comparable with those shown for FY 2003.

Table 3.3 (continued)

	Total small business		Small business distribution (percent)		Rank	
	FY 2004*	FY 2003	FY 2004*	FY 2003	FY 2004*	FY 2003
Department of Justice	1,271,135,195	903,591,865	1.84	1.51	8	10
Department of Labor	587,813,760	410,909,064	0.85	0.69	16	16
Department of State	946,842,559	982,884,028	1.37	1.64	10	8
Department of the Treasury	714,322,403	575,690,820	1.03	0.96	13	14
Department of Transportation	677,934,185	879,082,080	0.98	1.47	15	11
Department of Veterans Affairs	2,263,843,279	1,722,399,592	3.27	2.88	4	5
Environmental Protection Agency	398,490,413	295,867,425	0.57	0.49	17	17
Equal Employment Opportunity Commission	13,726,398	5,862,139	0.02	0.01	30	33
Executive Office of the President	28,005,947	39,560,087	0.04	0.07	26	22
Federal Election Commission	2,127,792	1,190,890	0.00	0.00	36	40
Federal Emergency Management Agency	17,619,592	18,280,230	0.03	0.03	29	28
Federal Maritime Commission	472,359	26,951	0.00	0.00	42	44
Federal Trade Commission	38,918	8,667,637	0.00	0.01	43	29
General Services Administration	3,161,604,640	6,201,129,970	4.57	10.37	2	2
International Trade Commission	4,992,441	3,371,994	0.01	0.01	33	37
National Aeronautics and Space Administration	1,804,891,570	1,524,160,449	2.61	2.55	6	7

(continued, next page)

* Through FY 2003, the contract dollars reflected in the data were in contracts over $25,000. For FY 2004, the new FPDS-NG data shown here reflect all contract actions available for small business competition (excluding some categories), not just those over $25,000. The figures are not strictly comparable with those shown for FY 2003.

Table 3.3 (continued)

	Total small business		Small business distribution (percent)		Rank	
	FY 2004*	FY 2003	FY 2004*	FY 2003	FY 2004*	FY 2003
National Archives and Records Administration	40,454,930	35,934,719	0.06	0.06	23	24
National Foundation on the Arts and the Humanities	1,664,093	1,120,947	0.00	0.00	38	41
National Labor Relations Board	1,074,647	4,246,127	0.00	0.01	40	35
National Mediation Board	—	668,973	—	0.00	—	42
National Science Foundation	22,343,855	7,589,001	0.03	0.01	28	31
National Transportation Safety Board	1,208,490	—	0.00	—	39	—
Nuclear Regulatory Commission	34,851,834	28,071,019	0.05	0.05	24	25
Office of Personnel Management	78,325,112	36,198,840	0.11	0.06	21	23
Peace Corps	5,950,269	6,846,102	0.01	0.01	31	32
Railroad Retirement Board	2,432,260	2,348,958	0.00	0.00	35	39
Securities and Exchange Commission	59,192,592	8,170,238	0.09	0.01	22	30
Small Business Administration	26,801,613	23,164,306	0.04	0.04	27	26
Smithsonian Institution	28,545,265	52,069,371	0.04	0.09	25	21
Social Security Administration	227,786,096	192,736,525	0.33	0.32	19	19

(continued, next page)

* Through FY 2003, the contract dollars reflected in the data were in contracts over $25,000. For FY 2004, the new FPDS-NG data shown here reflect all contract actions available for small business competition (excluding some categories), not just those over $25,000. The figures are not strictly comparable with those shown for FY 2003.

Table 3.3 (continued)

	Total small business		Small business distribution (percent)		Rank	
	FY 2004*	FY 2003	FY 2004*	FY 2003	FY 2004*	FY 2003
Trade and Development Agency	829,702	130,917	0.00	0.00	41	43
U.S. Information Agency	1,708,616	18,422,425	0.00	0.03	37	27
U.S. Soldiers' and Airmen's Home	—	423	—	0.00	—	45

* Through FY 2003, the contract dollars reflected in the data were in contracts over $25,000. For FY 2004, the new FPDS-NG data shown here reflect all contract actions available for small business competition (excluding some categories), not just those over $25,000. The figures are not strictly comparable with those shown for FY 2003.

Source: General Services Administration, Federal Procurement Data Center, and Eagle Eye Publishers.

Table 3.4 Small Business Share of Dollars in Contract Actions by Top 24 Major Procuring Agencies, Fiscal Year 2004

Agency	Contract dollars (thousands) Total	Contract dollars (thousands) Small business	Small business share (percent)	Share rank
Total	299,886,098	69,228,772	23.09	
Department of Defense	210,742,333	46,928,476	22.27	17
General Services Administration	7,470,718	3,161,604	42.32	8
Department of Health and Human Services	7,892,963	2,339,001	29.63	13
Department of Veterans Affairs	8,472,953	2,263,843	26.71	16
Department of Agriculture	3,996,408	1,957,588	48.98	5
National Aeronautics and Space Administration	12,456,469	1,804,892	14.49	20
Department of Homeland Security	4,435,595	1,706,076	38.46	9
Department of Justice	3,876,756	1,271,135	32.79	11
Department of the Interior	2,323,773	1,240,594	53.39	2
Department of State	1,871,751	946,843	50.59	4
Department of Energy	21,987,386	918,252	4.18	23
Department of Commerce	1,491,763	794,440	53.26	3
Department of the Treasury	2,450,891	714,322	29.15	15
Department of Housing and Urban Development	946,938	686,939	72.54	1
Department of Transportation	1,572,426	677,934	43.11	7
Department of Labor	1,681,304	587,814	34.96	10
Environmental Protection Agency	1,352,085	398,490	29.47	14
Social Security Administration	523,150	227,786	43.54	6
Department of Education	1,523,043	102,648	6.74	22
Office of Personnel Management	469,639	78,325	16.68	19
National Archives and Records Administration	126,259	40,455	32.04	12
Smithsonian Institution	140,780	28,545	20.28	18
Executive Office of the President	240,262	28,006	11.66	21
Agency for International Development (1152)	1,225,733	21,401	1.75	24

Note: For FY 2004, the new FPDS-NG data shown here reflect all contract actions available for small business competition (excluding some categories), not just those over $25,000. The figures are not strictly comparable with figures for previous years.

Note: All agencies are represented in the total dollars for FY 2004; the organizations listed are those agencies that awarded at least $100 million in individual contract actions over $25,000 in FY 2004.

Source: General Services Administration, Federal Procurement Data Center, and Eagle Eye Publishers.

awards overall declined steadily from 80 percent of these contract dollars in FY 1985 to 66.3 percent in FY 1992. Since the early 1990s, the DOD share has remained at about two-thirds of all dollars in contracts over $25,000. In 2004, some 70 percent of total contract dollars available for small business competition and 68 percent of the $69 billion in FY 2004 prime contract dollars awarded to small businesses resulted from Department of Defense awards.

The Department of Defense awarded $46.9 billion or 22.27 percent of its dollars available for small business competition in FY 2004 to small businesses *(Table. 3.4)*. The next largest source of federal contracting awards to small businesses was the General Services Administration, which awarded $3.16 billion or 42.32 percent of its dollars to small business in FY 2004. Third was the Department of Health and Human Services, which awarded $2.34 billion or 29.6 percent to small businesses.

Small Business Innovation Research

The Small Business Innovation Development Act requires the federal departments and agencies with the largest extramural research and development (R&D) budgets to award a portion of their R&D funds to small businesses. Ten government agencies with extramural research and development obligations over $100 million initially participated in this program: the Departments of Agriculture, Commerce, Defense, Education, Energy, Health and Human Services, and Transportation, and the Environmental Protection Agency, the National Aeronautics and Space Administration, and the National Science Foundation. A total of about $17.3 billion has been awarded to small businesses over the 22 years of the program *(Table 3.5)*.[9] Participating agencies received a total of 30,766 proposals in FY 2004.

Procurement from Minority- and Women-owned Businesses

Small women- and minority-owned businesses continue to increase their level of participation in the federal marketplace *(Tables 3.6–3.8)*. Small women-owned businesses constitute approximately 26 percent of the total nonagricultural

---

9   FY 2004 figures for the Small Business Innovation Research program are preliminary.

Table 3.5 Small Business Innovation Research Program, FY 1983–FY 2004

Fiscal year	Phase I Number of proposals	Phase I Number of awards	Phase II Number of proposals	Phase II Number of awards	Total awards (millions of dollars)
Total	409,327	60,210	47,272	22,872	17,307.3
2004	30,766	4,638	3,604	2,013	1,867.4
2003	27,992	4,465	3,267	1,759	1,670.1
2002	22,340	4,243	2,914	1,577	1,434.8
2001	16,666	3,215	2,566	1,533	1,294.4
2000	17,641	3,172	2,533	1,335	1,190.2
1999	19,016	3,334	2,476	1,256	1,096.5
1998	18,775	3,022	2,480	1,320	1,100.0
1997	19,585	3,371	2,420	1,404	1,066.7
1996	18,378	2,841	2,678	1,191	916.3
1995	20,185	3,085	2,856	1,263	981.7
1994	25,588	3,102	2,244	928	717.6
1993	23,640	2,898	2,532	1,141	698.0
1992	19,579	2,559	2,311	916	508.4
1991	20,920	2,553	1,734	788	483.1
1990	20,957	2,346	2,019	837	460.7
1989	17,233	2,137	1,776	749	431.9
1988	17,039	2,013	1,899	711	389.1
1987	14,723	2,189	2,390	768	350.5
1986	12,449	1,945	1,112	564	297.9
1985	9,086	1,397	765	407	199.1
1984	7,955	999	559	338	108.4
1983	8,814	686	127	74	44.5

Note: The FY 2004 numbers are preliminary. Phase I evaluates the scientific and technical merit and feasibility of an idea. Phase II expands on the results and further pursues the development of Phase I. Phase III commercializes the results of Phase II and requires the use of private or non-SBIR federal funding. The Phase II proposals and awards in FY 1983 were pursuant to predecessor programs that qualified as SBIR funding.

Source: U.S. Small Business Administration, Office of Innovation, Research and Technology (annual reports for FY 1983–FY 2004).

Table 3.6 Prime Contract Awards by Recipient Category (billions of dollars)

	FY 2003		FY 2004	
	Dollars	Percent	Dollars	Percent
Total to all businesses	**277.48**	**100.00**	**299.89**	**100.00**
Small businesses	65.51	23.61	69.23	23.08
Small disadvantaged businesses (SDBs)	19.46	7.01	18.54	6.11
8(a) businesses	10.11	3.64	8.44	2.81
Non-8(a) SDBs	9.35	3.37	10.09	3.30
HUBZone businesses	3.42	1.23	4.78	1.58
Women-owned small businesses	8.28	2.98	9.09	3.03
Service-disabled veteran-owned small businesses	0.55	0.20	1.15	0.38

Source: Federal Procurement Data System.

business population of the United States and their share of the federal procurement dollars grew from 2.98 percent in FY 2003 to 3.03 percent in FY 2004 *(Table 3.6)*. Small disadvantaged businesses achieved their 5 percent goal by reaching 6.11 percent or $18.54 billion. Participants in the SBA 8(a) program were awarded 2.8 percent of the total FY 2004 procurement dollars or $8.44 billion in contracts.

Service-disabled veteran business owners are now included in the socio-economic groups monitored in the federal procurement marketplace. Public Law 106-50 established a statutory goal of 3 percent of all prime and subcontracting dollars to be awarded to service-disabled veterans. In FY 2001 they were awarded 0.25 percent of direct federal contract dollars and in FY 2002 that percentage was 0.17 percent. In FY 2003 their share increased to $550 million or 0.20 percent and in FY 2004, small service-disabled veterans were awarded contracts valued at $1.15 billion or 0.38 percent of federal contracting dollars.

Table 3.7 Annual Change in the Dollar Volume of Contract Actions Over $25,000 Awarded to Small, Women-Owned, and Minority-Owned Businesses, FY 1980–FY 2004* (thousands of dollars)

	Total, all business			Small business			Women-owned business			Minority-owned business		
	Total (thousands of dollars)	Change from prior year		Total (thousands of dollars)	Change from prior year		Total (thousands of dollars)	Change from prior year		Total (thousands of dollars)	Change from prior year	
		Thousands of dollars	%		Thousands of dollars	%		Thousands of dollars	%		Thousands of dollars	%
2004*	299,886,098	NA	NA	68,228,772	NA	NA	9,091,919	NA	NA	18,538,012	NA	NA
2003	292,319,145	47,740,664	19.5	59,813,330	12,587,280	26.7	8,212,453	1,534,833	23.0	18,903,087	3,595,020	23.5
2002	244,578,481	21,476,465	9.6	47,226,050	461,545	9.9	6,677,620	-3,595	—	15,308,067	754,369	5.2
2001	223,338,280	17,490,979	8.5	46,764,505	7,983,057	20.6	6,681,215	2,226,212	50.0	14,553,698	1,966,900	15.6
2000	205,847,301	20,722,610	11.2	38,781,448	3,036,256	8.5	4,455,003	427,264	10.6	12,586,798	727,575	5.8
1999	185,124,691	1,013,686	0.6	35,745,192	1,485,753	4.3	4,027,739	485,838	13.7	11,859,223	414,203	3.6
1998	184,111,005	5,186,111	2.8	34,259,439	-7,013,742	-17.0	3,541,901	-48,406	-1.3	11,445,020	312,398	2.8
1997	178,924,894	-4,558,799	-2.5	41,273,181	8,082,760	24.4	3,590,307	621,845	20.9	11,132,622	491,851	4.6
1996	183,483,693	-1,636,299	-0.9	33,190,421	1,383,158	4.3	2,968,462	148,214	5.3	10,640,771	121,302	1.2
1995	185,119,992	3,619,653	2.0	31,807,263	3,384,230	11.9	2,820,248	508,700	22.0	10,519,469	1,459,981	16.1
1994	181,500,339	-2,926,609	-1.6	28,423,033	475,592	1.7	2,311,548	262,828	12.8	9,059,488	255,468	2.9
1993	184,426,948	1,345,741	0.7	27,947,441	-282,308	-1.0	2,048,720	56,155	2.8	8,804,020	1,007,913	12.9
1992	183,081,207	-10,469,218	-5.4	28,229,749	-617,609	-2.1	1,992,565	227,399	12.9	7,796,107	1,309,818	20.2
1991	193,550,425	14,263,523	8.0	28,847,358	3,445,732	13.6	1,765,166	287,272	19.4	6,486,289	796,229	14.0
1990	179,286,902	6,674,713	3.8	25,401,626	1,685,455	7.1	1,477,894	74,955	5.3	5,690,060	356,172	6.7

Year											
1989	172,612,189	-3,931,853	-2.2	23,716,171	-1,955,147	-7.8	1,402,939	75,215	5.7	5,333,888	141,382	2.7
1988	176,544,042	-5,206,284	-2.9	25,671,318	-2,256,401	-8.1	1,327,724	74,839	6.0	5,192,506	343,381	7.1
1987	181,750,326	-1,931,063	-1.1	27,927,719	-852,373	-3.0	1,252,885	56,034	4.7	4,849,125	563,200	13.1
1986	183,681,389	-4,505,240	-2.4	28,780,092	2,077,397	7.8	1,196,851	102,643	9.4	4,285,925	401,286	10.3
1985	187,985,466	20,085,235	11.9	26,702,695	1,196,672	4.7	1,094,208	238,077	27.8	3,884,639	-119,500	-3.0
1984	167,933,486	12,513,288	8.0	25,506,023	3,425,999	15.5	856,131	244,755	40.0	4,004,139	817,048	25.6
1983	155,588,106	3,190,222	2.1	22,080,024	-1,478,539	-6.3	611,376	60,775	11.0	3,187,091	328,180	11.5
1982	152,397,884	23,533,140	18.3	23,558,563	3,489,774	17.4	550,601	-534,772	-49.3	2,858,911	223,903	8.5
1981	128,864,744	27,971,359	27.7	20,068,789	4,742,668	30.9	1,085,373	297,844	37.8	2,635,008	813,087	44.6
1980	100,893,385	–	–	15,326,121	–	–	787,529	–	–	1,821,921	–	–

NA = Not applicable because figures are not comparable to previous years' figures.

* For FY 2004, the new FPDS-NG data shown here reflect all contract actions available for small business competition (excluding some categories), not just those over $25,000. The figures and are not strictly comparable with those shown for previous years; therefore, the change from the previous year is not shown.

Source: Federal Procurement Data System, "Special Report S89522C" (prepared for the U.S. Small Business Administration, Office of Advocacy, June 12, 1989); and idem., *Federal Procurement Report* (Washington, D.C.: U.S. Government Printing Office, July 10, 1990, March 13, 1991, February 3, 1994, January 13, 1997, 1998, 1999, 2000), and Eagle Eye Publishers.

Table 3.8 Contract Actions Over $25,000, FY 1984–FY 2003, and FY 2004 Total* with Annual 8(a) Set-Aside Breakout

Fiscal Year	Thousands of dollars		8(a) share (percent)
	Total	8(a) set-aside	
2004*	299,886,098	8,438,046	2.8
2003	292,319,145	10,043,219	3.4
2002	258,125,273	7,868,727	3.0
2001	248,985,613	6,339,607	2.5
2000	207,537,686	5,785,276	2.8
1999	188,865,248	6,125,439	3.2
1998	184,176,554	6,527,210	3.5
1997	179,227,203	6,510,442	3.6
1996	183,489,567	6,764,912	3.7
1995	185,119,992	6,911,080	3.7
1994	181,500,339	5,977,455	3.3
1993	184,426,948	5,483,544	3.0
1992	183,081,207	5,205,080	2.8
1991	193,550,425	4,147,148	2.1
1990	179,286,902	3,743,970	2.1
1989	172,612,189	3,449,860	2.0
1988	176,544,042	3,528,790	2.0
1987	181,750,326	3,341,841	1.8
1986	183,681,389	2,935,633	1.6
1985	188,186,629	2,669,174	1.4
1984	168,101,394	2,517,738	1.5

*For FY 2004, the new FPDS-NG data shown here reflect all contract actions available for small business competition (excluding some categories), not just those over $25,000. The figures are not strictly comparable with those shown for previous years.

Source: General Services Administration, Federal Procurement Data Center.

4 MINORITY ENTREPRENEURSHIP

Synopsis

Minority entrepreneurship continues to be an important facet of the American small business mainstream.[1] Of the various ethnic and racial groups in the United States, White non-Latinos and Asians have the highest self-employment rates. The likelihood of business ownership among Latinos is roughly 60 percent of that for White non-Latinos and the African-American self-employment rate is roughly 40 percent of the White non-Latino rate.

Trends among the groups differ by gender, so the analysis of trends in self-employment by race and ethnicity includes separate discussions for men and women. The White male self-employment rate rose by slightly more than 2 percentage points from 1979 to 1993, dropped the next year, and has essentially remained at the lower level. The male African-American self-employment rate remained roughly constant in the 1980s, increased in the early 1990s, decreased in the late 1990s, increased again in the 2000s, and hit a high point in 2003. Self-employment among Latino men has fluctuated around 8 percent, while the business ownership rate for Asian men declined by more than 2 percentage points from 1989 to 2003. Asian men continue to have the highest rate of business ownership among minority groups.

Female self-employment rates generally increased sharply from 1979 to the mid-1990s. Business ownership rates for African-American women and Latinas increased fairly steadily over the entire period. Self-employment rates for Asian women remained roughly constant over the period.

The research looks at causes for lower rates of minority business ownership, as well as the literature on racial differences in business outcomes and at contracting set-asides, a key public policy addressing minority business development.

---

1   This chapter was prepared under contract with the U.S. Small Business Administration, Office of Advocacy by Robert W. Fairlie, University of California, Santa Cruz, rfairlie@ucsc.edu, with review by Ying Lowrey of the Office of Advocacy.

Introduction

African-American and Latino business ownership rates, compared with White and Asian business ownership rates, reveal striking differences. Estimates from the 2000 Census indicate that 11.8 percent of White workers and 10.9 percent of Asian workers are self-employed business owners, whereas only 4.8 percent of Black workers and 7.2 percent of Latino workers are business owners. Furthermore, African-American/White differences in business ownership rates have remained roughly constant over most of the twentieth century.[2]

In addition to lower rates of business ownership, African-American and Latino firms are less successful on average than are White or Asian firms. In particular, businesses owned by African Americans and Latinos have lower sales, hire fewer employees, and have smaller payrolls than White-owned businesses.[3] African-American-owned firms also have lower profits and higher closure rates than White-owned firms.[4]

The relatively smaller number and weaker performance of minority-owned businesses in the United States is a major concern among policymakers. A large number of federal, state, and local government programs have provided set-asides and loans to minorities, women, and other disadvantaged groups.[5] In addition, many states and the federal government are promoting self-employment as a way for families to leave the welfare and unemployment insurance rolls.[6] The interest in entrepreneurship and business development programs has been spurred by arguments from academicians and policymakers that entrepreneurship provides a route out of poverty and an alternative to unemployment.[7] It has been argued, for example, that the economic success of several immigrant groups in the United States is in part because of their ownership of small businesses.[8]

---

2 Fairlie and Meyer, 2000.

3 U.S. Census Bureau, 2001, U.S. Small Business Administration, 2001.

4 U.S. Census Bureau, 1997, U.S. Small Business Administration, 1999.

5 See Bates, 1993a, for a description of programs promoting self-employment among minorities.

6 Vroman 1997, Kosanovich, et al., 2001, Guy, Doolittle, and Fink, 1991, and Raheim, 1997.

7 Glazer and Moynihan, 1970, Light, 1972, 1979, Sowell, 1981, and Moore, 1983.

8 Loewen, 1971, Light, 1972, Baron, et al., 1975, Bonacich and Modell, 1980, and Min, 1996.

Minority-owned firms hired more than 4.2 million employees in the United States in 1997, a disproportionate share of them minorities.[9] Self-employed business owners are also unique in that they create jobs for themselves, and it has been argued that political influence comes with success in small business.[10] Finally, business ownership is the main alternative to wage-and-salary employment for making a living, and thus has important implications for earnings and wealth inequality. Both African-American and White entrepreneurs are found to have more upward mobility and less downward mobility in the wealth distribution than wage-and-salary workers.[11]

This review of the recent and rapidly expanding literature on minority business ownership will focus on four major research topics:

- Current patterns and recent trends in business ownership and outcomes by race and ethnicity in the United States and internationally,
- The major causes of low rates of business ownership among disadvantaged minorities identified in the literature,
- The relatively young and growing literature on racial differences in business outcomes, and
- A key public policy addressing minority business development: contracting set-asides.

For all of these topics, the discussion will focus on new estimates and previous research using large, nationally representative individual- and business-level data.

Trends in Minority Business Ownership

Before discussing the more substantive literature on minority business ownership, it is useful to first lay out the basic facts. A number of major trends in minority business ownership have occurred in the past few decades. Microdata from the 1979 to 2003 Outgoing Rotation Group Files to the Current Population Survey (CPS) are used for this analysis. These data provide an up-to-date estimate of the

---

9 U.S. Census Bureau, 1997, 2001.

10 Brown, Hamilton, and Medoff, 1990

11 Bradford, 2003.

rate of self-employment in the United States. They improve on published estimates from the same source by the Bureau of Labor Statistics (BLS). Regularly published estimates from the BLS, such as those reported in *Employment and Earnings*, do not include incorporated business owners, which represent roughly one-third of all business owners—and that share is growing.[12]

These data may also provide a more accurate representation of recent trends in minority business ownership than the Survey of Minority-Owned Business Enterprises (SMOBE). The scope of businesses included in the SMOBE has changed over the past two decades and the data possibly include a large number of side or "casual" businesses owned by wage-and-salary workers or individuals who are not in the labor force.[13] The Current Population Survey (CPS) microdata include all individuals who identify themselves as self-employed in their own unincorporated or incorporated business on their main job, and thus capture only primary business owners.

Before discussing the trends by race and ethnicity, it is useful to compare overall rates of self-employment across groups *(Chart 4.1 and Table 4.1)*.[14] For this discussion of self-employment rates, the mean value from each of the last three years of the CPS is used to increase sample sizes and remove the emphasis placed on any specific year; therefore, the values will not correspond to any single year's self-employment rate shown in the table.[15] A clear ordering of self-employment propensities across ethnic and racial groups emerges. White non-Latinos and Asians have the highest self-employment rates. Among White non-Latinos, 10.7 percent of the work force is self-employed. The Asian self-employment rate is slightly lower, at 10.3 percent. Relative to these two groups, African Americans and Latinos are much less likely to be self-employed. The likelihood of business ownership among Latinos is roughly 60 percent of that

---

12 See Hipple (2004) for recent estimates of the number of unincorporated and incorporated business owners.

13 The data include individuals who file an IRS form 1040 Schedule C (individual proprietorship or self-employed person), 1065 (partnership), or 1120S (subchapter S corporation). Estimates from the confidential 1992 Characteristics of Business Owners (CBO), which is a sample partly drawn from the SMOBE, indicate that 44.2 percent of owners in the survey report that their businesses provided less than 25 percent of their total personal income (U.S. Bureau of the Census 1997).

14 See Fairlie, 2004c, for estimates for additional demographic groups.

15 In the discussion of trends that follows, the values do correspond to those shown in the tables for the years discussed.

Table 4.1 Self-Employment Rates by Race in Nonagricultural Industries (numbers in thousands; rates in percent)

Years	White, non-Latino Self-employment			Black Self-employment			Latino Self-employment			Asian Self-employment			Total Self-employment		
	Rate	Number	Labor force	Rate	Number	Labor force	Rate	Number	Labor force	Rate	Number	Labor force	Rate	Number	Labor force
1979	10.1	7,066	70,168	3.8	297	7,907	6.1	241	3,956				9.3	7,724	83,503
1980	10.4	7,298	69,988	3.8	300	7,960	6.4	270	4,205				9.6	8,016	83,694
1981	10.6	7,589	71,827	3.8	309	8,203	5.9	269	4,533				9.7	8,380	86,587
1982	10.8	7,663	70,896	3.8	300	7,960	6.6	292	4,430				9.9	8,460	85,405
1983	11.4	8,220	71,953	3.6	298	8,213	6.2	281	4,515				10.4	9,056	86,946
1984	11.4	8,608	75,386	4.0	352	8,908	6.9	337	4,868				10.4	9,568	91,568
1985	11.2	8,497	75,697	3.8	357	9,285	6.3	362	5,774				10.2	9,494	93,327
1986	11.2	8,670	77,401	3.9	374	9,627	7.2	450	6,248				10.2	9,786	95,998
1987	11.4	8,949	78,818	3.8	388	10,179	7.4	496	6,743				10.3	10,175	98,691
1988	11.5	9,294	80,533	4.1	429	10,446	7.4	533	7,203	11.7	319	2,734	10.5	10,617	101,292
1989	11.4	9,384	81,978	3.8	406	10,711	7.5	553	7,392	12.1	372	3,088	10.4	10,711	103,432
1990	11.5	9,381	81,861	4.3	471	11,040	6.9	594	8,588	12.1	381	3,147	10.3	10,881	105,248
1991	11.7	9,407	80,724	4.1	451	10,976	6.7	570	8,563	12.9	418	3,254	10.5	10,880	104,114
1992	11.4	9,217	81,041	3.9	424	11,007	6.6	573	8,675				10.2	10,690	104,687

(continued, next page)

Table 4.1 (continued)

Years	White, non-Latino Self-employment			Black Self-employment			Latino Self-employment			Asian Self-employment			Total Self-employment		
	Rate	Number	Labor force	Rate	Number	Labor force	Rate	Number	Labor force	Rate	Number	Labor force	Rate	Number	Labor force
1993	11.7	9,663	82,244	3.8	431	11,322	7.2	642	8,952	12.2	394	3,218	10.5	11,201	106,498
1994	11.6	9,714	84,005	4.3	507	11,704	6.8	632	9,342	12.2	362	2,953	10.4	11,287	108,801
1995	11.4	9,732	85,336	4.3	526	12,134	6.1	592	9,645	11.2	298	2,661	10.1	11,217	110,594
1996	11.2	9,550	85,032	4.3	538	12,386	6.6	661	9,953	11.3	460	4,074	10.0	11,258	112,238
1997	11.3	9,738	86,490	4.1	530	12,828	6.4	697	10,935	11.1	488	4,375	10.0	11,525	115,537
1998	11.1	9,710	87,353	4.1	544	13,407	6.4	734	11,466	10.8	494	4,595	9.8	11,557	117,730
1999	10.8	9,545	88,536	4.3	602	13,999	6.4	759	11,819	10.9	521	4,771	9.6	11,483	120,015
2000	10.7	9,510	89,108	4.9	697	14,220	5.9	732	12,490	9.4	466	4,977	9.4	11,460	121,743
2001	10.5	9,273	88,560	4.4	629	14,251	6.1	785	12,848	10.5	534	5,077	9.3	11,287	121,707
2002	10.6	9,290	87,788	4.4	621	14,062	6.1	782	12,842	9.9	502	5,077	9.3	11,268	120,803
2003	11.1	9,658	87,305	5.2	710	13,717	7.0	1,032	14,777	10.4	590	5,647	9.8	12,176	123,830

Notes: The sample includes individuals ages 16 and over who work 15 or more hours during the survey week. Agricultural industries are defined using the NAICS classifications and are excluded. Estimates for 1979 to 1991 also exclude veterinary services. Race and Spanish codes changed in 1989, 1996, and 2003, and the CPS was redesigned in 1994. Estimates for 2003 only include individuals reporting one race

Source: Author's calculations using microdata from the Current Population Survey, Outgoing Rotation Group Files (1979–2003).

Chart 4.1 Self-Employment Rates for All Workers
Current Population Survey, Outgoing Rotation Group Files (1979–2003)

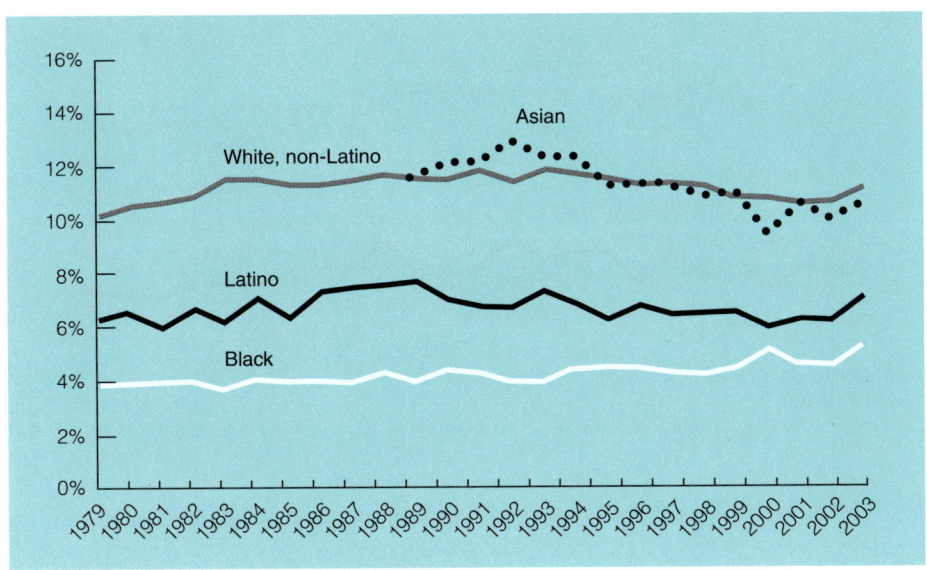

for White non-Latinos. Of the four ethnic/racial groups identified in this analysis, African Americans have the lowest rates of business ownership. For example, the African-American self-employment rate of 4.7 percent is roughly 40 percent of the White non-Latino rate. Similarly low rates of African-American business ownership relative to Whites date back to at least 1910.[16] Clearly, the two largest disadvantaged minority groups in the United States—African Americans and Latinos—are substantially underrepresented in business ownership.

Examining self-employed business ownership rates by race separately for men and women generally reveals similar differences, with women having lower rates than men for all groups *(Charts 4.2 and 4.3 and Tables 4.2 and 4.3).* The one exception is that Asian women have the highest business ownership rate at 8.3 percent instead of White women (7.3 percent). African-American and Latino men and women are much less likely to own businesses than White non-Latino men and women, respectively.

---

16   See Fairlie and Meyer, 2000.

Chart 4.2 Self-Employment Rates for Working Men
Current Population Survey, Outgoing Rotation Group Files (1979–2003)

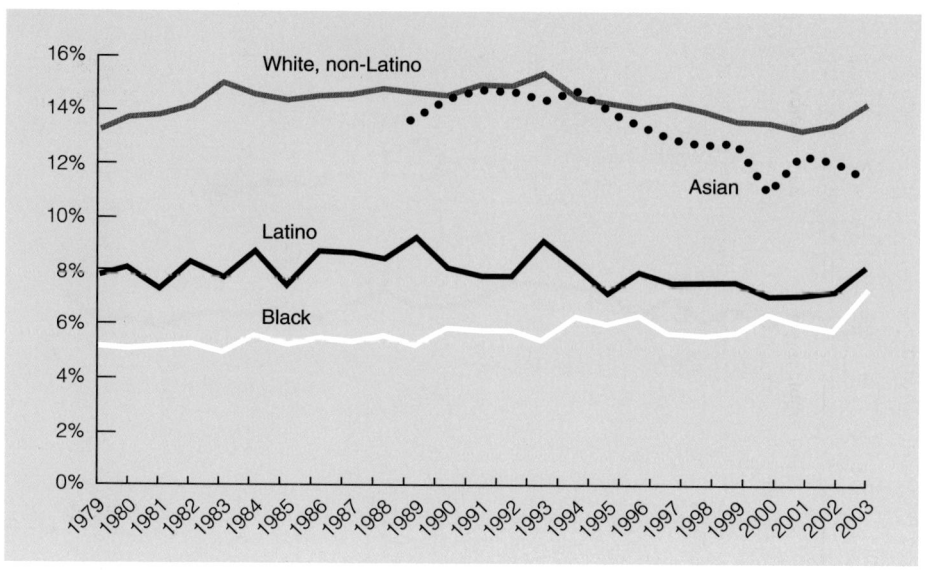

Chart 4.3 Self-Employment Rates for Working Women
Current Population Survey, Outgoing Rotation Group Files (1979–2003)

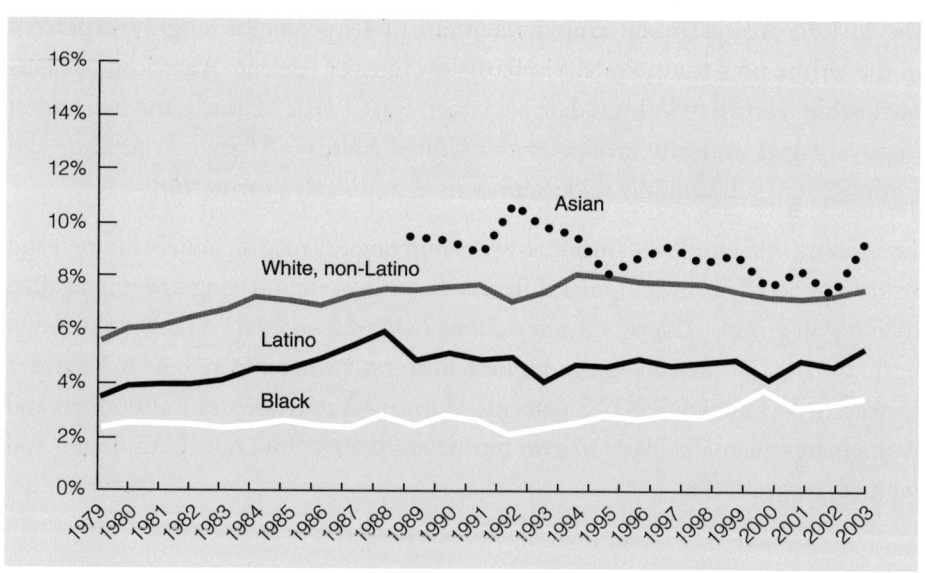

Table 4.2 Male Self-Employment Rates by Race in Nonagricultural Industries (numbers in thousands; rates in percent)

Years	White, non-Latino Self-employment			Black Self-employment			Latino Self-employment			Asian Self-employment			Total Self-employment		
	Rate	Number	Labor force	Rate	Number	Labor force	Rate	Number	Labor force	Rate	Number	Labor force	Rate	Number	Labor force
1979	13.1	5,496	41,888	5.1	213	4,182	7.8	191	2,456				12.1	5,982	49,318
1980	13.6	5,609	41,230	5.0	207	4,141	8.0	207	2,592				12.6	6,124	48,774
1981	13.8	5,784	41,998	5.1	216	4,244	7.2	200	2,782				12.7	6,349	50,155
1982	14.1	5,788	41,050	5.1	208	4,042	8.3	222	2,678				13.0	6,370	48,949
1983	14.9	6,178	41,390	4.9	207	4,203	7.6	207	2,707				13.7	6,777	49,553
1984	14.6	6,329	43,473	5.5	247	4,519	8.6	247	2,863				13.4	7,012	52,165
1985	14.4	6,216	43,246	5.2	242	4,698	7.4	262	3,550				13.0	6,900	52,907
1986	14.5	6,355	43,842	5.4	263	4,861	8.7	334	3,846				13.2	7,137	54,041
1987	14.5	6,461	44,460	5.3	273	5,143	8.6	357	4,138				13.2	7,318	55,331
1988	14.7	6,659	45,228	5.5	286	5,228	8.4	366	4,349				13.4	7,562	56,516
1989	14.6	6,693	45,862	5.2	280	5,374	9.2	412	4,497	13.7	199	1,454	13.2	7,619	57,540
1990	14.6	6,637	45,588	5.8	319	5,488	8.1	426	5,279	14.4	243	1,689	13.1	7,667	58,424
1991	14.9	6,668	44,782	5.7	313	5,451	7.8	408	5,242	14.7	259	1,761	13.4	7,693	57,622

(continued, next page)

Table 4.2 (continued)

Years	White, non-Latino Self-employment Rate	White, non-Latino Self-employment Number	White, non-Latino Labor force	Black Self-employment Rate	Black Self-employment Number	Black Labor force	Latino Self-employment Rate	Latino Self-employment Number	Latino Labor force	Asian Self-employment Rate	Asian Self-employment Number	Asian Labor force	Total Self-employment Rate	Total Self-employment Number	Total Labor force
1992	14.9	6,664	44,871	5.7	308	5,413	7.7	406	5,275	14.6	263	1,796	13.3	7,679	57,752
1993	15.3	6,942	45,374	5.3	298	5,576	9.1	502	5,511	14.3	250	1,751	13.7	8,038	58,624
1994	14.4	6,694	46,421	6.2	356	5,750	8.1	462	5,714	14.7	232	1,582	13.0	7,796	59,919
1995	14.2	6,693	47,213	6.0	354	5,946	7.1	418	5,861	13.9	197	1,412	12.7	7,711	60,890
1996	14.1	6,607	46,997	6.2	369	5,970	7.8	472	6,061	13.4	298	2,218	12.6	7,781	61,675
1997	14.2	6,736	47,568	5.6	346	6,137	7.5	500	6,677	12.9	305	2,371	12.6	7,939	63,257
1998	13.9	6,694	48,080	5.6	356	6,407	7.5	523	6,951	12.7	319	2,515	12.3	7,943	64,454
1999	13.5	6,614	48,869	5.7	373	6,575	7.5	525	6,995	12.8	326	2,560	12.0	7,869	65,472
2000	13.5	6,606	49,007	6.3	420	6,684	7.0	519	7,365	10.9	292	2,634	11.9	7,868	66,258
2001	13.2	6,422	48,675	5.9	398	6,699	7.1	529	7,508	12.3	343	2,793	11.7	7,738	66,189
2002	13.4	6,423	48,109	5.8	386	6,682	7.2	535	7,460	12.0	332	2,760	11.8	7,722	65,570
2003	14.1	6,668	47,317	7.2	461	6,399	8.1	731	9,053	11.5	351	3,058	12.4	8,336	67,080

Notes: The sample includes individuals ages 16 and over who work 15 or more hours during the survey week. Agricultural industries are defined using the NAICS classifications and are excluded. Estimates for 1979 to 1991 also exclude veterinary services. Race and Spanish codes changed in 1989, 1996, and 2003, and the CPS was redesigned in 1994. Estimates for 2003 only include individuals reporting one race

Source: Author's calculations using microdata from the Current Population Survey, Outgoing Rotation Group Files (1979–2003).

Table 4.3 Female Self-Employment Rates by Race in Nonagricultural Industries (numbers in thousands; rates in percent)

Years	White, non-Latino			Black			Latino			Asian			Total		
	Self-employment		Labor force	Self-employment		Labor force	Self-employment		Labor force	Self-employment		Labor force	Self-employment		Labor force
	Rate	Number		Rate	Number		Rate	Number		Rate	Number		Rate	Number	
1979	5.6	1,570	28,280	2.2	84	3,725	3.3	50	1,500				5.1	1,741	34,185
1980	5.9	1,689	28,758	2.4	93	3,819	3.9	62	1,613				5.4	1,892	34,921
1981	6.1	1,805	29,829	2.4	94	3,959	3.9	68	1,751				5.6	2,031	36,432
1982	6.3	1,875	29,847	2.4	92	3,918	4.0	69	1,752				5.7	2,089	36,456
1983	6.7	2,043	30,563	2.3	91	4,009	4.1	74	1,808				6.1	2,279	37,394
1984	7.1	2,279	31,912	2.4	105	4,388	4.5	90	2,005				6.5	2,556	39,403
1985	7.0	2,281	32,452	2.5	115	4,587	4.5	100	2,224				6.4	2,595	40,420
1986	6.9	2,315	33,559	2.3	112	4,766	4.8	116	2,402				6.3	2,649	41,957
1987	7.2	2,488	34,358	2.3	115	5,037	5.4	139	2,606				6.6	2,857	43,360
1988	7.5	2,635	35,305	2.7	143	5,218	5.8	167	2,853				6.8	3,055	44,776
1989	7.5	2,691	36,116	2.4	126	5,337	4.9	141	2,894	9.4	120	1,280	6.7	3,091	45,892
1990	7.6	2,743	36,273	2.7	152	5,551	5.1	168	3,308	9.3	130	1,399	6.9	3,213	46,824
1991	7.6	2,739	35,942	2.5	138	5,525	4.9	162	3,321	8.8	123	1,386	6.9	3,187	46,492

(continued, next page)

Table 4.3 (continued)

Years	White, non-Latino Self-employment			Black Self-employment			Latino Self-employment			Asian Self-employment			Total Self-employment		
	Rate	Number	Labor force	Rate	Number	Labor force	Rate	Number	Labor force	Rate	Number	Labor force	Rate	Number	Labor force
1992	7.1	2,553	36,170	2.1	116	5,593	4.9	167	3,400	10.6	155	1,459	6.4	3,011	46,935
1993	7.4	2,720	36,869	2.3	133	5,746	4.1	140	3,441	9.8	144	1,466	6.6	3,163	47,874
1994	8.0	3,020	37,585	2.5	151	5,954	4.7	170	3,628	9.4	129	1,371	7.1	3,491	48,883
1995	8.0	3,039	38,123	2.8	172	6,189	4.6	175	3,784	8.1	101	1,249	7.1	3,506	49,704
1996	7.7	2,943	38,035	2.6	169	6,416	4.9	189	3,892	8.7	162	1,856	6.9	3,478	50,563
1997	7.7	3,002	38,921	2.7	184	6,692	4.6	197	4,258	9.1	182	2,004	6.9	3,586	52,279
1998	7.7	3,016	39,273	2.7	188	7,000	4.7	211	4,515	8.4	175	2,080	6.8	3,613	53,276
1999	7.4	2,932	39,667	3.1	230	7,425	4.8	234	4,824	8.8	195	2,211	6.6	3,615	54,544
2000	7.2	2,904	40,101	3.7	277	7,536	4.1	213	5,125	7.6	174	2,293	6.5	3,592	55,485
2001	7.1	2,851	39,886	3.1	231	7,553	4.8	255	5,340	8.3	190	2,284	6.4	3,549	55,518
2002	7.2	2,867	39,680	3.2	235	7,380	4.6	247	5,382	7.3	170	2,317	6.4	3,546	55,233
2003	7.5	2,990	39,989	3.4	249	7,318	5.3	301	5,724	9.2	239	2,589	6.8	3,839	56,750

Notes: The sample includes individuals ages 16 and over who work 15 or more hours during the survey week. Agricultural industries are defined using the NAICS classifications and are excluded. Estimates for 1979 to 1991 also exclude veterinary services. Race and Spanish codes changed in 1989, 1996, and 2003, and the CPS was redesigned in 1994. Estimates for 2003 only include individuals reporting one race

Source: Author's calculations using microdata from the Current Population Survey, Outgoing Rotation Group Files (1979–2003).

The ordering of self-employment rates across ethnic/racial groups is similar to that reported in previous studies using alternative data sources and years. These include, but are not limited to, estimates for some or all groups from the 1980 Census,[17] the 1990 Census,[18] the General Social Survey,[19] the Panel Study of Income Dynamics,[20] and the Survey of Income and Program Participation.[21]

Because the trends differ by gender, the analysis of trends in self-employment by race and ethnicity includes separate discussions for men and women. The White male self-employment rate rose by slightly more than 2 percentage points from 1979 to 1993.[22] It then dropped by a percentage point the next year and has essentially remained at this lower level. Some caution is warranted, however, in interpreting the drop from 1993 to 1994 as it may simply be a result of the 1994 CPS redesign.[23] Although the rate was relatively flat in the late 1990s and dipped in the early 2000s, the White male business ownership rate of 14.1 percent is very similar to the rate of 14.4 percent in 1994. Over the entire period, the self-employment rate rose by 1 percentage point.

The male African-American self-employment rate remained roughly constant in the 1980s, increased in the early 1990s and decreased in the late 1990s *(Chart 2.2)*. In the 2000s the rate of business ownership increased again and hit a high point in 2003. The 2003 estimate appears to be an outlier. Overall, business ownership rates have increased over the past 24 years by a full percentage point, from roughly 5 to 6 percent. These trends indicate that business ownership for African-American men is rising at a faster rate than for White men, suggesting that the racial gap is closing in percentage terms. At the same time, it is clear that African-American men had lower self-employment rates than any other group of men for the entire period.

---

17 Borjas, 1986, Borjas and Bronars,1989, Light and Rosenstein,1995.

18 Fairlie and Meyer, 1996 and Razin and Light, 1998.

19 Hout and Rosen, 2000.

20 Fairlie, 1999.

21 Meyer, 1990, Bates, 1997.

22 Estimates reported in Aronson, 1991, Blau, 1987, and Fairlie and Meyer, 2000, indicate that the upward trend in the male self-employment rate dates back to the early 1970s.

23 See Polivika and Miller, 1998, and Fairlie and Meyer, 2000, for more discussion.

Over the past 24 years, the self-employment rate among Latino men has fluctuated around 8 percent. The self-employment rate was 7.8 percent in 1979 and 8.1 percent in 2003. The constancy of the business ownership rate is somewhat surprising in light of the rapid increase in the Latino work force over this period. These two trends have led to a large increase in the total number of Latino business owners over the past 24 years.

The business ownership rate for Asian men declined by more than 2 percentage points from 1989 to 2003. Unfortunately, the CPS does not allow identification of Asians prior to 1989. In 1989, the self-employment rate was 13.7 percent and by 2003 the rate dropped to 11.5 percent. Although the group's self-employment rate has declined over the past decade, Asian men continue to have the highest rate of business ownership among minority groups and have rates only slightly lower than those of White men.

Several previous studies provide evidence that levels of female self-employment have been increasing rapidly in recent decades.[24] In contrast to the male trends, female self-employment rates increased sharply from 1979 to the mid-1990s *(Chart 4.3)*. The White female self-employment rate was 5.6 percent in 1979 and rose to 7.4 percent in 1993 and 8.0 percent in 1994. The rapid convergence of male and female business ownership rates, however, appears to have ended or at least flattened. Since the late 1990s, the White female self-employment rate has declined slightly from the mid-1990s highs.

Trends for minority women are different. For African-American women and Latinas, the business ownership rate increased fairly steadily over the entire period. African-American self-employment rates were 2.2 percent in 1979 and 3.4 percent by 2003, and Latina rates rose from 3.3 percent to 5.3 percent. In relative terms, African-American women and Latinas made gains on both White women and minority men over this period. In contrast to these sharp trends, self-employment rates for Asian women remained roughly constant over the period.

---

24 See Aronson, 1991, Devine, 1994 and U.S. Small Business Administration, 1998, for example.

Although there is little evidence in the literature on what has contributed to these trends, especially in the past few years, there is some evidence on the causes of racial differences in trends from 1979 to 1998. Using a dynamic decomposition technique, Fairlie explores the causes of racial differences in trends in self-employment rates over this period.[25] Several interesting patterns are revealed. For example, increasing levels of education among African-American men relative to White men may have contributed to the narrowing of the White/African-American self-employment rate gap between the 1979–1981 and 1996–1998 periods. In contrast, the White/Latino gap increased over the period partly because Latino men did not experience gains in education relative to White men. Differential trends in the age distribution of the work force across racial groups may also have contributed to relative trends in self-employment rates. For all minority groups, the work force aged less rapidly than for Whites, reducing the self-employment rates of these groups relative to the White self-employment rate.

International Comparison

Are the ethnic and racial differences in business ownership unique to the United States? The answer to this question has important implications for the thinking about the causes and potential solutions to racial disparities in business ownership. Using aggregate data from the 2001 Canadian and United Kingdom Censuses and microdata from the 2000 U.S. Census, the researcher provides estimates of self-employment rates by ethnicity and race *(Table 4.4)*. All ethnic/racial groups that are roughly comparable for at least two of the three countries are selected. Black self-employment rates are higher in the United Kingdom than in Canada and the United States, but remain relatively low. Even in the United Kingdom, where 8.3 percent of Blacks are self-employed business owners, this represents less than two-thirds of the White rate of business ownership. Latinos have similarly low self-employment rates in both Canada and the United States. For example, only 7.2 percent of Latinos are self-employed business owners in the United States and 7.9 percent of Latinos in Canada are self-employed. Finally, Asians have substantially higher rates of business ownership in the United Kingdom than in Canada and the United States. In the United Kingdom, they also have higher rates than Whites.

---

25   See Fairlie, 2004b.

Table 4.4 Self-Employment Rates by Race/Ethnicity for Selected Countries, 2000–2001

	Canada		United Kingdom		United States	
	Self-employment rate (percent)	Workers (thousands)	Self-employment rate (percent)	Workers (thousands)	Self-employment rate (percent)	Workers (thousands)
Total	12.0	15,516	13.7	22,796	10.6	115,146
White	12.4	13,208	13.6	21,277	11.8	85,743
Black	6.1	315	8.3	424	4.8	11,368
Latino	7.9	114			7.2	10,696
Asian	11.0	1,284	18.7	849	10.9	4,034

Notes: Canadian minority groups include multiracial responses to the race question. Canadian Whites, and all U.S. and U.K. groups include only monoracial responses to the race question.

Sources: Estimates are from the Canadian 2001 Census, the United Kingdom 2001 Census and the U.S. 5 Percent Public Use Microdata Sample from the 2000 Census.

The estimates indicate a clear pattern in ethnic/racial entrepreneurship—disadvantaged groups, such as Blacks and Latinos, have relatively low rates of business ownership in all of the countries reported. Thus, low rates of business ownership among these ethnic/racial groups are not peculiar to the United States or one country. Although more cross-country research is needed, disadvantaged groups may have similar characteristics associated with lower levels of entrepreneurship or face similar institutional barriers such as consumer or lending discrimination in each of the countries.

Minority Business Outcomes

Although racial disparities in business ownership have been the focus of many previous studies, there is less evidence in the literature on whether the businesses created by disadvantaged minorities are also less successful. In this section, the researcher presents results from firm-level datasets. Estimates from the 1997 Survey of Minority Owned Business Enterprises (SMOBE) indicate that African-American and Latino firms have lower sales, hire fewer employees, and have smaller payrolls than White or Asian-owned firms

(Table 4.5).[26] Average sales and receipts are $86,478 for African-American-owned firms and $155,242 for Latino-owned firms. In contrast, White-owned firms have average sales of $448,294 and Asian-owned firms have average sales of $338,852. For each reported measure of employment, White-owned businesses are significantly larger than African-American- and Latino-owned businesses. Asian-owned businesses are more likely to hire at least one employee than White-owned businesses, but hire fewer employees on average and have a much lower average payroll.

Estimates from other data sources paint a similar picture for the state of minority business. Estimates from the 1992 Characteristics of Business Owners (CBO) indicate that African-American-owned firms have lower revenues and profits, hire fewer employees, and are more likely to close than White-owned businesses.[27] Latino-owned firms are also less successful than White-owned firms, but the differences are smaller and, for profits and closure rates, the differences are negligible. Estimates from the 1998 Survey of Small Business Finances indicate that African-American- and Latino-owned businesses hire fewer employees than White-owned businesses.[28] Minority-owned businesses also have lower sales and end-of-year assets, and are younger than businesses owned by Whites. Additional evidence indicates that closure rates are high among African-American-owned firms.[29] Finally, Asian-owned firms have somewhat lower average sales than White-owned firms, but slightly higher survival rates and profits than White-owned firms.[30]

Focusing on employer firms, two recent studies use special administrative panel data on minority-owned businesses to examine survival and other dynamic outcomes. Robb links Business Information Tracking Series (BITS) data from 1992 to 1996 to SMOBE microdata from 1992 and examines firm survival

---

26 See U.S. Bureau of the Census, 2001 and U.S. Small Business Administration, 1999, 2001 for more details including recent trends in business outcomes.

27 U.S. Department of Commerce, 1997.

28 Bitler, Robb, and Wolken, 2001.

29 Bates, 1997, Boden and Headd, 2002, and Robb, 2000, 2002.

30 Bates, 1997.

Table 4.5 Business Outcomes by Race

	White- owned firms	African- American- owned firms	Latino- owned firms	Asian- owned firms
Total number of firms	17,316,796	823,499	1,199,896	893,590
Mean sales and receipts (dollars)	448,294	86,478	155,242	338,852
Firms with paid employees (percent)	25.3	11.3	17.7	32.1
Mean number of paid employees	3.1	0.9	1.2	2.4
Mean annual payroll for employer firms (dollars)	319,051	153,615	140,785	158,185

Source: U.S. Department of Commerce, Bureau of the Census, Company Summary, Economic Census, Survey of Minority Business Enterprises (2001).

rates by race.[31] She finds that 48.7 percent of White employer firms and 51.7 percent of Asian employer firms survived from 1992 to 1996. In contrast, only 34.8 percent of African-American employer firms and 43.7 percent of Latino employer firms survived over this period. Lowrey uses a special Census dataset that tracks 1997 SMOBE respondents over time to examine racial differences in survival, contraction, and expansion among employer firms from 1997 to 2001.[32] She also finds lower survival rates among African-American- and Latino-owned establishments than among nonminority and Asian-owned establishments. In contrast to these results, however, she finds that Latino-owned establishments had a higher expansion rate, and African-American- and Latino-owned establishments had lower contraction rates than White-owned establishments. Asian-owned establishments had a higher expansion rate, but a slightly higher contraction rate than firms owned by Whites.

31 Robb, 2004.

32 Lowrey, 2005.

Explanations for Racial Differences in Business Ownership

What are the causes of lower business ownership rates among African Americans and Latinos in the United States? A number of factors are addressed in the previous literature. Emphasis is placed here on previous research that provides estimates of the magnitude of explanatory factors in explaining racial differences in business ownership rates in addition to identifying these factors.

The Opportunity Cost of Owning a Business

The standard economic model of the self-employment decision posits that individuals choose the work sector that provides the highest utility—wage-and-salary work or self-employment.[33] The main component of this comparison is potential earnings in the two sectors. Minorities may be less likely to choose self-employment than Whites because of lower relative earnings in the self-employment sector. Opportunities in self-employment may be less attractive for minorities and/or opportunities in the wage-and-salary sector may be more attractive relative to those for Whites. Previous research focusing on highly educated workers finds that African-American scientists and engineers were less likely than Asian scientists and engineers to enter business ownership because of more favorable returns in the wage-and-salary sector.[34]

The mean, median, and standard deviation of total annual earnings of self-employed and wage-and-salary workers by race provide some useful information *(Table 4.6)*. Only full-year, full-time workers are included in the sample to control for differences in hours worked. For all groups of men, the self-employed earn substantially more on average than do wage-and-salary workers. Self-employed African American and Latino men earn $9,444 and $11,052 more than their wage-and-salary counterparts, respectively.[35] These differences are large, representing roughly 25–30 percent of average wage-and-salary earnings. A comparison of means can create a distorted picture, however,

---

33 Kihlstrom and Laffont, 1979, and Evans and Jovanovic, 1989.

34 Tang, 1995.

35 Higher average self-employment earnings are also found after controlling for individual characteristics (see Portes and Zhou 1999 and Fairlie 2004a for example).

Table 4.6 Self-Employment and Wage-and-Salary Earnings by Race and Ethnicity (dollars, except sample sizes)

	Men		Women	
	Self-employed	Wage/salary	Self-employed	Wage/salary
White, non-Latinos				
Mean	71,695	57,105	36,349	39,223
Median	45,000	44,878	25,570	32,729
Standard deviation	83,024	51,483	46,622	32,607
Sample size (number sampled)	14,163	96,058	5,057	72,885
Blacks				
Mean	48,775	39,331	30,716	31,924
Median	36,000	32,590	20,779	27,451
Standard deviation	60,359	32,645	44,413	25,796
Sample size (number sampled)	682	12,073	413	14,624
Latinos				
Mean	45,442	34,390	28,164	27,726
Median	30,300	27,013	20,779	22,439
Standard deviation	64,428	33,984	37,782	24,800
Sample size (number sampled)	1,436	19,614	579	12,934
Asians				
Mean	64,266	58,349	39,653	41,114
Median	44,178	44,178	25,570	33,133
Standard deviation	76,439	53,464	56,588	36,252
Sample size (number sampled)	800	6,104	445	5,067

Notes: (1) The sample consists of individuals who work at least 40 weeks and 35 hours per usual week in the previous year. (2) All calculations use sample weights provided by the CPS.

Source: Author's calculations using microdata from the Current Population Survey. Annual Demographic Files (2000–04).

if a few business owners are extremely successful. Comparing median income levels removes these concerns. For both African American and Latino men, median self-employment earnings are substantially higher than median wage-and-salary earnings; however, the differences are much smaller.

Although average and median earnings are higher for self-employed African American and Latino men, it is important to also compare the variance of earnings in the two sectors. For both races, the standard deviation of self-employment income is substantially higher than that of wage-and-salary income, suggesting that a much larger percentage of the self-employed men have very high or very low earnings than male wage-and-salary workers.

The researcher also reports characteristics of the earnings distribution for White men. The most notable difference is that White men earn substantially more than either African-American or Latino men in both the self-employment and wage-and-salary sectors. Of interest to this analysis, however, is the difference between the two sectors. Using mean earnings, self-employed White men earn substantially more than their wage-and-salary counterparts, whereas in median earnings there is essentially no difference. Asian men also experience higher average self-employment earnings, but similar median self-employment earnings to those of Asian wage-and-salary workers.

For men, the earnings estimates do not shed light on why African Americans and Latinos have substantially lower business ownership rates than Whites and Asians. The most consistent differences between self-employment and wage-and-salary earnings are for African Americans and Latinos. The self-employed earn substantially more than wage-and-salary workers for these two groups, and even for average earnings, the differences in percentage terms are comparable for African Americans and larger for Latinos than for Whites.

Estimates of the mean, median, and standard deviation for self-employment and wage-and-salary earnings for women by race offer insight into the earnings picture for women *(Table 4.6)*. In contrast to men, self-employed White, African-American, Latina, and Asian women earn less than women working in the wage-and-salary sector.[36] The only exception is that mean self-employment

---

36 Fairlie (2004a) finds higher average self-employment earnings after controlling for individual characteristics for Latinas and no difference for African-American women.

earnings are higher for Latinas than mean wage-and-salary earnings. Similar to the results for men, African-American women and Latinas earn substantially less than White and Asian women in both the self-employment and wage-and-salary sectors. Another interesting finding is that the self-employment/wage-and-salary earnings difference is very similar in percentage terms for African Americans, Whites, and Asians. The self-employment/wage-and-salary earnings differential is positive or smaller for Latinas. These patterns clearly do not provide an answer to why substantially lower rates of business ownership are observed among African-American women and Latinas than White and Asian women.

Although the earnings comparison is a key component of the standard theoretical model of entrepreneurship, the decision between wage-and-salary work and self-employment is actually based on a comparison of utility in the two sectors. In addition to earnings in the two sectors, characteristics of the type of work may be important. Theoretical models by Rees and Shah (1986) and Blanchflower and Oswald (1998) specifically take into account "the flexibility associated with hours worked and the independence entailed," and "the nonpecuniary utility from being independent and one's own boss" from self-employment, respectively. A potential explanation for low rates of business ownership may be that minorities have less preference for entrepreneurship.

Overall, the desire for entrepreneurship is strong in the United States and many other countries in the world. When individuals are asked the question of whether they would prefer "being an employee or being self-employed" a large percentage report "self-employment."[37] Slightly more than 70 percent of respondents in the United States express a desire to be self-employed. Interest in self-employment is also strong among minorities. More than 75 percent of young African Americans report being interested in starting their own business.[38] For comparison, 63 percent of young Whites are interested in starting a business.[39] Interestingly, these findings suggest that minorities may have a stronger desire for self-employment, suggesting that different preferences cannot explain racial disparities in business ownership.

---

37 Blanchflower, Oswald, and Stutzer, 2001.

38 Walstad and Kourilsky, 1998.

39 African-American youth are also more likely than White youth to report that it is important "for our nation's schools to teach students about entrepreneurship and starting a business" (Walsted and Kourilsky 1998).

Assets

The importance of assets has taken center stage in the literature on the determinants of self-employment. Numerous studies using various methodologies, measures of assets, and country microdata explore the relationship between assets and self-employment. Several recent studies estimate the relationship by modeling the decision of wage-and-salary workers or other non-business owners to switch into self-employment over a fixed period of time.[40] These studies generally find that asset levels (such as net worth or asset income) measured in one year increase the probability of entering self-employment by the following year, suggesting that entrepreneurs face liquidity constraints.[41]

A few recent studies use inheritances, gifts, lottery winnings or insurance settlements as a measure of assets.[42] Inheritances and other unanticipated, or at least less anticipated, lump sum payments represent a more exogenous or externally derived measure of assets than net worth. Inheritances and other lump sum payments are found to increase the probability of entering or being self-employed, suggesting that entrepreneurs face liquidity constraints.[43] Additional studies find that home prices and home ownership, among other things, increase the likelihood of business creation and self-employment.[44]

---

40 For examples, see Evans and Jovanovic, 1989, Evans and Leighton, 1989, Meyer, 1990, Holtz-Eakin, Joulfaian, and Rosen, 1994, Dunn and Holtz-Eakin, 1999, and Fairlie, 1999; and Hurst and Lusardi, 2004, for evidence from U.S. microdata; Holtz-Eakin and Rosen, 2004, for the United States and Germany; and Johansson, 2000, for Finland.

41 The focus on transitions to self-employment attempts to avoid the endogeneity problem of including assets in a static model of self-employment. A positive relationship found in a cross-sectional analysis may simply reflect the possibility that business owners accumulate more wealth, instead of wealth increasing the likelihood of owning a business.

42 See Holtz-Eakin, Joulfaian, and Rosen, 1994, Fairlie, 1999, and Hurst and Lusardi, 2004, for U.S. microdata; Blanchflower and Oswald, 1998, and Taylor, 2001, for British microdata; and Lind and Ohlsson, 1994, for Swedish data.

43 Hurst and Lusardi, 2004, however, find that future inheritances also increase the probability of self-employment entry, suggesting that liquidity constraints are not the underlying cause of the positive relationship.

44 Fairlie, 2005b, Black, de Meza, and Jeffreys, 1996, Johansson, 2000, and Earle and Sakova, 2000.

Several previous studies also show that African Americans have substantially lower levels of assets than Whites.[45] Although less research focuses on Latinos, disparities in asset levels may be large and may explain why this group is also less likely to become business owners. Indeed, a few recent studies indicate large disparities in wealth between Latinos, especially Mexican-Americans, and White non-Latinos.[46] Estimates from the Survey of Income and Program Participation indicate that the median levels of net worth among native-born and foreign-born Mexicans are $28,690 and $6,276, respectively.[47] The median net worth for African Americans is $23,278. Clearly, all three groups have median levels of net worth that are substantially lower than the median net worth for White non-Latinos, at $76,685.

These findings in the previous literature suggest that relatively low levels of assets among African Americans and Latinos may be a source of racial differences in rates of business ownership. Recent research provides evidence supporting this hypothesis. Using matched CPS Annual Demographic Files (ADF) data from 1998 to 2003, Fairlie finds that the largest single factor explaining racial disparities in business creation rates are differences in asset levels.[48] Lower levels of assets among African Americans account for 15.5 percent of the White/African-American gap in the probability of entry into self-employment. This finding is consistent with the presence of liquidity constraints and low levels of assets limiting opportunities for African Americans to start businesses. The finding is very similar to estimates reported in Fairlie for men using the Panel Study of Income Dynamics (PSID).[49] Estimates from the PSID indicate that 13.9 to 15.2 percent of the African-American/White gap in the transition rate into self-employment can be explained by differences in assets.

---

45 See Blau and Graham, 1992, Oliver and Shapiro, 1995, Menchik and Jianakoplos, 1997, Altonji and Doraszelski, 2001, and Gittleman and Wolff, 2004, for a few recent studies on racial differences in asset levels, and Bradford, 2003, on wealth holding among African-American and White entrepreneurs.

46 See Wolff, 2000, and Cobb-Clark and Hildebrand, 2004.

47 Cobb-Clark and Hildebrand, 2004.

48 Fairlie, 2005a.

49 Fairlie, 1999.

Fairlie also reports separate estimates for native-born and immigrant Latinos.[50] The most important factor in explaining the gaps between the two Latino groups and native-born Whites is also assets. Relatively low levels of assets explain more than half of the entry rate gap for native-born Latinos and slightly less than half of the gap for immigrant Latinos. Apparently, low levels of assets are limiting opportunities for Latinos to start businesses and this factor, at least in percentage terms, is more important for Latinos than for African Americans.

Also contributing to the low rate of business ownership among minorities is a higher rate of exit from self-employment. In fact, the steady-state self-employment rate is simply equal to $E / (E+X)$, where E is the entry rate into self-employment and X is the exit rate from self-employment. Investigating the causes of the higher rate of self-employment exit for African Americans than Whites, Fairlie finds that racial differences in asset levels explain 7.3 percent of the gap using CPS data.[51] This estimate is in the range of estimates from the PSID reported in Fairlie's earlier work.[52] Estimates from the PSID indicate that 1.8 to 11.1 percent of the male African-American/White gap in exit rates from self-employment is explained by differences in asset levels. Recent estimates from the CBO survey indicate that 43.2 percent of the gap in business closure rates is explained by differences in the amount of required startup capital,[53] but the focus on businesses, startup capital, and closure rates makes the results difficult to compare.[54]

Both native-born and immigrant Latinos have substantially higher exit rates than native-born Whites. Lower levels of assets partly explain why Latinos are more likely to leave self-employment. Racial differences in assets explain roughly 10 percent of the gap in self-employment exit rates for each Latino group.

Overall, low levels of assets limit entry into business ownership and increase business exit among minorities. These two patterns combine to create lower rates of business ownership among African Americans and Latinos.

---

50   Fairlie, 2005a.

51   Fairlie, 2005a.

52   Fairlie, 1999.

53   Fairlie and Robb, 2003,

54   Using the 1982 CBO, Bates, 1989, finds that racial differences in levels of financial capital partly explain racial patterns in business failure rates.

Human Capital

Education has been found in the literature to be a major determinant of business ownership. Are relatively low levels of education among African Americans and Latinos partly responsible for limiting opportunities in entrepreneurship? Using CPS data, Fairlie finds that 6.0 percent of the African-American/White gap in self-employment entry rates is explained by racial differences in education levels.[55] African Americans are found to have lower levels of education than Whites. For example, 14.3 percent of African Americans are high school dropouts compared with only 6.2 percent of Whites. Estimates from the PSID reported in Fairlie are similar in one specification and close to zero in another specification.[56]

Latinos, especially immigrants, have very low levels of education, which may translate into a limiting factor in business creation. A surprisingly high 53.1 percent of immigrant Latinos and 20.4 percent of native-born Latinos did not complete high school. Estimates from the CPS indicate that education differences account for 44.8 percent of the entry rate gap for Latino immigrants and 34.3 percent of the entry rate gap for Latino natives.[57] The only factor more important in explaining Latino/White differences in business entry rates is assets.

Examining exit rates using the CPS, Fairlie finds that education plays only a minor role in explaining high exit rates for African Americans.[58] Education explains 3.2 percent of the gap in exit rates. Estimates from the PSID are similar.[59] In contrast, estimates from the Characteristics of Business Owners indicate a larger role for differences in education levels in explaining racial differences in business closure rates. Fairlie and Robb find that group differences in education levels explain 6.5 to 7.8 percent of the African-American/White gap in business closure rates.[60]

---

55 Fairlie, 2005a.

56 Fairlie, 1999.

57 Fairlie, 2005a.

58 Fairlie, 2005a.

59 Fairlie, 1999.

60 Fairlie and Robb, 2003.

Using earlier CBO data from 1982, Bates finds that differences in failure rates between African-American-, nonminority-, and Asian male-owned businesses are partly attributable to the fact that Asian owners tend to be more educated.[61]

Education plays a stronger role in explaining Latino/White differences in exit rates. Group differences in education explain 6.8 and 20.7 percent of the gap in exit rates for native-born Latinos and Latino immigrants, respectively.

Another measure of human capital relevant for Latinos is language ability. Difficulty speaking English may limit opportunities in the wage-and-salary sector, resulting in an increased likelihood of becoming self-employed for some Latinos. In fact, previous research indicates that English language ability affects earnings in the wage-and-salary sector.[62] Interestingly, however, Fairlie and Meyer find that better command of the English language is associated with more self-employment among men, whereas the opposite holds among women.[63] Recent research focusing on Mexican immigrants also finds that English language ability is associated with self-employment rates among men but not among women.[64] The male self-employment rate among those with lower English language ability is 4.7 percent; the comparable number among those who speak English well or fluently is 7.3 percent. The raw differences among women are much smaller. Women with lower language ability have self-employment rates of 5.4 percent; those with fluency or near fluency have self-employment rates of 5.7 percent. The differences do not change substantially after controlling for differences in observable characteristics such as education, age, marital status and children.

Intergenerational Progress and Family Business Capital

A major reason for concern about the lack of business success among African Americans is that they have made little progress in rates of business ownership, even in light of the substantial gains in education, earnings, and civil rights made during the twentieth century. Estimates from Census microdata

---

61 Bates, 1989.

62 McManus, Gould, and Welch, 1983, Dustman and van Soest, 2002, Bleakley and Chin, 2003.

63 Fairlie and Meyer, 1996.

64 Fairlie and Woodruff, 2005.

reported in Fairlie and Meyer (2000) indicate that the 3 to 1 ratio of White to African-American self-employment rates has remained roughly constant over the past 90 years. The question of why there was no convergence in racial self-employment rates over the twentieth century is an important one. Early researchers emphasized the role that past inexperience in business played in creating low rates of business ownership among African Americans. In particular, Du Bois (1899), and later Myrdal (1944), Cayton and Drake (1946), and Frazier (1957) identify the lack of African-American traditions in business enterprise as a major cause of low levels of African-American business ownership at the time of their analyses.

Arguments about the lack of tradition in business ownership for African Americans rely on a strong intergenerational link in business ownership. Theoretically, we might expect the link to be strong because of the transmission of general business or managerial experience in family-owned businesses ("general business human capital"), the acquisition of industry-or firm-specific business experience in family-owned businesses ("specific business human capital"), the inheritance of family businesses, and the correlation among family members in preferences for entrepreneurial activities.[65] Past empirical research supports this conjecture. The probability of self-employment is substantially higher among the children of the self-employed.[66] These studies generally find that an individual who had a self-employed parent is roughly two to three times as likely to be self-employed as someone who did not have a self-employed parent.

Recent research has examined directly whether the strong intergenerational link in business ownership is detrimental to disadvantaged minorities. Hout and Rosen note a "triple disadvantage" faced by African-American men in terms of business ownership.[67] They are less likely than White men to have self-employed fathers, to become self-employed if their fathers were not self-employed, and to follow their fathers in self-employment. Fairlie provides evidence from the PSID that current racial patterns of self-employment are in part determined by

---

65 Dunn and Holtz-Eakin, 2000, consider an additional explanation. Successful business owners may be more likely to transfer financial wealth to their children, potentially making it easier for them to become self-employed. Their empirical results, however, suggest that this plays only a modest role.

66 Lentz and Laband, 1990, Fairlie, 1999, Dunn and Holtz-Eakin, 2000, and Hout and Rosen, 2000.

67 Hout and Rosen, 2000.

racial patterns of self-employment in the previous generation.[68] Finally, Fairlie and Robb find related evidence that the lack of prior work experience in a family business among African-American business owners, perhaps by limiting their acquisition of general and specific business human capital, increases the probability of business closure.[69] They also find that racial differences in business inheritances are negligible and cannot explain differences in closure rates.

Networks and Ethnic Enclaves

The finding that having a self-employed family member increases the likelihood of owning a business and the finding that working for that family member's business increases business success suggest that racial differences in networks more generally may be important in creating disparities in ownership. Previous research indicates that the size and composition of social networks is associated with self-employment.[70] If minority firms have limited access to business, social, or family networks, or have smaller networks, they may be less likely to enter business and create successful businesses. These networks may be especially important in providing financing, customers, technical assistance, role models, and contracts. These same networks, however, are likely to also be useful for finding employment in the wage-and-salary sector, creating a dampening effect on self-employment.

In an earlier study, Fratoe finds that African-American business owners were less likely to have business role models, obtain loans from other family members and use family members as unpaid labor.[71] Social networks may be especially important in industries such as construction, in which deals are often made in informal settings.[72] If minorities are blocked from these industries, perhaps because of discrimination (as discussed below), their business networks may be restricted. Examining the retail industry in New York, Rauch finds evidence that African-American-owned businesses were less able to organize "mutual

---

68 Fairlie, 1999.

69 Fairlie and Robb, 2003.

70 See Allen, 2000, for example.

71 Fratoe, 1988.

72 Feagin and Imani, 1994.

self-help" than immigrant businesses.[73] On the other hand, Bates finds evidence that less successful Asian immigrant-owned businesses were associated with extensive use of social support networks.[74]

Ethnic and racial groups may differ, not only in the size of their networks, but also in their ability to transfer information related to running a business among co-ethnics. Experience as an employee of a small business and transfers of information can be important.[75] Strong patterns of industry concentrations for businesses owned by many ethnic groups are consistent with this explanation.[76] Interestingly, however, the industry concentration of African-American-owned businesses has become more similar to that of White-owned businesses over time, while there has been no convergence in rates of business ownership.

A major limitation of these explanations is that they are difficult to analyze empirically. The problem is that success in business for some groups may simply create larger and more efficient business and social networks. Thus, it is difficult to identify the direction of causation between networks and success. Co-ethnic networks may also create a multiplier effect, whereby small differences in initial business success between groups may lead to large differences in future business success. This point is related to the argument that the lack of a tradition of business enterprise among African Americans is a major cause of current low levels of African-American business ownership.[77]

Ethnic enclaves represent one method of creating and facilitating entry into networks. Of particular importance is that locating in an ethnic enclave may provide a market for special products and services and access to co-ethnic labor.[78] Using a measure of enclave at the Standard Metropolitan Statistical Area (SMSA) level, Borjas finds that self-employment among Mexicans, Cubans, and "other Hispanics" is increasing in the percentage of Hispanics in

---

73 Rauch, 2001.

74 Bates, 1994.

75 Portes and Zhou, 1992, and Meyer, 1990.

76 Fairlie and Meyer, 1994.

77 Du Bois, 1899, Myrdal, 1944, Cayton and Drake, 1946, and Frazier, 1957.

78 Earlier studies making this argument include Kinzer and Sagarin, 1950, Glazer and Moynihan, 1970, and Light, 1972.

an SMSA.[79] The effect is larger among the immigrant population than among the population born in the United States. Using 2000 Census data, Fairlie and Woodruff find that Mexican immigrant self-employment rates are higher for men, but not for women, who live in ethnic enclaves.[80] Ethnic enclaves may explain why some immigrant groups are successful in business, but enclaves can also dampen opportunities for entrepreneurs by creating intense competition among co-ethnics.[81] Ethnic enclaves also cannot explain why native-born African Americans and Latinos have lower rates than native-born Whites.

Discrimination

Additional factors that might explain differing rates of business ownership across ethnic and racial groups are labor market, lending, and consumer discrimination. Unlike the other forms of discrimination, labor market discrimination may increase business entry for some minority groups. Wage and employment discrimination represent disadvantages in the labor market causing some groups to favor self-employment.[82] On the other hand, Coate and Tennyson present a theoretical model positing that labor market discrimination can reduce the incentive for minorities to enter self-employment.[83] This happens because lenders provide less favorable terms in the credit market, such as higher interest rates, to the discriminated group because of the difficulty in observing entrepreneurial ability. Empirical evidence for 60 detailed ethnic/racial groups indicates that more advantaged ethnic/racial groups—measured by wage-and-salary earnings, self-employment earnings and unearned income—and not the more disadvantaged groups—have the highest self-employment rates.[84] Finally, discrimination may occur directly in self-employment through limited opportunities to penetrate networks, such as those in construction.[85]

---

79 Borjas, 1986.

80 Fairlie and Woodruff, 2005.

81 Aldrich and Waldinger, 1990, and Razin and Langlois, 1994.

82 Light, 1972, 1979, Sowell 1981, and Moore, 1983.

83 Coate and Tennyson, 1993.

84 Fairlie and Meyer, 1996.

85 Bates, 1993b, Feagin and Imani, 1994, Bates and Howell, 1997.

Using microdata from the 1980 Census, Borjas and Bronars explore whether the large observed variance in self-employment rates across racial groups is partly due to consumer discrimination.[86] They find that minorities negatively select into self-employment, with the most able minorities remaining in the wage-and-salary sector, whereas Whites positively select into self-employment and negatively select into wage-and-salary work. These findings are consistent with White consumers having a distaste for purchasing goods and services from minority-owned businesses. Using recent panel data from the CPS, Kawaguchi finds that among African Americans, low earners are the most likely to enter into business ownership, whereas both low- and higher-earning Whites are the most likely to enter self-employment.[87] He notes that this finding is consistent with the theoretical predictions of consumer and credit market discrimination against African Americans. In contrast to these results, Meyer does not find evidence supporting the consumer discrimination hypothesis.[88] Using data from the 1987 Characteristics of Business Owners, he finds that African-American-owned businesses are relatively more common in industries in which White customers more frequently patronize African-American-owned businesses.

Several previous studies use data from the Federal Reserve's Survey of Small Business Finances (SSBF) to study lending discrimination and find that minority-owned businesses experience higher loan denial probabilities and pay higher interest rates than White-owned businesses even after controlling for differences in creditworthiness, and other factors.[89] For example, a comparable loan application filed by a firm owned by African Americans is twice as likely to be denied than if the application was filed by a White owner.[90] Minorities are found to have higher denial rates even after controlling for personal net worth, home ownership, underwriting standards, and selection.[91] Research

86 Borjas and Bronars, 1989.

87 Kawaguchi, 2004.

88 Meyer, 1990.

89 Blanchard, Yinger, and Zhao, 2004, Blanchflower, Levine, and Zimmerman, 2003, Cavalluzzo, Cavalluzzo, and Wolken, 2002, Cavalluzzo and Wolken, 2004, Coleman, 2002, 2003.

90 Evidence from the CBO indicates that Black and Latino firms are substantially less likely to use bank loans for startup capital than White firms. See Christopher, 1998.

91 Cavalluzzo and Wolken, 2004, and Blanchard, Yinger, and Zhao, 2004.

using the SSBF also indicates that African-American and Latino owners were less likely to apply for loans because they believed they would be denied, and denial rates for African-American-owned businesses appear to decrease with lender market concentration.

Cavalluzzo and Wolken also estimate the magnitude of contributions from group differences in characteristics to racial gaps in loan denial rates.[92] They find that group differences in personal wealth play only a modest role in explaining African-American/White differences in denial rates. Credit history differences are found to explain most of the difference. Personal wealth, however, is found to explain more of the Latino/White and Asian/White gaps in denial rates.

Overall, consumer and lending discrimination are likely to discourage would-be minority entrepreneurs and reduce the longevity of minority-owned businesses. These patterns are consistent with relatively low rates of business ownership among discriminated-against groups. The theoretical predictions and empirical evidence on the effects of labor market discrimination on minority business ownership, however, are less clear. The hypothesis is also not consistent with the finding of low current and historical rates of business ownership among African Americans and Latinos.

Explanations for Racial Differences in Business Outcomes

The extensive literature on minority business ownership provides evidence that access to financial capital and lower levels of family, business, and human capital limit opportunities for African Americans and Latinos to start businesses. A much smaller body of literature focuses on why these businesses are less successful than White- or Asian-owned businesses. Relatively few studies focus specifically on explaining disparities in business outcomes.

Using data from the 1992 CBO, Fairlie and Robb explore why African-American-owned firms have lower profits and sales, hire fewer employees, and are more likely to close than White-owned businesses.[93] They find that

---

92 Cavalluzzo and Wolken, 2004.

93 Fairlie and Robb, 2003.

African-American business owners have a relatively disadvantaged family business background compared with White business owners. African-American business owners are much less likely than White business owners to have had a self-employed family member prior to starting their business and are less likely to have worked in that family member's business.[94] The finding is that racial differences in small business outcomes are more linked to the lack of prior work experience—which may limit African Americans' acquisition of general and specific business human capital—than to their relatively lower probability of having a self-employed family member prior to business startup.

Estimates from the 1992 CBO also indicate that worse business outcomes are also related to African Americans' limited opportunities for acquiring specific business human capital through work experience in businesses providing similar goods and services. Lower levels of education among African-American business owners relative to White business owners explain a modest portion (2.4 to 6.5 percent) of the African-American/White gaps in small business outcomes (closure, profits, employment, and sales). Finally, lower levels of startup capital among African-American-owned firms are associated with less successful businesses. Racial differences in startup capital explain 14.5 to 43.2 percent of the gaps in small business outcomes. The results should be interpreted with caution because of endogeneity issues.

Using earlier CBO data, Bates also finds evidence that business outcomes are associated with higher levels of education and startup capital.[95] He finds that the success of Asian-owned firms relative to African-American-owned firms is related to these two factors. Asian immigrant-owned firms have average startup capital of $53,550 compared with $14,226 for African-American-owned firms. Interestingly, however, he finds that firms owned by Koreans have lower sales and profits per dollar of invested capital than African-American-owned firms.[96]

---

94 Only 12.6 percent of African-American business owners had prior work experience in a family member's business compared with 23.3 percent of White business owners.

95 Bates, 1994, 1997.

96 Bates, 1994.

The small body of literature on the causes of racial differences in business outcomes is expanding. Although much of the literature focuses on differences in the roles of financial and human capital, a few studies have examined additional inputs. For example, the use of technology varies substantially by the race of the business owner. Using data from the 1998 SSBF, Bitler finds that 76 percent of all small businesses use computers.[97] In comparison, 62 percent of African-American-, 66 percent of Asian-, and 70 percent of Latino-owned businesses use computers. The evidence on the relationship between computer use and entrepreneurship and firm performance, however, is mixed.[98]

Affirmative Action Programs

In the late 1970s and 1980s, the value of federal, state, and local government contracts reserved for minority-owned businesses grew substantially. The purpose of these minority business set-aside programs was to develop minority enterprise, counter the effects of past discrimination, and reduce unemployment among minorities in urban communities. These programs originated in government policies that attempted to strengthen the viability of small businesses. Initially, set-asides were focused on economically disadvantaged entrepreneurs with the goal of increasing the number of minority-owned firms during the late 1960s and early 1970s. During the following 15 years, however, set-asides were increasingly targeted to businesses that had greater future growth potential.[99]

In general, there are two types of set-aside programs. In one type, a specified percentage of the number or total dollar value of government contracts is allotted to minority-owned businesses. In the other type, prime contractors are required to allot a specified percentage of the total amount of government contracts to minority-owned subcontractors and/or suppliers.[100] Data on local set-aside programs listed in a report by the Minority Business Enterprise Legal Defense and Education Fund (MBELDEF) indicate that these goals

---

97 Bitler, 2004.

98 Fairlie, 2005, and Bitler, 2002.

99 Bates, 1985.

100 Rice, 1991, and Myers, 1997.

range from 1 to 50 percent, with most programs having goals of 5 to 15 percent.[101] A large proportion of the program coverage appears to be targeted towards the construction sector. Set-aside programs are also often complemented with procurement officials who aid minority-owned businesses in obtaining assistance.[102]

Set-aside programs exist at the federal, state, city, county, and special district (airport, water, sanitary, park, and school) levels. Minority business set-asides were mandated for federal transportation and highway construction; national defense; National Aeronautics and Space Administration contracts; international development grants; and for the development, construction, and operation of the super collider.[103] The federal government reported $4.4 billion in contract awards to minority and disadvantaged firms in FY 1986.[104] Most states also created set-aside programs for minority-owned businesses, and more than 200 local governments created minority business set-aside programs.[105] Most of the local government programs were created in the early to mid-1980s,[106] and many of them, especially in large central cities, were quite substantial.[107]

Although minority business set-asides represent a multi-billion-dollar annual governmental expenditure, relatively little is known about their effectiveness. The first obvious question is whether set-aside programs actually increased the number and/or total dollar amount of government contracts received by minority-owned businesses. Myers and Chan examine the award of public procurement and construction contracts to minority- and nonminority-owned firms before, during, and after the implementation of the state of New Jersey's set-aside program.[108] They

---

101   Minority Business Enterprise Legal Defense and Education Fund, 1988.

102   Bates and Williams, 1993.

103   Myers, 1997.

104   Rice, 1991.

105   Rice, 1991, Myers, 1997.

106   MBELDEF, 1988.

107   Rice, 1991, Bates, 1985, and Boston, 1998.

108   See Myers and Chan, 1996. New Jersey's set-aside program started in 1985 and was suspended in 1989 because of the *City of Richmond v. Croson* decision. The authors define the pre-, during, and post-periods as 1980–1984, 1985–1988, and 1989–1990, respectively.

find that the average number of contract awards going to African-American-owned firms submitting bids remained unchanged from the period before set-asides (1980–1984) to the period during set-asides (1985–1988) and decreased from the period during set-asides to the period after set-asides (1989–1990). In contrast, average contract awards for White male-owned firms increased from the 1980–1984 to the 1985–1988 period and decreased markedly over the period from 1985–1988 to 1989–1990. The authors conclude that New Jersey's set-aside program did not have a substantial impact on the average number of contracts awarded to African-American-owned firms submitting bids on state contracts.

Some additional evidence on the "first-stage" relationship between set-aside programs and contract awards is provided in a recent review of 58 disparity studies conducted in response to the *Richmond v. Croson* decision by the Urban Institute.[109] Disparity is defined as the ratio of the percentage of total contract dollars awarded to minority-owned firms to the percentage of all available firms that are minority-owned. The study finds evidence of greater disparity in contract awards (i.e., lower disparity ratios) in jurisdictions without affirmative action programs, suggesting that such programs positively affect the amount of government contracts received by minority-owned firms.

The next natural question is whether set-aside programs had an effect on the growth and viability of minority-owned firms. Boston uses published data from the Survey of Minority-Owned Business Enterprises (SMOBE) to examine the growth rate in the number of African-American-owned businesses in cities that implemented affirmative action programs in the 1980s relative to cities that did not.[110] He finds that the average growth rate from 1982 to 1992 was 65 percent in cities with programs and 61 percent in cities without programs and that this difference is not statistically significant.

Bates and Williams provide additional indirect evidence on the effectiveness of minority business set-asides.[111] They find that from 1982 to 1987, total sales by African-American-owned businesses and the number of African-American-owned firms increased more in cities with than without African-American mayors.

---

109 Enchautegui, et al., 1996.

110 Boston, 1998.

111 Bates and Williams, 1993.

Citing evidence from case studies suggesting that African-American mayors place a high priority on contracting with minority-owned businesses, Bates and Williams argue that the positive effect of these mayors on African-American business outcomes is partly due to their support of minority business set-aside programs.

In a later study, Bates and Williams use data from the U.S. Census Bureau's Characteristics of Business Owners survey to examine the survival rates of minority-owned enterprises that sell to state and local governments relative to minority-owned firms that do not.[112] Controlling for many owner and firm characteristics, they find that minority firms with local government sales are no more likely to survive than minority-owned firms with no local government sales from 1987 to the end of 1991. They also find that minority-owned firms that derive at least 25 percent of their sales from state and local government are less likely to survive than minority-owned enterprises that are less reliant on state and local government.

Bates and Williams also explore whether the characteristics of preferential procurement programs have an effect on survival among minority-owned businesses.[113] The authors and the Joint Center for Political and Economic Studies (JCPES) collected detailed information on minority business set-aside programs in 28 large cities in the United States.[114] They find higher survival rates among minority-owned businesses that derive 1–24 percent of their sales from state and local governments in cities with affirmative action programs that have a rigorous certification process and a staff assigned to assist minority firms, that routinely waive bonding requirements or provide bonding, and/or that provide working capital assistance to minority firms receiving contracts. Their results are less clear for minority-owned firms that derive at least 25 percent of their sales from state and local governments.

More recently, Chatterji, Chay, and Fairlie use the staggered introduction of set-aside programs across U.S. cities during the 1980s to estimate their impact on minority self-employment rates.[115] They find large increases in African-American

---

112 Bates and Williams, 1996.

113 Bates and Williams, 1995.

114 Joint Center for Political and Economic Studies, 1994.

115 Chatterji, Chay, and Fairlie, 2004.

self-employment soon after program implementation concentrated in industries most heavily affected by contract set-asides from city governments. Blanchflower and Wainwright provide evidence from a series of natural experiments indicating that once the programs are removed—which often occurs by court injunction following the Supreme Court's finding in the case of *City of Richmond v. Croson* in 1989—utilization of minority and women's business enterprises drops precipitously.[116] Finally, Marion explores the costs of set-aside programs using program changes attributable to California's Proposition 209.[117] Proposition 209 ended preferences for minority-owned businesses on state-funded contracts, but had no effect on federally-funded contracts. He finds that after Proposition 209, the value of the winning bid on state-funded contracts for highway construction projects fell by 4–6 percent relative to federally-funded contracts, which continued to include preferences.

Conclusions

African Americans and Latinos are less likely to own businesses than are Whites and Asians. Minority-owned businesses are also less successful than White-owned businesses, on average. Recent trends indicate some improvement in the state of minority entrepreneurship, but a major convergence in racial patterns in business ownership and outcomes is unlikely in the near future.

Three major barriers to minority-owned business are identified in the literature. First, relatively low asset levels appear to be limiting business entry among minorities. Higher rates of business closure, lower sales and profits, and less employment are also found to be associated with low levels of startup capital among minorities. Second, relatively disadvantaged family business backgrounds appear to limit entry and success in small business. In terms of business success, the lack of prior work experience in a family business among minority business owners may be severely limiting their acquisition of general and specific business human capital useful to running successful businesses.

---

116   Blanchflower and Wainwright, 2004.

117   Marion, 2004.

Lack of access to business, social, and co-ethnic networks may also represent an impediment to business creation for some groups. Finally, other forms of human capital, such as education and prior work experience in a related business, appear to limit the potential for minority business creation and success.

In light of these findings and the trend toward reducing and eliminating affirmative action contracting programs, future policies promoting minority entrepreneurship need to be creative. Programs targeted toward alleviating financial constraints and providing opportunities for work experience in small businesses may be especially useful. In particular, programs that directly address deficiencies in family business experience, possibly through an expansion of apprenticeship-type entrepreneurial training programs, may be needed to break the cycle of low rates of business ownership and negative business outcomes being passed from one generation of minorities to the next.

Barriers to business entry and success for minority-owned businesses that are created by imperfect capital markets, discrimination, and lack of opportunities to acquire business human capital may impose a large efficiency loss in the overall U.S. economy. Furthermore, the potential benefits of promoting minority business ownership in terms of increasing minority employment should not be overlooked. In 1997, there were 2.9 million minority-owned firms hiring 4.3 million employees in the United States. Estimates from the CBO indicate that more than 40 percent of African-American and Latino employer firms hire at least 90 percent minority employees.[118]

References

Aldrich, Howard E., and Roger Waldinger. 1990. "Ethnicity and Entrepreneurship." *Annual Review of Sociology*, 16(1): 111–135.

Allen, W. David. 2000. "Social Networks and Self-Employment," *Journal of Socio-Economics*, 29: 487–501.

Altonji, Joseph G., and Ulrich Doraszelski. 2001. "The Role of Permanent Income and Demographics in Black/White Differences in Wealth," NBER Working Paper No. 8473.

---

118   U.S. Census Bureau, 1997. Estimates from the CBO also indicate that more than 30 percent of other minority-owned employer firms hire at least 90 percent minority employees.

Aronson, Robert L. 1991. *Self-Employment: A Labor Market Perspective*, Ithaca: ILR Press.

Baron, Salo W., Arcadius Kahan, and others. 1975. *Economic History of the Jews*, ed, Nachum Gross. New York: Schocken Books.

Bates, Timothy. 1985. "Impact of Preferential Procurement Policies on Minority-Owned Businesses," *Review of Black Political Economy*, Summer: 51–65.

Bates, Timothy. 1989. "The Changing Nature of Minority Business: A Comparative Analysis of Asian, Nonminority, and Black-Owned Businesses." *The Review of Black Political Economy*, 18, Fall: 25–42.

Bates, Timothy. 1993. *Assessment of State and Local Government Minority Business Development Programs*. Report to the U.S. Department of Commerce Minority Business Development Agency. Washington, D.C.: U.S. Department of Commerce.

Bates, Timothy. 1993. *Banking on Black Enterprise*. Washington, D.C.: Joint Center for Political and Economic Studies.

Bates, Timothy. 1994. "An Analysis of Korean-Immigrant-Owned Small-Business Start-Ups with Comparisons to African-American and Nonminority-Owned Firms," *Urban Affairs Quarterly*, 30(2): 227–248.

Bates, Timothy. 1994. "Social Resources Generated by Group Support Networks May Not be Beneficial to Asian Immigrant-Owned Small Businesses," *Social Forces*, 72(3): 671–689.

Bates, Timothy. 1997. *Race, Self-Employment and Upward Mobility: An Illusive American Dream*, Washington, D.C.: Woodrow Wilson Center Press and Baltimore: John Hopkins University Press.

Bates, Timothy, and David Howell. 1997. "The Declining Status of African American Men in the New York City Construction Industry. In *Race, Markets, and Social Outcomes*, edited by Patrick Mason and Rhonda Williams. Boston: Kluwer.

Bates, Timothy, and Darrell L. Williams. 1993. "Racial Politics: Does It Pay?" *Social Science Quarterly*, 74(3): 507–22.

Bates, Timothy, and Darrell Williams. 1995. "Preferential Procurement Programs and Minority-Owned Businesses," *Journal of Urban Affairs*, 17(1): 1–17.

Bates, Timothy, and Darrell Williams. 1996. "Do Preferential Procurement Programs Benefit Minority Business?" *American Economic Review*, 86(2): 294–97.

Bitler, Marianne, 2002. "Does PC Use Pay? Computers and Small Firm Performance," Rand Working Paper.

Bitler, Marianne, 2004. "Racial and Ethnic Differences in Computer Adoption: Evidence from Small Businesses," Paper Presented at Economics and Technology Workshop at UC Santa Cruz.

Bitler, Marianne, Alicia Robb, and John Wolken, 2001. "Financial Services Used by Small Businesses: Evidence from the 1998 Survey of Small Business Finances," *Federal Reserve Bulletin*, Vol. 87, April 2001.

Black, Jane, David de Meza, and David Jeffreys. (1996). "House Prices, The Supply of Collateral and the Enterprise Economy," *The Economic Journal*. 106 (434):60–75.

Blanchard, Lloyd, John Yinger and Bo Zhao. 2004. "Do Credit Market Barriers Exist for Minority and Women Entrepreneurs?" Syracuse University Working Paper.

Blanchflower, David G., P. Levine and D. Zimmerman. 2003. "Discrimination in the small business credit market," *Review of Economics and Statistics*, November, 85(4), 930–943.

Blanchflower, David G., and Andrew J. Oswald. 1998. "What Makes an Entrepreneur?" *Journal of Labor Economics*, 16 (1), 26–60.

Blanchflower, David G., Andrew Oswald, and Alois Stutzer. 2001. "Latent entrepreneurship across nations." *European Economic Review*. 45:680–691.

Blanchflower, D. G. and Wainwright, J. (2004), "Minority and female self-employment in the USA," Dartmouth College.

Blau, David M. (1987), "A Time-series analysis of self-employment in the United States," *Journal of Political Economy*, 95, 445–467.

Blau, Francine, and David Graham (1990): "Black-White Differences in Wealth and Asset Composition," *Quarterly Journal of Economics*, 321–339.

Bleakley, Hoyt and Aimee Chin, 2003, "Language Skills and Earnings: Evidence from Childhood Immigrants," working paper UCSD.

Boden, Rick and Brian Headd. 2002. "Race and Gender Differences in Business Ownership and Business Turnover." *Business Economics*, October.

Bonacich, Edna and John Modell. 1980. *The Economic Basis of Ethnic Solidarity in the Japanese American Community*. Berkeley: University of California Press.

Borjas, George. 1986. "The Self-Employment Experience of Immigrants." *Journal of Human Resources*, 21, Fall: 487–506.

Borjas, George, and Stephen Bronars (1989): "Consumer Discrimination and Self-Employment," *Journal of Political Economy*, 97, 581–605.

Boston, Thomas D. 1998. "Trends in Minority-Owned Businesses," Paper presented at the National Research Council Research Conference on Racial Trends in the United States.

Bradford, William D. 2003. "The Wealth Dynamics of Entrepreneurship for Black and White Families in the U.S.," *Review of Income and Wealth*, 49(1): 89–116.

Brown, Charles, James Hamilton, and James Medoff (1990): *Employers Large and Small*, Cambridge: Harvard University Press.

Cavalluzzo, Ken, Linda Cavalluzzo, and John Wolken. 2002. "Competition, Small Business Financing, and Discrimination: Evidence from a New Survey," *Journal of Business*, Vol. 25 no. 4.

Cavalluzzo, Ken and John Wolken. 2005. "Small Business Loan Turndowns, Personal Wealth and Discrimination." *Journal of Business* (forthcoming).

Cayton, Horace R. and St. Clair Drake. 1946. *Black Metropolis*. London: Jonathan Cape.

Chay, Kenneth Y., Ronnie Chatterji and Robert W. Fairlie, "The Impact of Contracting Set-Asides on Minority Business Ownership,"

Christopher, Jan E. 1998. "Minority Business Formation and Survival: Evidence on Business Performance and Viability," *The Review of Black Political Economy*. 26 (3), Summer: 37–72.

Coate, Stephen and Tennyson, Sharon. "Labor Market Discrimination, Imperfect Information and Self-Employment." *Oxford Economic Papers* 44 (April 1992): 272–288.

Cobb-Clark, Deborah A., and Vincent Hildebrand. 2004. "The Wealth of Mexican Americans," IZA Discussion paper No. 1150.

Coleman, Susan. 2002. "The Borrowing Experience of Black and Hispanic-Owned Small Firms: Evidence from the 1998 Survey of Small Business Finances." *The Academy of Entrepreneurship Journal* 8, no. 1: 1–20.

Coleman, Susan. 2003. "Borrowing Patterns for Small Firms: A Comparison by Race and Ethnicity." *The Journal of Entrepreneurial Finance & Business Ventures* 7, no. 3: 87–108.

Devine, Theresa J. 1994 "Changes in Wage-and-Salary Returns to Skill and the Recent Rise in Female Self-Employment." *American Economic Review* 84(2):108–13.

Du Bois, W.E.B. 1899. *The Philadelphia Negro*, Philadelphia: University of Pennsylvania.

Dunn, Thomas A. and Douglas J. Holtz-Eakin (2000), "Financial capital, human capital, and the transition to self-employment: evidence from intergenerational links," *Journal of Labor Economics* 18 (2): 282–305.

Dustmann, Christian and Arthur van Soest, 2002, "Language and the Earnings of Immigrants," *Industrial and Labor Relations Review* 55:3, 473–492.

Enchautegui, Maria E., Michael Fix, Pamela Loprest, Sarah von der Lippe, and Douglas Wissoker. 1996. *Do Minority-Owned Businesses Get a Fair Share of Government Contracts.* Washington, D.C.: Urban Institute.

Earle, John S., and Zuzana Sakova. 2000. "Business start-ups or disguised unemployment? Evidence on the character of self-employment from transition economies," *Labour Economics*, 7:(5): 575–601.

Evans, David and Boyan Jovanovic. 1989. "An Estimated Model of Entrepreneurial Choice Under Liquidity Constraints." *Journal of Political Economy* 97(4):808–27.

Evans, David, and Linda Leighton (1989): "Some Empirical Aspects of Entrepreneurship," *American Economic Review*, 79, 519–535.

Fairlie, Robert W. 1999. "The Absence of the African-American Owned Business: An Analysis of the Dynamics of Self-Employment." *Journal of Labor Economics*, 17(1): 80–108.

Fairlie, Robert W. 2004. "Does Business Ownership Provide a Source of Upward Mobility for Blacks and Hispanics?," *Entrepreneurship and Public Policy*, ed., Doug Holtz-Eakin, Cambridge: MIT Press.

Fairlie, Robert W. 2004. "Recent Trends in Ethnic and Racial Business Ownership." *Small Business Economics*, 23: 203–218.

Fairlie, Robert W. 2004. *Self-Employed Business Ownership Rates in the United States: 1979–2003*, Washington, D.C.: U.S. Small Business Administration, Office of Advocacy.

Fairlie, Robert W. 2005. "The Personal Computer and Entrepreneurship." *Management Science*, forthcoming.

Fairlie, Robert W. 2005. "Entrepreneurship among Disadvantaged Groups: An Analysis of the Dynamics of Self-Employment by Gender, Race and Education," *Handbook of Entrepreneurship, Volume 2*, eds. Simon C. Parker, Zoltan J. Acs, and David R. Audretsch, Kluwer Academic Publishers (forthcoming).

Fairlie, Robert W., and Bruce D. Meyer. 1996. "Ethnic and Racial Self-Employment Differences and Possible Explanations," *Journal of Human Resources*, 31, Fall 1996, 757–793.

Fairlie, Robert W., and Bruce D. Meyer. 2000. "Trends in Self-Employment among Black and White Men: 1910-1990." *Journal of Human Resources*, 35(4): 643–669.

Fairlie, Robert W., and Alicia Robb. 2003. "Why are Black-Owned Businesses Less Successful than White-Owned Businesses: The Role of Families, Inheritances, and Business Human Capital," Joint Center for Poverty Research Working Paper 336.

Fairlie, Robert W., and Christopher Woodruff. 2005. "Mexican Entrepreneurship: A Comparison of Self-Employment in Mexico and the United States," *Mexican Immigration*, ed. George Borjas, Cambridge: National Bureau of Economic Research (forthcoming).

Feagin, Joe R., and Nikitah Imani. 1994. "Racial barriers to African American entrepreneurship: an exploratory study," *Social Problems*, November, 41(4): 562–585.

Fratoe, F. (1988). "Social Capital of Black Business Owners," *The Review of Black Political Economy*, Spring, 33–50.

Frazier, E. Franklin (1957): *The Negro in the United States*, 2nd Edition, New York: McMillan.

Gittleman, Maury, and Edward N. Wolff. 2004. "Racial Differences in Patterns of Wealth Accumulation," *Journal of Human Resources*, 34(1): 193–227.

Glazer, Nathan and Daniel P. Moynihan. 1970. *Beyond the Melting Pot: the Negroes, Puerto Ricans, Jews, Italians, and Irish of New York City*, 2nd Edition. Cambridge: MIT Press.

Guy, Cynthia, Fred Doolittle, and Barbara Fink. 1991. *Self-Employment for Welfare Recipients: Implementation of the SEID Program*. New York: Manpower Demonstration Research Corporation.

Hipple, Steven. 2004. "Self-Employment in the United States: an Update," *Monthly Labor Review*, 127(7): 13–23.

Holtz-Eakin, Douglas, and Harvey Rosen (2004): "Cash Constraints and Business Start-Ups: Deutschmarks Versus Dollars," Syracuse University Working Paper.

Holtz-Eakin, Douglas, David Joulfaian and Harvey Rosen (1994a): "Entrepreneurial Decisions and Liquidity Constraints," *Rand Journal of Economics*, 23, 2, 334–347.

Hout, Michael and Harvey S. Rosen. 2000. "Self-Employment, Family Background, and Race," *Journal of Human Resources*, 35(4): 670–92.

Hurst, Erik, and Annamaria Lusardi (2004): "Liquidity Constraints, Household Wealth, and Entrepreneurship," *Journal of Political Economy*, 112(2): 319–347.

Johansson, Edvard. 2000. "Self-employment and Liquidity Constraints: Evidence from Finland." *Scandinavian Journal of Economics*, 102 (1):123–134.

Joint Center for Political and Economic Studies. 1994. Assessment of Minority Business Development Programs, Report to the U.S. Department of Commerce Minority Business Development Agency, Washington, D.C.

Kawaguchi, Daiji. 2005. "Negative Self Selection into Self-Employment among African Americans," *Topics in Economic Analysis & Policy*, Berkeley Electronic Press Journals, 5(1): Article 9, 1–25.

Kihlstrom, Richard, and Jean-Jacques Laffont. 1979. "A General Equilibrium Entrepreneurial Theory of Firm Formation Based on Risk Aversion." *Journal of Political Economy*, 87(4):719–48.

Kinzer, Robert H., and Edward Sagarin. 1950. *The Negro in American Business: the Conflict between Separatism and Integration*, New York: Greenberg.

Kosanovich, William T., Heather Fleck, Berwood Yost, Wendy Armon, and Sandra Siliezar. 2001. Comprehensive Assessment of Self-Employment Assistance Programs, U.S. Department of Labor Report.

Lentz, Bernard, and David Laband. 1990. "Entrepreneurial Success and Occupational Inheritance among Proprietors," *Canadian Journal of Economics*, 23, No. 3, 563–579.

Lindh T., and H. Ohlsson (1996). "Self-employment and windfall gains: evidence from the Swedish lottery," *Economic Journal*, 106: (439), November, pp.1515–1526.

Light, Ivan. 1972. *Ethnic Enterprise in America*. Berkeley: University of California Press.

Light, Ivan. 1979. "Disadvantaged Minorities in Self Employment." *International Journal of Comparative Sociology* 20(1–2):31–45.

Light, Ivan, and Carolyn Rosenstein. 1995. *Race, Ethnicity, and Entrepreneurship in Urban America*. New York: Aldine de Gruyter.

Loewen, James W. 1971. *The Mississippi Chinese: Between Black and White*. Cambridge: Harvard University Press.

Lowrey, Ying. 2005. *Dynamics of Minority-Owned Employer Establishments, 1997–2001: An Analysis of Employer Data from the Survey of Minority-Owned Business Establishments*, Washington, D.C.: U.S. Small Business Administration, Office of Advocacy.

Marion, Justin. 2004. "How Costly is Affirmative Action? Government Contracting and California's Proposition 209." University of Chicago Working Paper.

McManus, Walter, William Gould and Finish Welch, 1983, "Earnings of Hispanic Men: The Role of English Language Proficiency," *Journal of Labor Economics* 1(2): 101–130.

Menchik, Paul L. and Nancy A. Jianakoplos. 1997. "Black-White Wealth Inequality: Is Inheritance the Reason?," *Economic Inquiry*, 35(2), p. 428–442.

Meyer, Bruce 1990. "Why Are There So Few Black Entrepreneurs?," National Bureau of Economic Research, Working Paper No. 3537.

Min, Pyong Gap. 1996. *Caught in the Middle: Korean Merchants in America's Multiethnic Cities*. Berkeley: University of California Press.

Minority Business Enterprise Legal Defense and Education Fund. 1988. *Report on the Minority Business Enterprise Programs of State and Local Governments*.

Moore, Robert L. 1983. "Employer Discrimination: Evidence form Self-employed Workers," *Review of Economics and Statistics*, 65 (August 1983): 496–501.

Myers, Samuel L., Jr. 1997. "Minority Business Set-Asides," Entry in *Encyclopedia of African-American Business History*. Greenwood Press.

Myers, Samuel L. Jr., and Tsze Chan. 1996. "Who Benefits from Minority Business Set-Asides? The Case of New Jersey," *Journal of Policy Analysis and Management*, 15(2): 202–26.

Myrdal, Gunnar. 1944. *An American Dilemma*, New York: Harper and Brothers.

Oliver, Melvin L. and Thomas M. Shapiro. 1995. *Black Wealth/White Wealth: A New Perspective on Racial Inequality*, New York: Routledge.

Polivka, Anne E. and Stephen M. Miller (1998): "The CPS After the Redesign: Refocusing the Economic Lens." In *Labor Statistics Measurement Issues*. eds. John Haltiwanger, Marilyn E. Manser, and Robert Topel, 249–286. Chicago: University of Chicago Press.

Portes, Alejandro, and Min Zhou. 1992. "Gaining the Upper Hand: Economic Mobility among Immigrants and Domestic Minorities," *Ethnic and Racial Studies*, October, 15 (4): 491–523.

Portes, Alejandro, and Min Zhou. 1999. "Entrepreneurship and Economic Progress in the 1990s: A Comparative Analysis of Immigrants and African Americans," in *Immigration and Opportunity: Race, Ethnicity, and Employment in the United States*," eds., Frank D. Bean and Stephanie Bell-Rose, New York: Russell Sage Foundation.

Raheim, Salome. 1997. "Problems and prospects of selfemployment as an economic independence option for welfare recipients," *Social Work*, 42, 1, 44–53.

Rauch, James E. 2001. "Black Ties Only? Ethnic Business Networks, Intermediaries, and African-American Retail Entrepreneurship," in James E. Rauch and Alessandra Casella, eds., *Networks and Markets*, New York: Russell Sage Foundation.

Razin, Eran and Andre Langlois. 1996. "Metropolitan Characteristics and Entrepreneurship among Immigrants and Ethnic Groups in Canada, *International Migration Review*, 30(3): 703–727.

Razin, Eran and Ivan Light. 1998. "Ethnic Entrepreneurs in America's Largest Metropolitan Areas." *Urban Affairs Review*, 33(3): 332–360.

Rees, Hedley, and Anup Shah (1986), "An empirical analysis of self-employment in the U.K.," *Journal of Applied Econometrics* 1(1): 95–108.

Rice, Mitchell F. 1991. "Government Set-Asides, Minority Business Enterprises, and the Supreme Court," *Public Administration Review*, 51(2): 114–22.

Robb, Alicia. 2000. "The Role of Race, Gender, and Discrimination in Business Survival," Doctoral Dissertation, University of Michigan Press.

Robb, Alicia. 2002. "Entrepreneurship: A Path for Economic Advancement for Women and Minorities?," *Journal of Developmental Entrepreneurship*, Volume 7, No. 4.

Robb, Alica M. 2004. "Entrepreneurial Performance by Women and Minorities: The Case of New Firms," Working Paper.

Sowell, Thomas. 1981. *Markets and Minorities*. New York: Basic Books.

Taylor, Mark. 2001. "Self-Employment and Windfall Gains in Britain: Evidence from Panel Data." *Economica*. 63, 539–565.

U.S. Bureau of Labor Statistics. 2005. "Table A-2. Employment status of the civilian population by race, sex, and age" and "Table A-3. Employment status of the Hispanic or Latino population by sex and age." http://stats.bls.gov/news. release/empsit.toc.htm.

U.S. Census Bureau. 1997. *1992 Economic Census: Characteristics of Business Owners*. Washington, D.C.: U.S. Government Printing Office.

U.S. Census Bureau. 2001. *1997 Economic Census: Company Summary*. Washington, D.C.: U.S. Government Printing Office.

U.S. Small Business Administration. 1998. *Women in Business*. Washington, D.C.: U.S. Small Business Administration, Office of Advocacy.

U.S. Small Business Administration. 1999. *Minorities in Business*. Washington, D.C.: U.S. Small Business Administration, Office of Advocacy.

U.S. Small Business Administration. 2001. *Minorities in Business*. Washington, D.C.: U.S. Small Business Administration, Office of Advocacy.

Vroman, Wayne. 1997. "Self-Employment Assistance: Revised Report." Urban Institute.

Walstad, William B. and Marilyn L. Kourilsky. 1998. "Entrepreneurial Attitudes and Knowledge of Black Youth," *Entrepreneurship Theory & Practice*, 23(2): 5–18.

5 ENTREPRENEURSHIP *and* BUSINESS OWNERSHIP *in the* VETERAN *and* SERVICE-DISABLED VETERAN COMMUNITY

Synopsis

A study by Waldman Associates and REDA International provides insights on veteran and service-disabled veteran entrepreneurship. Among the findings were the following:

- More than one-third of both new veteran entrepreneurs[1] and current veteran business owners had gained skills from their active duty service that were directly relevant to business ownership.

- Prior business ownership and employment experience had a positive impact on an even higher percentage of both new veteran entrepreneurs and current veteran business owners than did military experience.

- A focus on addressing the challenges of home-based business ownership and Internet use in veteran-owned businesses would be useful.

Introduction

In recent years, increasing attention has been called to the entrepreneurial needs of America's veterans, particularly those who have sustained a disability as a result of their active-duty service in the armed forces. Growing concerns about services to veterans and service-disabled veterans who either own or wish to start a small

---

1 "New veteran entrepreneurs" in this study are defined as the 22.1 percent of veterans in a residential survey conducted during the summer of 2003 who said they were either purchasing or starting a new business or considering doing so.

business climaxed with the enactment of the Veterans Entrepreneurship and Small Business Development Act of 1999.[2] This legislation included many recommendations of the Task Force for Veterans Entrepreneurship, an umbrella group including representatives of veteran organizations, as well as individual veteran business owners, originally created to advise the U.S. Small Business Administration (SBA) on how it and other federal agencies could better serve the veteran community. The task force continues to make recommendations to federal agencies on how to best assist veterans, but it has also taken on a proactive role in advocacy for veteran entrepreneurship before the Congress and in the private sector.

A study by Waldman Associates and REDA International supported by the SBA's Office of Advocacy provides insights on veteran and service-disabled veteran entrepreneurship.[3] At the center of the study is a survey instrument that was administered nationwide to a residential population of veterans who began their active duty service after the Korean conflict period,[4] and to a population of veteran business owners from all conflicts and peacetime periods.[5] The research team considered that those who served their active duty during and before the Korean conflict were in an age bracket that rendered them less likely to be starting new firms or self-employment activities. However, it was recognized that veterans in that age bracket were likely to be *current* small business owners.

In addition to collecting the survey data, the research team conducted informal conversations with policymakers and program staff in government agencies that administer programs for veterans and/or small business owners, as well as with congressional staff and program and policy staff in a number of state governments. These consultations were held in order to provide context on the status of programs focused on veteran entrepreneurship.

---

2 Public Law 106–50; August 17, 1999.

3 Waldman Associates and REDA International, *Entrepreneurship and Business Ownership in the Veteran Population*, 2004. See summary at *http://www.sba.gov/advo/research/rs242.pdf*. The complete study can be accessed at *http://www.sba.gov/advo/research/rs242tot.pdf*.

4 Specifically, after January 31, 1955.

5 Because this research was federally sponsored, the surveys constituted an "information collection" subject to provisions of the Paperwork Reduction Act, as amended (44 U.S.C. 3501 et seq.), and its implementing regulations (5 C.F.R. 1320). Accordingly, after a thorough review of this project's purposes, methodology and response burden, approval to conduct these surveys was obtained from the Office of Management and Budget (OMB), Office of Information and Regulatory Affairs under OMB Approval Number 3245-0340 (Expiration date: April 30, 2006).

The Survey

This project relies on a survey administered to two separate populations: veterans in the U.S. residential population, and veteran business owners drawn from a subset of the Dun and Bradstreet national database of businesses.

Each respondent was first asked a series of questions to assess his/her veteran status. These included questions on periods of active duty service; branch of the military served in; and service-connected disability rating, if any. A number of these questions were modeled after similar questions in the Department of Veterans Affairs' National Survey of Veterans.[6] The respondent was then asked basic demographic questions regarding gender, marital status, children, age, location and education. Published small business studies have shown that, within a given population, these parameters influence both the number of entrepreneurs from that population and the potential for successful business ownership. For example, there is evidence that men under the age of 35 who have married are much more likely to become self-employed than men who have never married. Further, it has been found that males under the age of 35 with some college experience have a greater prospect for success than those with 12 or fewer years of schooling.[7] Respondents were then queried about computer ownership and Internet access. This was important for many reasons, especially because of the accelerating development of government programs and public information on the web.

Veterans in the residential population were then asked whether they were considering starting or purchasing a new business (or were in the process of doing so). The survey differentiated between starting and purchasing a new firm, as the small business literature suggests that the purchase of a firm could be a negative success indicator.[8] Those who answered "no" to this question were asked no further questions. Veterans in the business owners' survey were asked if they were currently self-employed or currently owned or operated a small business concern.

---

6   For more information, *see http://www.va.gov/vetdata/SurveyResults/index.htm.*

7   Schiller, Bradley R. and Crewson, Phillip E., "Entrpreneurial Origins: A Longitudinal Inquiry," *Economic Inquiry*, July 1997, 523–531.

8   Duchesneau, Donald A. and Gartner, William B. (1990), "A Profile of New Venture Success and Failure in An Emerging Industry," *Journal of Business Venturing*, vol. 5, 297–312.

Those who were either considering or in the process of starting or purchasing a new business were asked questions about the new business itself.[9] Would it be home-based? Would it be computer-oriented? Would it employ people initially? In the business owners' survey, respondents were asked similar questions about their current business and were also asked when they purchased or started their new business. In both surveys, respondents were asked if they had partners in their business. There is some evidence that teams tend to have a greater chance of success than firms started by single founders, at least in manufacturing and high-tech start-ups.[10]

In both surveys, respondents were then asked to identify the problems they had encountered in starting or operating their businesses (a somewhat different list of questions was used for the two populations). This question was modeled after a similar question that produces data for *Small Business Problems and Priorities*, a periodic publication of the National Federation of Independent Business (NFIB) Education Foundation.[11]

Next, both populations were asked a series of questions that, in conjunction with the demographic parameters outlined above, gauged their members' potential for business ownership success. These questions were developed using characteristics of successful entrepreneurs previously identified in the small business literature. For example, respondents were asked about prior business ownership experience, as well as skills needed for business success, such as managing employees, anticipating business trends, etc. Relevant experience—specific knowledge of various functional aspects of the business—has been shown to be an important predictor of business ownership success.[12]

Respondents were also asked about business ownership skills gained from military service, for example, if they supervised others while on active duty and if they

---

9   Where veteran respondents owned more than one business, they were queried about each business currently owned.

10   Arnold C. Cooper, Carolyn Y. Woo, and William C. Dunkelberg (1988), "Entrepreneurs Perceived Chances for Success," *Journal of Business Venturing*, vol.3, 97–108.

11   This publication is authored by William C. Dennis, senior research fellow of the NFIB Education Foundation. General information on this series can be accessed by using the Research Foundation link at *http://www.nfib.com/*. See *http://www.nfib.com/object/IO_16191.html* for the full 2004 report.

12   Cooper, Woo, and Dunkelberg; *op.cit.*, 100.

were required to teach or reinforce new skills of those they supervised. Further, respondents were asked if they had technology training or other types of courses while on active duty that were of direct relevance to the management of their new or current business enterprise.

Finally, both populations were asked about their use of and experience with government programs in general, as well as programs for entrepreneurs generally and for veteran entrepreneurs in particular. They were first asked whether they had used or planned to use such programs. If they answered "yes," they were asked to identify the specific programs they had used. If they answered "no," they were asked to identify the reasons. Questions were asked to gauge the proclivity of the respondent to use government programs at all—even those designed to meet their needs. For example, respondents were asked if they had used veterans' benefits to fund all or part of their education or career training. Those who had used general small business programs, or programs specifically for veterans, were asked to rate their satisfaction with these programs.

The data generated by the survey will aid policymakers in three areas. First, new data on the level of entrepreneurship activity in the veteran and service-disabled veteran population, the potential for business ownership success in the veteran community, and the propensity of veterans to use government resources will guide policymakers on the rational level of resources to commit to the veteran program area. Second, new data on the characteristics of businesses that veterans start, the obstacles and problems they have faced, and their prior experience with government entrepreneurship programs will guide policymakers on the types of programs in which to invest. Finally, policymakers should be able to understand the differences in many of the parameters referenced above between the general veteran community and the service-disabled veteran community.

Residential Survey Results

The residential survey conducted during the summer of 2003 revealed that a significant 22.1 percent of veterans in the household population were either purchasing or starting a new business or considering doing so *(Table 5.1)*.[13]

---

13   This population will henceforth be referred to as "new veteran entrepreneurs."

Table 5.1 Veterans in the Population of U.S. Households Starting or Purchasing a New Business Enterprise or Considering Doing So (percent)

Veteran Cohort	Purchasing or Starting	Starting	Purchasing
Service-Connected Disability Status			
Service-disabled	28.0	25.4	2.6
Non-service-disabled	21.4	16.9	4.5
Gender			
Male	21.6	17.5	4.1
Female	26.6	20.5	6.1
Marital Status			
Single	22.2	17.8	4 4
Married	22.5	18.1	4.4
Living with a partner	22.6	22.6	0.0
Legally separated	28.6	14.3	14.3
Divorced	16.5	15.1	1.4
Age of Veteran			
20 to 29	29.9**	26.1**	3.8**
30 to 39	41.1**	35.9**	5.2**
40 to 49	35.4**	24.4**	11.0**
50 to 64	17.0**	14.3**	2.7**
65 and older	1.6**	1.6**	0.0**
Dependents			
Dependent children	33.8**	25.5**	8.3**
No dependent children	14.3**	12.7**	1.6**
Education			
High school graduate	15.4	11.8	3.6
One year of college	25.3	20.3	5.0
Two years of college	26.0	21.8	4.2
Three years of college	22.8	17.1	5.7
College graduate	30.8	25.1	5.7
College graduate, post graduate course(s)	18.1	18.1	0.0
Post graduate degree	21.6	10.8	10.8
Other	18.9	18.9	0.0
Full Sample	**22.1**	**17.8**	**4.3**

* Chi-square for the difference in the means is significant at the 10 percent level or less and greater than the 5 percent level.

** Chi-square for the difference in the means is significant at the 5 percent significance level or less.

Starting a new business was the dominant activity over purchasing a new business by a wide margin (17.8 percent versus 4.3 percent). Evidence has shown this to be a positive success indicator.[14]

The difference in start-up activity between service-disabled and non-service-disabled veterans was not statistically significant. However, the difference among the age cohorts was statistically significant, with older veterans exhibiting a lesser degree of interest and/or activity in starting a business. Only 17 percent of veterans in the age 50 to 64 cohort indicated that they were either purchasing or starting a new business or considering doing so, compared with 29.9 percent of veterans in their 20s, 41.1 percent of veterans in their 30s, and 35.4 percent of veterans in their 40s.

A larger percentage of veterans with dependents (33.8 percent) were purchasing or starting a new business or were considering doing so at the time of the survey than were those without dependents (14.3 percent).[15]

Of veterans starting or purchasing a new business at the time of the survey, 31.6 percent were doing so with at least one partner, a sizable enough figure to be considered a modest plus for the overall success of this population, as evidence has shown that partnership is a positive success indicator *(Table 5.2)*.[16]

Of new veteran entrepreneurs, 62.1 percent planned to initially locate their business entirely in their residence, but 67.4 percent of these planned to expand their business partially or entirely beyond their residence in the "foreseeable future" *(Table 5.3)*.

---

14 Duchesneau, Donald A. and Gartner, William B. (1990), "A Profile of New Venture Success and Failure in An Emerging Industry," *Journal of Business Venturing*, vol. 5, 297–312.

15 For the purposes of this study, dependents are children who depend on the veteran for at least half of their support.

16 Cooper, Arnold C.; Woo, Carolyn Y.; and Dunkelberg, William C. (1988); "Entrepreneurs Perceived Chances for Success," *Journal of Business Venturing*, vol.3, 97–108.

Table 5.2 New Veteran Entrepreneurs Forming or Purchasing Their New Business Enterprise With Partners (percent)

Veteran Cohort	Share Starting or Purchasing With One or More Partners
Service-Connected Disability Status	
Service-disabled	33.3
Non-service-disabled	31.3
Gender	
Male	31.0
Female	38.3
Age of Veteran	
20 to 29	12.7
30 to 39	31.3
40 to 49	42.2
50 to 64	27.6
65 and Older	0.0
Full Sample	**31.6**

Table 5.3 Home-based Startup and Relocation Plans of New Veteran Entrepreneurs in the U.S. Residential Population (percent)

Veteran Cohort	Share of Planned Startup Firms Initially Locating Entirely in Residence	Share of Planned Home-based Startups Planning to Relocate Firm
Service-Connected Disability Status		
Service-disabled	52.4	72.7
Non-service-disabled	63.6	66.7
Gender		
Male	61.4	69.8
Female	69.1	44.6
Marital Status		
Single	59.8	83.3
Married	62.6	62.5
Living with a partner	50.0	100.0
Legally separated	100.0	100.0
Divorced	49.8	66.7
Dependents		
Dependent children	57.5	66.1
No dependent children	68.9	69.1
Full Sample	**62.1**	**67.4**

Veteran entrepreneurs are motivated to create jobs. Almost 72 percent of new veteran entrepreneurs planned to employ at least one individual besides themselves at the outset of their new venture *(Table 5.4)*. Further analysis revealed that the share of veteran business owners who planned to initially locate their business in their home and who planned to initially employ at least one individual was nearly identical to the share of those who planned to initially locate their business outside of their residence.

The Internet was not unimportant to veteran start-ups. Eleven percent of new veteran entrepreneurs believed that they would be entirely dependent on the web *(Table 5.5)*. But 31.7 percent indicated that their business would be 50 percent or more dependent on the Internet.

The availability of resources and government programs ranked high on the list of problems and obstacles that new veteran entrepreneurs face *(Table 5.6)*. The populations of both service-disabled and non-service-disabled veterans ranked "Access to financing" their number one problem of 10. But a much higher proportion of service-disabled veterans (52.4 percent) viewed it as a "critical" problem than did non-service-disabled veterans (34.3 percent).

Veterans were concerned about government and private small business programs. "The existence of useful government and private programs for entrepreneurs" and "The existence of useful government and private programs for veterans and/or service-disabled veteran entrepreneurs" ranked second and third on the problem list of both service-disabled and non-service-disabled veteran entrepreneurs. "My disability" and "My status as a veteran or service-disabled veteran" were at the bottom of the list for both non-service-disabled and service-disabled veteran entrepreneurs.

Active duty service appeared to provide a training ground for business ownership. Most veteran entrepreneurs supervised others while on active duty, 74.3 percent being the lowest share with supervisory experience among the four entrepreneurship categories *(Table 5.7)*.[17] Most of those who did have supervisory experience were required to teach those they supervised new skills or reinforce existing skills.

---

17   The design of the survey prohibited the generation of an estimate for the sum of all four entrepreneurship categories (i.e., starting or purchasing a new business, or considering starting or purchasing a new business).

Table 5.4 New Veteran Entrepreneurs Planning to Hire at Least One Person Besides Themselves at the Beginning of Their Venture (percent)*

Veteran Cohort	Share of Start-ups Planning to Hire at Least One Person
Service-Connected Disability Status	
Service-disabled	61.9
Non-service-disabled	73.1
Gender	
Male	71.1
Female	77.0
Age of Veteran	
20 to 29	87.3
30 to 39	56.2
40 to 49	84.4
50 to 64	68.1
65 and older	100.0
Full Sample	**71.6**

* Includes part-time, temporary and contract workers

Table 5.5 Anticipated Internet Dependence for the Prospective Business Ventures of New Veteran Entrepreneurs (percent)

Veteran Cohort	Dependence Level (percent)			
	0 to 24	25 to 49	50 to 99	100
Service-Connected Disability Status				
Service-disabled	23.8	23.8	38.1	14.3
Non-service-disabled	49.3	22.4	17.9	10.4
Full Sample	**45.7**	**22.6**	**20.7**	**11.0**

Table 5.6 Measures of Veteran Entrepreneurship Problem Importance (percent)

Problem	Non-Service-Disabled			Service-Disabled		
	Rank	Mean	Percent Critical	Rank	Mean	Percent Critical
Access to financing	1	3.490	34.3	1	3.669	52.4
Useful government and private programs for entrepreneurs	2	3.393	33.3	2	3.381	38.1
Useful government and private programs for veteran entrepreneurs	3	3.378	29.9	3	3.092	23.8
Retaining qualified employees	4	2.550	10.4	6	2.333	4.8
Developing a network of contacts	5	2.450	6.0	4	2.619	9.5
Finding qualified employees	6	2.444	13.4	7	2.239	4.8
Developing and implementing a marketing strategy	7	2.415	3.0	5	2.569	9.5
Understanding the competition	8	2.256	7.5	9	1.906	4.8
My status as a veteran or service-disabled veteran	9	1.497	3.0	8	2.139	9.5
My disability	10	1.227	1.5	10	1.572	0.0

Table 5.7 Veteran Entrepreneurs Who Supervised Others While on Active Duty and Who Taught New Skills To Those They Supervised (percent)

Category of Entrepreneurship Activity	Supervised Others			As Supervisors Taught Skills		
	Full Sample	Service-Disabled	Non-service-Disabled	Full Sample	Service-Disabled	Non-service-Disabled
Considering starting a new business	81.1	78.6	81.6	90.4	90.9	90.3
In process of starting a new business	74.3	80.0	73.3	92.3	100.0	90.9
Considering purchasing new business	79.0	100.0	77.8	100.0	100.0	100.0
In process of purchasing new business	100.0	100.0	100.0	81.9	100.0	80.0

Of new veteran entrepreneurs, 36.4 percent indicated that they made use of one or more technologies while on active duty service that were of "direct relevance to the operation" of their new business enterprise or self-employment activity *(Table 5.8)*. Thirty-two percent of new veteran entrepreneurs had classes while on active duty (other than to learn the use of new technologies) that would be "of direct relevance to the operation" of their new business enterprise or self-employment activity.

Many new veteran entrepreneurs gained skills of relevance to their ventures while on active duty, but the share of new veteran entrepreneurs with previous business experience was even greater. Almost 61 percent of new veteran entrepreneurs have owned at least one business in the past or own one currently.[18] Such owners were significantly more common among non-service-disabled veterans (63.6 percent) than in the population of service-disabled veterans (42.9 percent). Prior business owners were also far more common among male veterans (64.2 percent) than among female veterans (23.0 percent).

Most new veteran entrepreneurs had gained some experience in key business skills from previous employment or business ownership experience *(Table 5.9)*. For example, 86.8 percent indicated that they had gained experience managing employees, and 96 percent indicated experience in dealing with customers. The smallest proportion, 48.3 percent, had gained experience in the area of dealing with tax laws.

---

18   New veteran entrepreneurs surveyed in the residential population could include current or past business owners, including self-employed persons, who were considering the purchase or start-up of a new enterprise.

Table 5.8 New Veteran Entrepreneurs with Prior Relevant Experience or Classes (percent)

Veteran Cohort	Used Technologies[1]	Formal Classes[2]	Previous Business[3]
Service-Connected Disability Status			
Service-disabled	33.3	38.1	42.9**
Non-service-disabled	36.9	30.8	63.6**
Gender			
Male	37.6	31.9	64.2**
Female	23.5	30.9	23.0**
Age of Veteran			
20 to 29	25.3	38.0*	62.0
30 to 39	15.7	12.5*	37.5
40 to 49	55.8	51.2*	62.7
50 to 64	35.8	28.4*	69.5
65 and older	0.0	0.0*	100.0
Full Sample	**36.4**	**31.8**	**60.7**

* Chi-square for the difference in the means is significant at the 10 percent level or less and greater than the 5 percent level.

** Chi-square for the difference in the means is significant at the 5 percent significance level or less.

1 Used one or more technologies while on active duty of direct use to new business enterprise.

2 Had formal classes while on active duty that were of direct relevance to new venture.

3 Previously owned at least one business or had self-employment activity.

Table 5.9 New Veteran Entrepreneurs Who Have Gained Key Business Ownership Skills From Previous Employment and/or Previous Business Ownership (percent)

Veteran Cohort	Managing Employees	Dealing With Customers	Marketing Products or Services	Managing Tax Laws	Anticipating Business Trends
Service Disability Status					
Service-disabled	90.5	100.0	71.4	42.9	61.9
Non-service-disabled	86.2	95.4	69.2	49.2	66.2
Age of Veteran					
20 to 29	62.7	100.0	74.7	0.0	50.0
30 to 39	90.6	93.8	56.2	25.1	43.8
40 to 49	86.1	100.0	62.9	67.5	67.5
50 to 64	88.1	94.1	79.1	52.2	76.0
65 and older	100.0	100.0	100.0	100.0	100.0
Education					
High school graduate	79.4	94.1	52.9	26.5	73.5
One year of college	100.0	90.0	74.9	45.0	35.0
Two years of college	85.4	95.1	75.6	43.8	58.5
Three years of college	100.0	100.0	75.0	75.0	100.0
College graduate	88.0	100.0	64.2	56.0	63.9
Post graduate courses	100.0	100.0	100.0	100.0	100.0
Post graduate degree	100.0	100.0	75.0	75.0	100.0
Other	63.7	100.0	81.9	63.7	63.7
Full Sample	**86.8**	**96.0**	**69.5**	**48.3**	**65.5**

Those who had gained experience from formal on-the-job training "that will be directly relevant" to the running of their new business enterprise constituted 57.3 percent of veteran entrepreneurs, while 88.2 percent had gained such experience through informal on-the-job training *(Table 5.10)*. Apprenticeship programs provided such experience to 24.2 percent of new veteran entrepreneurs.

Of new veteran entrepreneurs, 5.3 percent had made use of a public or private small business program designed for veterans, in spite of the fact that 24 percent of service-disabled veterans and 30 percent of non-service-disabled veterans indicated that the lack of such programs was a "critical" problem *(Table 5.11)*.

Table 5.10 New Veteran Entrepreneurs Who Have Gained Education and/or Experience Directly Relevant to Their New Business Enterprise from Apprenticeship Programs or On-the-Job Training (percent)

Veteran Cohort	Apprenticeship Programs	On-the-Job Training (Formal Classes)	On-the-Job Training (Informal)
Service-Connected Disability Status			
Service-disabled	15.0	50.0	90.0
Non-service-disabled	25.9	58.6	87.9
Age of Veteran			
20 to 29	49.6	66.4	100.0
30 to 39	18.6	48.1	92.6
40 to 49	25.6	64.2	82.0
50 to 64	23.8	57.1	88.9
65 and older		0.0	100.0
Education			
High school graduate	42.3	51.5	94.0
One year of college	16.8	66.8	88.9
Two years of college	21.5	62.1	83.9
Three years of college	25.0	50.0	100.0
College graduate	14.3	57.1	80.9
Post graduate course(s)	0.0	50.0	100.0
Post graduate degree	0.0	100.0	100.0
Other	33.5	22.2	77.8
Full Sample	**24.2**	**57.3**	**88.2**

Also, 65.9 percent of new veteran entrepreneurs planned to make use of a veterans small business program in the foreseeable future.

When those who did not use these programs were asked why, 36.8 percent said that they did not have a need for "any of these" program services and 35.5 percent said that they were not aware that veteran small business programs even existed *(Table 5.12)*. Almost 20 percent said that they were confused as to what was available.[19]

---

19 Respondents were allowed to choose more than one response category. Thus the categories are not mutually exclusive.

Table 5.11 New Veteran Entrepreneurs Using Veterans and Small Business Programs (percent)

Veteran Cohort	Used a Veterans Program[1]	Plan to Use a Veterans Program[1]	Would Use Veterans Program if Aware[2]	Used a Small Business Program[3]	Plan to Use a Small Business Program[3]
Service Disability Status					
Service-disabled	0.0	52.4	91.7	4.8	47.4
Non-service-disabled	6.2	68.3	97.1	15.6	51.9
Gender					
Male	5.8	67.9	95.9	15.4	50.9
Female	0.0	46.1	100.0	0.0	53.9
Age of Veteran					
20 to 29	0.0	87.3	100.0	12.7	43.5
30 to 39	0.0	46.7	94.3	6.6	39.2
40 to 49	4.6	68.3	93.9	23.2	51.5
50 to 64	8.9	70.3	100.0	11.9	56.8
65 and older	0.0	100.0	100.0	0.0	100.0
Education					
High school graduate	5.9	78.1	94.0	17.6	53.5
One year of college	0.0	55.0	87.5	25.1	39.9
Two years of college	9.7	59.9	100.0	15.3	39.4
Three years of college	0.0	75.0	100.0	0.0	50.0
College graduate	0.0	63.0	100.0	7.9	56.6
Post graduate course(s)	0.0	50.0	100.0	0.0	50.0
Post graduate degree	0.0	75.0	100.0	0.0	75.0
Other	18.1	66.5	100.0	18.1	75.0
Full Sample	**5.3**	**65.9**	**96.3**	**14.1**	**51.2**

1 Have used or plan to use a public or private small business program specifically designed for veterans.

2 Unaware of small business programs for veterans and would use such programs if aware of them.

3 Have used or plan to use a public or private small business program not specific to veterans.

Of veterans who indicated some degree of unawareness or confusion regarding the existence or the structure of veteran-oriented small business programs, 96.3 percent would use them if they became aware of them and if the programs met their needs, with no significant difference between the proportion of service-disabled and non-service-disabled veterans who indicated this propensity *(Table 5.11)*.

Table 5.12 Reasons Given by New Veteran Entrepreneurs Who Had Not Used Any Veteran Small Business Programs (percent)

Reason for Nonuse of Veterans Programs	Service-Disabled	Non-service-Disabled	Full Sample
Didn't have a need for these program services	28.6	38.3	**36.8**
Had a need but nothing in these programs meets my needs	4.8	15.0	**13.4**
Programs serving both veterans and non-veterans are adequate	0.0	6.7	**5.7**
Perception that program service delivery is inadequate	9.5	11.7	**11.3**
Confused as to what is available	19.0	20.0	**19.9**
Wasn't aware that small business programs for veterans existed	38.1	35.0	**35.5**
I don't qualify	0.0	6.7	**5.7**
Other	14.3	13.3	**13.5**

Note: Respondents were allowed to select multiple response options. Thus, shares do not total 100.

New veteran entrepreneurs did not appear to have any fundamental bias against small business programs *per se*, as further evidenced by the finding that 66 percent planned to use such programs.

While 5.3 percent of new veteran entrepreneurs had used veteran-specific programs, 14.1 percent of veteran entrepreneurs had used a general, non-veteran-specific public or private small business program and 51.2 percent planned to make use of a non-veteran-specific small business program in the foreseeable future, compared with the 65.9 percent of new veteran entrepreneurs who planned to make use of a veteran-specific program.

The reasons for non-usage of general small business programs were qualitatively similar to those for non-use of veteran-specific programs: 42.9 percent said that they simply "didn't have a need for these program services" *(Table 5.13)*. Among these new veteran entrepreneurs, 22.7 percent were confused as to what was available, and 26.5 percent were not aware that these programs even existed.

Of new veteran entrepreneurs who said that they did not plan to use a general small business program, 40.2 percent indicated that they did not have a need for these program services, and 22.6 percent were confused as to what was available *(Table 5.14)*.

Table 5.13 Reasons Given by New Veteran Entrepreneurs Who Had Not Used Any Small Business Program Not Specific to Veterans (percent)

Reason for Past Non-use of Small Business Programs	Service-Disabled	Non-service-Disabled	Full Sample
Didn't have a need for these program services	35.0	44.4	**42.9**
Had a need but nothing in these programs meets my needs	5.0	3.7	**3.9**
Perception that program service delivery is inadequate	5.0	3.7	**3.9**
No time for training	0.0	0.0	**0.0**
Confused as to what is available	25.0	22.2	**22.7**
I don't qualify for program services because I am a veteran	0.0	3.7	**3.1**
I don't qualify for program services for other reasons	5.0	1.9	**2.4**
Wasn't aware that small business programs existed	10.0*	29.6*	**26.5***
Other	15.0	16.7	**16.4**

Note: Respondents were allowed to select multiple response options. Thus, shares do not total 100.

* Chi-square for the difference in the means is significant at the 10 percent level or less and greater than the 5 percent level.

Table 5.14 Reasons Given by New Veteran Entrepreneurs Who Did Not Plan to Use Any Small Business Program Not Specific to Veterans (percent)

Reason for No Plans to Use Small Business Programs	Service-Disabled	Non-service-Disabled	Full Sample
Didn't have a need for these program services	10.0**	46.2**	**40.2***
Have needs but these programs don't meet them	10.0	11.5	**11.3**
Need small business program designed for veterans	0.0	3.8	**3.2**
Perception that program service delivery is inadequate	10.0	0.0	**1.6**
Found these programs to be inadequate in the past	0.0	0.0	**0.0**
Confused as to what is available	20.0	23.1	**22.6**
I don't qualify for program services because I am a veteran	0.0	3.8	**3.2**
I don't qualify for program services for other reasons	0.0	7.7	**6.4**
Wasn't aware that small business programs existed	20.0	15.4	**16.1**
Other	50.0*	19.2*	**24.3***

Note: Respondents were allowed to select multiple response options. Thus, shares do not total 100.

* Chi-square for the difference in the means is significant at the 10 percent level or less and greater than the 5 percent level.

** Chi-square for the difference in the means is significant at the 5 percent significance level or less.

Business Owner Survey Results

Among the most striking findings about the demographics of the veteran business owner respondent pool was that 95.0 percent were age 40 or over, and that 77.9 percent were age 50 or over *(Table 5. 15)*. Also of interest was the finding that 96.3 percent of veteran business owners had a high school or higher degree, while 49.3 percent had a college degree, with or without additional postgraduate studies.

A significant percentage owned more than one business *(Table 5.16)*. Nearly one in six, or 15.7 percent, owned two businesses; and 2.1 percent owned three businesses.[20]

Of these businesses, 38.7 percent were home-based *(Table 5.17)*. A greater proportion of service-disabled than non-service-disabled owners had a home-based business (52.1 percent versus 37.7 percent). Also, a larger percentage of veterans with dependent children (46.1 percent) had businesses that were entirely located in their residence than did those without dependent children (35.4 percent).

The home-based business status appeared to be dynamic: 35.6 percent of veteran business owners who had home-based businesses intended to move some or all of their business operations outside of their residence in the "foreseeable future" *(Table 5.18)*. Cross-tabulation analysis suggests that the proportion of owners who intended to expand beyond the home declined with the age of the business enterprise, although the differences were not statistically significant at the 10 percent level.[21]

---

20 The results presented in this section will be based on the first business of those owning more than one.

21 The mean differences are substantial, likely because of the inadequate sample size.

Table 5.15 Demographics of Veteran Business Owner Respondent Pool (percent)

Veteran Cohort	Respondent Share
Service-Connected Disability Status	
Service-disabled	6.6
Non-service-disabled	93.4
Gender	
Male	90.1
Female	9.9
Marital Status	
Single	13.0
Married	77.4
Living with a partner	0.8
Legally separated	1.1
Divorced	7.8
Age of Veteran	
20 to 29	1.3
30 to 39	3.7
40 to 49	17.1
50 to 64	54.5
65 and older	23.4
Dependents	
Dependent children	30.3
No dependent children	69.7
Education	
High school graduate	18.4
One year of college	6.3
Two years of college	16.7
Three years of college	5.7
College graduate	25.3
Post graduate course(s)	5.2
Post graduate degree	18.8
Other	3.7

Table 5.16 Veteran Business Owners Owning More than One Business (percent)

Veteran Cohort	Share Who Own Two Businesses	Share Who Own Three Businesses
Service-Connected Disability Status		
Service-disabled	11.0	1.6
Non-service-disabled	16.0	2.1
Age of Veteran		
20 to 29	26.2	0.0
30 to 39	0.0	0.0
40 to 49	13.1	0.0
50 to 64	17.7	2.6
65 and older	13.5	2.7
Education		
High school graduate	12.6	1.7
One year of college	25.3	5.3
Two years of college	11.8	1.9
Three years of college	17.6	1.9
College graduate	13.2	1.3
Post graduate course(s()	20.9	6.4
Post graduate degree	18.0	1.8
Other	26.1	0.0
Full Sample	**15.7**	**2.1**

Table 5.17 Veteran Business Owners Whose Enterprise is Located Entirely in Their Residence (percent)

Veteran Cohort	Share of Enterprises Located Entirely In Residence
Service-Connected Disability Status	
Service-disabled	52.1**
Non-service-disabled	37.7**
Dependents	
Dependent children	46.1**
No dependent children	35.4**
Full Sample	38.7

** Chi-square for the difference in the means is significant at the 5 percent significance level or less.

Table 5.18 Home-Based Veteran Business Owners Planning to Relocate Some or All of Operations Outside of Their Residence in the "Foreseeable Future" (percent)

Veteran Cohort	Share Planning to Expand Beyond Their Residence
Service-Connected Disability Status	
Service-disabled	42.1
Non-service-disabled	34.9
Gender	
Male	34.3
Female	45.6
Marital Status	
Single	37.7
Married	34.2
Living with a partner	0.0
Legally separated	50.0
Divorced	43.5
Dependents	
Dependent children	39.6
No dependent children	33.3
Full Sample	**35.6**

There was an impressive longevity to veteran-owned small businesses: 68.1 percent of veteran business owners had owned their concerns for 10 years or more *(Table 5.19)*. Although a smaller share of service-disabled veterans were in this category than non-service-disabled veterans (48.7 percent versus 69.4 percent), the share was still nearly half.

Most owners started their business rather than purchasing an existing business (84.7 percent versus 15.3 percent) *(Table 5.20)*. Evidence suggests that this is a positive success indicator.[22] However, only 15.6 percent of owners had partners, their relative scarcity suggesting a negative success indicator *(Table 5.21)*.[23] The

---

22   Duchesneau, Donald A. and Gartner, William B. (1990), "A Profile of New Venture Success and Failure in An Emerging Industry," *Journal of Business Venturing*, vol. 5, 297–312.

23   Cooper, Arnold C.; Woo, Carolyn Y.; and Dunkelberg, William C. (1988); "Entrepreneurs Perceived Chances for Success," *Journal of Business Venturing*, vol.3, 97–108.

Table 5.19 Age Distribution of Business Enterprises Owned By Veterans (percent)

Business Age from Start or Purchase	All Owners	Service-disabled	Non-service-disabled
Less than six months	0.1	1.6**	0.0**
Six months or more but less than one year	0.6	4.7**	0.3**
One year or more but less than three years	6.6	16.0**	5.9**
Three years or more but less than five years	7.6	6.5**	7.7**
Five years or more but less than 10 years	17.1	22.5**	16.7**
Ten years or more	68.1	48.7**	69.4**

** Chi-square for the difference in the means is significant at the 5 percent significance level or less.

Table 5.20 Veteran Business Owners Starting or Purchasing a Business (percent)

Veteran Cohort	Share Starting	Share Purchasing
Service-Connected Disability Status		
Service-disabled	90.2	9.8
Non-service-disabled	84.3	15.7
Gender		
Male	84.5	15.5
Female	86.6	13.4
Age of Veteran		
20 to 29	73.8	26.2
30 to 39	80.9	19.1
40 to 49	89.5	10.5
50 to 64	85.5	14.5
65 and older	81.8	18.2
Full Sample	**84.7**	**15.3**

Table 5.21 Veteran Business Owners Beginning with Partners (percent)

Veteran Cohort	Share With Partners
Service-Connected Disability Status	
Service-disabled	13.1
Non-service-disabled	15.8
Dependents	
Dependent children	7.5**
No dependent children	19.1**
Education	
High school graduate	20.1**
One year of college	15.6**
Two years of college	5.9**
Three years of college	9.3**
College graduate	17.0**
Post graduate course(s)	34.6**
Post graduate degree	14.4**
Other	17.2**
Full Sample	**15.6**

** Chi-square for the difference in the means is significant at the 5 percent significance level or less.

partner situation appeared to be a dynamic one through the life of the business in that 32 percent of new entrepreneurs originally formed or purchased their new business enterprise with one or more partners *(Table 5.2)*. Partners may or may not stay through the life of the business.

Internet-dependent businesses did not dominate the population of existing veteran-owned businesses; but they were not unimportant, either. Only 5.8 percent of owners indicated that their business was 100 percent dependent on the Internet *(Table 5.22)*. However, 22.5 percent indicated that their business was 50 percent or more dependent on the Internet. The fact that almost 32 percent of the veteran entrepreneur population in the residential survey indicated that their business would be 50 percent or more dependent on the Internet in the future suggests that web dependence might grow in the veteran business population *(Tables 5.5 and 5.22)*.

Table 5.22 Internet Dependence of Current Veteran-Owned Businesses (percent)

Veteran Cohort	0 to 24 Percent	25 to 49 Percent	50 to 99 Percent	100 Percent
Service-Connected Disability Status				
Service-disabled	45.9**	20.6**	25.6**	7.9**
Non-service-disabled	65.6**	12.7**	16.1**	5.6**
Age of Veteran				
20 to 29	24.6**	0.0**	75.4**	0.0**
30 to 39	66.3**	15.2**	0.0**	18.5**
40 to 49	57.7**	10.1**	25.1**	7.0**
50 to 64	60.8**	16.1**	17.0**	6.0**
65 and older	78.8**	9.1**	9.4**	2.8**
Education				
High school graduate	66.5	20.7	11.1	1.7
One year of college	73.1	10.3	10.0	6.6
Two years of college	62.8	18.2	14.4	4.6
Three years of college	68.4	9.1	15.1	7.4
College graduate	60.6	11.8	22.9	4.7
Post graduate course(s)	64.9	6.4	16.2	12.5
Post graduate degree	57.2	9.6	22.4	10.8
Other	97.1	2.9	0.0	0.0
Full Sample	**64.3**	**13.2**	**16.7**	**5.8**

** Chi-square for the difference in the means is significant at the 5 percent significance level or less.

As was the case with new veteran entrepreneurs, military service was of great value in providing business ownership skills: 69.2 percent of business owners supervised others while on active duty *(Table 5.23)*. These owners included a significantly higher proportion of service-disabled veterans than non-service-disabled veterans (87.6 percent versus 67.9 percent). Of those who had supervisory experience while on active duty, 88.9 percent taught those they supervised new skills or reinforced existing skills *(Table 5.24)*.

Beyond supervisory experience, active duty taught business-related skills: 37.5 percent of veteran business owners indicated that they learned or made use of one or more technologies while on active duty that were of "direct use in their current business enterprise" *(Table 5.25)*. A higher percentage of service-disabled veterans benefited from business-relevant technological training while on active duty

Table 5.23 Veteran Business Owners Supervising Others On Active Duty (percent)

Veteran Cohort	Share With Active Duty Supervisory Experience
Service-Connected Disability Status	
Service-disabled	87.6**
Non-service-disabled	67.9**
Gender	
Male	70.1
Female	61.3
Full Sample	**69.2**

** Chi-square for the difference in the means is significant at the 5 percent significance level or less.

Table 5.24 Veteran Business Owners With Active Duty Supervisory Experience Who Taught or Reinforced Skills to Those They Supervised (percent)

Veteran Cohort	Share Who Taught Those They Supervised
Service-Connected Disability Status	
Service-disabled	96.5*
Non-service-disabled	88.2*
Full Sample	**88.9**

* Chi-square for the difference in the means is significant at the 10 percent level or less and greater than the 5 percent level.

than non-service-disabled veterans (51.6 percent versus 36.8 percent). Beyond pure technology training, 34.0 percent of veteran business owners indicated that while on active duty they had one or more formal classes (*other* than to learn new technologies) that were of direct relevance to the ownership and operation of their business enterprise. Again, a greater proportion of service-disabled veterans benefited: 49.3 percent versus 33.0 percent for veteran business owners who were not service-disabled. Experience gained from previous business ownership and from the labor market benefited a greater proportion of veteran business owners than business-relevant experience gained while on active duty service: 83.2 percent of veteran business owners had owned at least one business in the past. This appeared to be an increasing function of age, while approximate gender equality appeared to be the case.

Table 5.25 Veteran Business Owners Who Learned Business Skills of Use in Their Current Business While on Active Duty or Owned a Business Previously (percent)

Veteran Cohort	Used Learned Technologies of Direct Use	Took One or More Classes of Direct Relevance	Owned a Business in the Past
Service-Connected Disability Status			
Service-disabled	51.6**	49.3**	73.2*
Non-service-disabled	36.8**	33.0**	83.9*
Gender			
Male	39.1**	32.5	83.6
Female	25.1**	48.3	79.9
Age of Veteran			
20 to 29	24.6**	0.0*	24.6**
30 to 39	62.6**	27.1*	54.1**
40 to 49	53.5**	48.6*	84.7**
50 to 64	36.2**	33.6*	84.7**
65 and older	26.3**	27.9*	86.2**
Full Sample	**37.5**	**34.0**	**83.2**

* Chi-square for the difference in the means is significant at the 10 percent level or less and greater than the 5 percent level.

** Chi-square for the difference in the means is significant at the 5 percent significance level or less.

A high proportion of veteran owners gained key business skills from previous employment or business ownership experience: 91.6 percent gained experience in managing employees; 96.6 percent gained experience in dealing with customers; 84.5 percent gained experience in marketing; 73.4 percent gained experience in managing tax issues; and 72.3 percent of owners gained experience in anticipating business trends from previous business ownership or employment *(Table 5.26)*.

Informal, on-the-job training gave 83.4 percent of veteran business owners skills directly related to the running of their current business enterprise, while 57.0 percent gained such skills from formal on-the-job training, and 16.9 percent from apprenticeship programs *(Table 5.27)*.

Table 5.26 Veteran Business Owners Who Have Gained Key Business Ownership Skills From Previous Employment and/or Previous Business Ownership (percent)

Veteran Cohort	Managing Employees	Dealing with Customers	Marketing Products or Services	Managing Tax Laws	Anticipating Business Trends
Service Disability Status					
Service-disabled	87.9	96.5	86.0	77.3	77.4
Non-service-disabled	91.9	96.6	84.4	73.1	72.1
Age of Veteran					
20 to 29	100.0	100.0	100.0	100.0	100.0
30 to 39	76.3	89.2	72.4	73.1	69.2
40 to 49	99.3	94.9	89.8	79.6	79.9
50 to 64	89.6	96.7	86.3	69.9	69.8
65 and older	93.1	98.4	77.3	75.8	72.3
Education					
High school graduate	82.7	96.1	76.2	67.6	66.5
One year of college	94.4	94.4	88.9	58.8	51.4
Two years of college	92.9	97.8	80.8	71.9	75.7
Three years of college	91.9	94.1	90.2	73.9	59.8
College graduate	93.7	98.1	88.5	78.1	79.8
Post graduate courses	93.9	100.0	93.6	74.6	68.9
Post graduate degree	94.5	93.8	88.3	75.8	76.6
Other	91.4	100.0	65.1	82.8	74.3
Full Sample	**91.6**	**96.6**	**84.5**	**73.4**	**72.3**

Note: Respondents were allowed to select multiple response options. Thus, shares do not total 100.

Non-service-disabled veteran business owners ranked the affordability of health insurance as their number one concern among a choice of 17 problems *(Table 5.28)*. Nearly half (46.9 percent) indicated that health insurance affordability was a "critical" problem. The non-service-disabled veterans ranked problems related to government resources and programs just below health insurance affordability. The number 2 problem was "Knowledge of helpful government and private programs for small business owners in general," followed by "Obtaining resources of various types from the government" and "Knowledge of helpful government and private programs geared toward veteran small business owners." The two lowest-ranked problems were "My status as a veteran

Table 5.27 Veteran Business Owners with Business-Relevant Education and/or Experience from Apprenticeship Programs or On-the-Job Training (percent)

Veteran Cohort	Apprenticeship Programs	On-the-Job Training (Formal Classes)	On-the-Job Training (Informal)
Service-Connected Disability Status			
Service-disabled	8.6	49.8	87.2
Non-service-disabled	17.4	57.5	83.1
Age of Veteran			
20 to 29	50.0	100.0**	50.0
30 to 39	0.0	100.0**	52.8
40 to 49	13.6	59.0**	82.5
50 to 64	18.5	59.6**	85.6
65 and older	16.6	43.2**	84.2
Education			
High school graduate	19.2	58.8	74.0
One year of college	18.4	46.7	91.7
Two years of college	11.5	60.7	85.3
Three years of college	19.5	53.4	77.2
College graduate	17.4	57.3	85.1
Post graduate course(s)	6.9	54.0	83.5
Post graduate degree	16.8	61.4	83.7
Other	38.2	37.4	100.0
Full Sample	**16.9**	**57.0**	**83.4**

** Chi-square for the difference in the means is significant at the 5 percent significance level or less.

or service-disabled veteran" and "My disability," which, interestingly, were also fairly low in the problem rankings of the service-disabled veteran population.

Service-disabled veteran business owners ranked government program and resource issues at the top of their list of problems, while health insurance affordability, the top problem for non-service-disabled veteran owners, ranked number 5 *(Table 5.29)*. Of current veteran business owners, 5.8 percent indicated that they had made use of a public or private small business program specifically designed for veterans, nearly the same as the 5.3 percent share of new veteran entrepreneurs in the residential survey using such programs

Table 5.28 Measures of Veteran Business Owner Problem Importance: Non-service-disabled Veteran Business Owners

Problem	Rank	Mean	Percent "Critical"
Affordability of health insurance	1	3.443	46.9
Knowledge of programs for small business owners in general	2	3.171	26.0
Obtaining resources from the government	3	3.137	30.3
Knowledge of programs for veteran small business owners	4	3.018	30.5
Finding qualified employees	5	2.975	22.2
Access to health insurance	6	2.895	34.7
Understanding tax law	7	2.488	17.5
Access to financing	8	2.423	15.8
Disadvantages in government contracting	9	2.353	18.5
Managing time	10	2.326	10.4
Understanding regulations	11	2.239	10.4
Retaining qualified employees	12	2.175	8.8
Developing and implementing a marketing strategy	13	2.166	5.3
Managing employees	14	1.643	4.4
Business interruptions due to military deployment	15	1.260	3.6
My status as a veteran or service-disabled veteran	16	1.237	2.6
My disability	17	1.089	1.4

(Tables 5.11 and 5.30). A larger share of service-disabled than non-service-disabled business owners used veteran small business programs (16.7 percent versus 5.1 percent). A significant 36.3 percent of current owners *planned* to make use of veteran small business programs in the "foreseeable future," with the 30 to 39 age cohort being most likely to have had such a plan (56.6 percent).

Of those who have not used a veteran small business program, 41.0 percent indicated that they did not need such programs, and 36.3 percent were not aware that veteran small business programs existed *(Table 5.31)*. Of those who were not planning to use small business programs for veterans, 53.0 percent indicated that they did not have a need for such program services, 22.5 percent did not know such programs existed, and 12.8 percent were confused as to what was available *(Table 5.32)*.[24] But, as with new veteran entrepreneurs, there

---

24 Respondents were allowed to choose more than one response category to this question.

Table 5.29 Measures of Veteran Business Owner Problem Importance: Service-Disabled Veteran Business Owners

Problem	Rank	Mean	Percent "Critical"
Obtaining resources from the government	1	3.391	37.2
Knowledge of programs for veteran small business owners	2	3.237	31.7
Knowledge of programs for small business owners in general	3	3.192	28.3
Disadvantages in government contracting	4	2.875	35.4
Affordability of health insurance	5	2.803	31.6
Finding qualified employees	6	2.800	26.0
Access to financing	7	2.790	26.3
Understanding tax law	8	2.693	18.1
Access to health insurance	9	2.539	24.9
Retaining qualified employees	10	2.338	14.0
My disability	11	2.304	16.6
Understanding regulations	12	2.292	10.2
Managing time	13	2.229	9.9
Developing and implementing a marketing strategy	14	2.124	1.7
My status as a veteran or service-disabled veteran	15	1.926	11.8
Managing employees	16	1.646	5.4
Business interruptions due to military deployment	17	1.223	3.5

still was an interest in using these programs: 95.2 percent of those who were confused about the existence or structure of veteran small business programs indicated that, if they knew more about them, they would use such programs if they met their needs *(Table 5.30)*.

Of the business owners, 21.6 percent indicated that they had used a public or private small business program other than those specifically designed for veterans (with similar proportions of the service-disabled and non-service-disabled populations indicating such program usage). This level was more than 50 percent larger than the 14.1 percent share of new veteran entrepreneurs who indicated such past program usage *(Tables 5.11 and 5.30)*. Conversely, a significantly smaller share of the veteran business owners, 31.9 percent, than the new veteran entrepreneurs, 51.2 percent, planned to make use of a non-veteran-specific small business program in the foreseeable future.

Table 5.30 Veteran Business Owners Who Have Used or Plan to Use a Small Business Program for Veterans or for Small Businesses in General (percent)

Veteran Cohort	Used a Veterans Program[1]	Plan to Use a Veterans Program[1]	Would Use Veterans Program if Aware[2]	Used a Small Business Program[3]	Plan to Use a Small Business Program[3]
Service Disability Status					
Service-disabled	16.7**	46.0	90.6	26.7	37.1
Non-service-disabled	5.1**	35.8	95.4	21.2	31.5
Gender					
Male	6.1	34.3**	94.6	21.5	32.1
Female	3.3	55.0**	100.0	22.8	29.9
Age of Veteran					
20 to 29	0.0	49.2**	100.0	49.2	0.0*
30 to 39	14.1	56.6**	100.0	21.0	39.0*
40 to 49	3.9	51.2**	97.6	21.9	45.4*
50 to 64	6.3	35.0**	92.9	23.2	33.1*
65 and older	5.3	23.9**	96.9	16.4	20.3*
Education					
High school graduate	4.5	39.9	100.0**	19.4	28.5
One year of college	8.3	25.4	65.4**	20.0	18.7
Two years of college	6.6	41.1	100.0**	14.7	44.7
Three years of college	5.6	42.0	100.0**	25.8	27.6
College graduate	6.2	33.3	93.9**	24.9	32.1
Post graduate course(s)	0.0	30.4	100.0**	35.0	28.6
Post graduate degree	7.9	38.8	95.8**	21.6	29.0
Other	0.0	26.1	100.0**	17.7	31.1
Full Sample	**5.8**	**36.3**	**95.2**	**21.6**	**31.9**

* Chi-square for the difference in the means is significant at the 10 percent level or less and greater than the 5 percent level.

** Chi-square for the difference in the means is significant at the 5 percent significance level or less.

1 Have used or plan to use a public or private small business program specifically designed for veterans.

2 Unaware of small business programs for veterans and would use such programs if aware of them.

3 Have used or plan to use a public or private small business program not specific to veterans.

Table 5.31 Reasons Given by Veteran Owners Who Had Not Used Any Veteran Small Business Programs (percent)

Reason for Non-use of Veterans Programs	Service-Disabled	Non-service-Disabled	Full Sample
Didn't have a need for these program services	35.7	41.3	**41.0**
Had a need but nothing in these programs meets my needs	8.0	4.5	**4.7**
Programs serving both veterans and non-veterans are adequate	2.1	3.0	**3.0**
Perception that program service delivery is inadequate	10.1	6.4	**6.6**
Confused as to what is available	13.8	10.9	**11.0**
Wasn't aware that small business programs for veterans existed	26.1	36.9	**36.3**
I don't qualify	4.1	3.8	**3.8**
Other	14.3	9.4	**9.7**

Note: Respondents were allowed to select multiple response options. Thus, shares do not total 100.

Table 5.32 Reasons Given by Veteran Business Owners Who Did Not Plan to Use a Veteran Small Business Program (percent)

Reason for No Plans to use Veteran Small Business Programs	Service-Disabled	Non-service-Disabled	Full Sample
Didn't have a need for these program services	51.7	53.0	**53.0**
Have needs but these programs don't meet them	3.8	4.1	**4.1**
Non veteran-specific small business programs are adequate	0.0	0.6	**0.6**
Negative experience with these programs in the past	15.1**	2.9**	**3.5****
Perception that program service delivery is inadequate	7.2	3.6	**3.8**
Confused as to what is available	10.8	12.9	**12.8**
Wasn't aware that small business programs existed	11.3	23.0	**22.5**
Other	7.4	11.1	**11.0**

Note: Respondents were allowed to select multiple response options. Thus, shares do not total 100.

** Chi-square for the difference in the means is significant at the 5 percent significance level or less.

Table 5.33 Reasons Given by Veteran Business Owners Who Had Not Used Any Small Business Programs Non-Specific to Veterans (percent)

Reason for Non-use of Veterans Programs	Service-Disabled	Non-service-Disabled	Full Sample
Didn't have a need for these program services	50.2	51.0	**50.9**
Had a need but these programs don't meet my needs	2.2	3.2	**3.1**
Perception that program service delivery is inadequate	6.8	2.8	**3.1**
Don't have time for training	2.4	1.4	**1.5**
Confused as to what is available	15.5	15.5	**15.5**
Don't qualify for program due to my veteran status	0.0	0.4	**0.4**
Don't qualify for program for reasons other than being a veteran	0.0	1.3	**1.3**
Wasn't aware that small business programs existed	25.0	28.1	**27.9**
Other	9.2	6.4	**6.6**

Note: Respondents were allowed to select multiple response options. Thus, shares do not total 100.

More than half, 50.9 percent, of veteran business owners who did not make use of general, non-veteran-specific small business programs indicated that they did not have a need for these program services *(Table 5.33)*. Further, 27.9 percent did not know such programs existed, and 15.5 percent were confused as to what was available.

Of those who did need program services but did not use general, non-veteran-specific small business programs because those programs did not meet their needs, 23.3 percent indicated that the entire problem was the need for a veteran-specific program; 15.4 percent said that the need for a veteran-specific program was only part of the problem *(Table 5.34)*.[25]

Of those who were not planning to make use of a general, non-veteran-specific small business program, 61.6 percent indicated that they simply did not have a need for these program services, while 19.9 percent were unaware that these programs existed, and 10.9 percent were confused as to what was available *(Table 5.35)*.

---

25 The researchers were unable to obtain good data on this question for the population of new veteran entrepreneurs from the residential survey.

Table 5.34 Veteran Business Owners Who Rejected the Use of General Small Business Programs Due to the Need for a Veteran-Specific Program (percent)

Veteran Cohort	Share Rejecting Entirely Due to the Need for a Veteran-Specific Program	Share Rejecting Partially Due to the Need for a Veteran-Specific Program
Service-Connected Disability Status		
Service Disabled	0.0	100.0
Non-service Disabled	24.2	12.1
Gender		
Male	36.3	5.8
Female	0.0	32.6
Full Sample	**23.3**	**15.4**

Table 5.35 Reasons Given by Veteran Business Owners Who Did Not Plan to Use Any Small Business Program Not Specific to Veterans (percent)

Reason for No Plans to use Small Business Programs	Service-Disabled	Non-service-Disabled	Full Sample
Didn't have a need for these program services	53.7	62.1	**61.6**
Have needs but these programs don't meet them	0.0	1.3	**1.2**
Need small business program designed for veterans	0.0	0.7	**0.6**
Perception that program service delivery is inadequate	3.5	4.0	**4.0**
Found these programs to be inadequate in the past	7.4*	1.4*	**1.7**
Confused as to what is available	14.3	10.7	**10.9**
I don't qualify for program services because I am a veteran	0.0	0.6	**0.6**
I don't qualify for program services for other reasons	7.2**	0.0**	**0.4**
Wasn't aware that small business programs existed	17.4	20.0	**19.9**
Other	7.4	4.0	**4.2**

Note: Respondents were allowed to select multiple response options. Thus, shares do not total 100.

* Chi-square for the difference in the means is significant at the 10 percent level or less and greater than the 5 percent level.

** Chi-square for the difference in the means is significant at the 5 percent significance level or less.

Conclusion

The data presented here have been excerpted from an Advocacy study published in 2004. A wealth of additional information and source references helpful to those working on veteran entrepreneurship issues can be accessed in this and other Advocacy-sponsored studies available. Statistical information on the estimated number of veteran-owned firms is presented in *Evaluating Veteran Business Owner Data*.[26] The Census Bureau's pending 2002 Survey of Business Owners and Self-Employed Persons (SBO)[27] included questions on veteran status and, for the first time, on whether responding veteran business owners had a service-connected disability. When the SBO veteran data become available, they should provide a wealth of new information on veterans in business and be a primary source on this subject for researchers and policymakers.

---

26 *Evaluating Veteran Business Owner Data* was prepared in 2004 by the Office of Advocacy in collaboration with Jack Faucett Associates, Eagle Eye Publishers, Waldman Associates, and REDA International, Advocacy contractors and subcontractors. See *http://www.sba.gov/advo/research/rs244tot.pdf* for the complete study and summary.

27 For further information on the U.S. Census Bureau's *2002 Survey of Business Owners and Self-Employed Persons (SBO)*, see *http://www.census.gov/csd/sbo*.

6 A DISCOURSE *on* TAX COMPLEXITY *and* UNCERTAINTY *and their* EFFECTS *on* SMALL BUSINESS

Synopsis

The complexity of the U.S. tax code and its uncertainty have each, on their own, been studied and analyzed at length. This study attempts to link the two concepts in order to clarify the proper fiscal climate for healthy small business growth.

Introduction

Public finance economists have traditionally concentrated on the tradeoff between efficiency and equity in prescribing tax policy. The third leg of the normative tax policy framework is most often overlooked: complexity and its opposite, simplicity. An ideal tax system should balance the equity and efficiency of taxes while being as simple as possible. Simplification of the tax code often involves sacrificing equity, or at least perceived equity. The lack of emphasis on simplicity in recent times has led to a bloated tax code where compliance costs are now a significant portion of many taxpayers' overall tax burden.

Uncertainty over future tax obligations also imposes costs on those covered by the tax. It affects taxpayers' planning horizons, and reduces both their optimality and feasibility. Taxpayers thus face uncertainty from two directions: tax complexity and tax rates. Given that complexity raises compliance costs, taxpayers then become uncertain as to the total future burden of taxes.

Research by Crain (2005) details the small business compliance burden of income taxes. American small businesses in 2004 spent $1,304 per employee to comply with federal income taxes, or almost two times as much per employee as the average large business. One reason for the high per-employee cost to small businesses is the level of complexity in the tax code. There is a substantial burden in paperwork and recordkeeping for any firm with a payroll, even before the first paycheck is cut. These setup costs are largely fixed, and bigger firms are able to spread them over a greater number of employees than smaller firms, reducing the average cost per employee. For small firms these costs can be significant, and they increase with the complexity of the tax code. Furthermore, because significant changes in the code from year to year entail new fixed costs, uncertainty in the code can have a deterrent effect on small firm hiring and investment. Clearly, complexity and uncertainty in the tax code are important issues for small businesses in particular.

This discussion will focus on tax complexity and uncertainty within the context of the U.S. federal income tax. Income tax simplification has been a policy goal of the current administration as a part of an overall economic plan. Examples include making the code easier to understand, reducing the number of forms required for compliance, and reducing the number of deductions, loopholes, and programs and/or the complex qualifications for each. It is worth emphasizing at the outset that simplification is not unambiguously beneficial to all small businesses: if one were to unilaterally simplify the code, some small businesses might face higher effective tax rates, and their overall tax burden could increase, despite the fact that the code would then require fewer forms and less time to comply. Simplification, in this vein, needs further qualification. However, overall burdens will fall as compliance becomes simple and unambiguous. Reduced complexity also has benefits through the reduction of future tax uncertainty.

The existing literature on tax complexity and tax uncertainty, or predictability, tend to treat these two phenomena in isolation. The tax complexity literature has focused on either straightforward compliance cost estimates that measure the hours or dollars required to administer the income tax system, or on the distortionary effects of complexity. The uncertainty literature has concentrated on the distortionary effects of unpredictable changes in the tax code. Saade (2002), for example, models the effects of uncertainty in the rules-versus-discretion framework of Barro and Gordon (1981–1982). While they often measure the same things under different names, none of these approaches addresses the issue of how uncertainty and complexity are related. This paper takes on that issue.

The concept of simplification as a normative goal is expanded here by tying it to the concept of permanence to alleviate uncertainty. The goal is to specifically identify why complexity and uncertainty in the tax code are so interrelated and to bridge the gap between analyses of these two issues in the economics literature.

Uncertainty refers to the year-to-year stability of the tax code. While at first blush complexity and uncertainty hardly seem related at all, the two are actually critically related, with uncertainty determined by complexity. That is to say, increasing the simplicity of the tax code will, at the same time, decrease uncertainty, carrying benefits forward. Even without a policy commitment to permanent tax rules, reduced complexity would lead to clearer sets of possibilities for changes in the tax code. Employing the rules-versus-discretion framework of Saade (2002), lower complexity carries many of the same benefits that a rules-based tax setting system would. Adding a rules-based system on top of a simpler tax code would then further enhance the benefits, as rules permanence is a complement to the uncertainty reduction of simplification. These reinforcing effects provide a greater benefit to small businesses than increasing either in isolation. The conduit for this joint effect is through the decision making of small business owners: a simple and stable tax code has a greater impact on reducing the excess burden of taxation than the sum of the parts.

The remainder of this paper is organized as follows: the next section discusses the issue of tax complexity and lays out a very simple model for the concept of complexity, which, it is hypothesized, is the foundation of uncertainty. The following section illustrates uncertainty as it relates to and stems from complexity, and demonstrates the simple, yet powerful interrelatedness of these concepts. In addition the section looks at the normative issue of tax permanence in the familiar rules-versus-discretion framework. The final section offers some concluding remarks.

Complexity and Simplification

Concerns about the complexity of the tax code are not new in American public policy debates. Indeed, nearly as soon as the income tax was reinstated in 1913, talk turned to the unnecessary complexity of the code. By 1926 Congress had created the Joint Committee on Taxation to study the simplification of taxes. Throughout the remainder of the twentieth century, periodic cries for tax simplification became the norm. However, it is debatable whether any genuine simplification ever took place. For instance, during the Reagan administration, a significant tax reform movement gained momentum, culminating with the Tax Reform Act of 1986, which entailed some nominal simplifications but did little to reduce actual compliance costs.[1]

Given the apparent concern about complexity in the public eye, it is useful to investigate the question of whether the tax system really is complex, and whether complexity has been increasing. Exactly what is meant by complexity? A tax system is characterized by a few very simple parameters: first, what is taxed, commonly called the tax base, including the number of different tax bases; second, at what rate the base is taxed, and how many different rates are assessed; third, what contingent provisions exist that modify the calculation of either the tax base or the tax rate. For instance, in the U.S. income tax code, income from wages and salaries, interest, and business income are all taxed at the same rate, despite being different tax bases. Capital gains on asset transactions are another tax base, and are taxed differently. Further, there are a number of different tax rates in the federal code, with rates increasing on marginal income across a number of brackets, in other words, a progressive income tax. While the U.S. code is fairly simple with respect to the number of bases and rates compared with many foreign codes, the number of deductions, exemptions, credits, and other tax expenditure programs is rather large. Deductions and exemptions modify the tax base, while credits reduce the actual tax bill. To take advantage of most tax expenditure programs the taxpayer must do a certain amount of recordkeeping and fill out appropriate paperwork to be appended to the tax return. Both the number of restrictions on the various tax expenditure programs as well as the burdens one incurs to avail oneself of contribute to the observed complexity of the income tax code. Research sponsored by the Office of Advocacy further highlights and supports the position that this study takes.[2] Advocacy's research was initially conducted to investigate whether or not incorporated small businesses were taking advantage of tax credits that were available to their form of corporate structure. Not surprisingly, the researchers concluded that small firms were not as likely as their larger counterparts to benefit from many expenditure programs.

---

1 Slemrod, 1992.

2 *The Impact of Tax Expenditure Policies on Incorporated Small Businesses*, Office of Advocacy, SBA, 2004, available at *www.sba.gov/advo/research/rs237tot.pdf*.

While a qualitative description of tax complexity is relatively straightforward, it is difficult to describe a quantitative complexity metric. Perhaps this is why compliance costs, an imperfect complexity metric, are so commonly accepted as the relevant measure. The relationship between tax complexity and the paperwork and recordkeeping burden of taxes is a well-documented one. Slemrod (1992) equates tax complexity with the sum of compliance costs, which fall on taxpayers, and administrative costs, which fall on the government. Using this simple metric, it is possible to measure the compliance costs to American taxpayers and relate this burden back to complexity.[3]

These cost calculations are direct and simply measure the opportunity cost of engaging in tax compliance activities. It is largely assumed in this literature that compliance costs accurately map tax complexity, which may be true for any given year. However, technological innovations can drastically reduce compliance costs over time even while the tax code remains largely intact. If the structure of the tax has not changed, its complexity has not changed, even if the direct compliance costs have declined.[4] Tax preparation software, for instance, has produced massive time savings for many individual taxpayers and at the same time reduced reporting and calculation errors that stem from complexity, even while the tax code has arguably moved in the direction of greater complexity.

Tax complexity affects taxpayer behavior by constraining choices and changing incentives for undertaking certain activities. Incentives change whenever there are multiple tax bases and rates, as resources are shifted in response to relative prices modified by effective tax rates. The same is true of complexities in obtaining deductions and credits: in some cases the cost of availing oneself of relief negates the incentive to engage in the said activity.[5] This facet of complexity will

---

3 On measuring compliance costs, see, for example, Slemrod and Sorum, 1984; Arthur D. Little, 1988; Blumenthal and Slemrod, 1992; Slemrod, 1992.

4 Compliance cost estimates in burden hours will tend to fall over time as technology speeds data processing by quickly combining records and performing calculations. The IRS must occasionally resubmit Information Collection Requests (ICR) to the U.S. Office of Management and Budget under the Paperwork Reduction Act for all of its tax forms. Each ICR must include current burden hour estimates, and these will tend to be declining insofar as taxpayers are employing available tax compliance technology.

5 For example, see the discussion of the home-office deduction in *Home-Based Business and Government Regulations*. Office of Advocacy, 2004. The research is available at *www.sba.gov/advo/research/rs235tot.pdf*.

be juxtaposed here with uncertainty to show how the two concepts are related, and how tax simplification carries greater benefits than a mere reduction in the number of hours Americans spend filling out tax paperwork.

Equating complexity and compliance burden is an oversimplification, but for lack of a better metric it must suffice to shed some light on the issue. Thus, compliance burden estimates represent the most straightforward complexity measure. In its most recent compliance burden study, the Tax Foundation estimated that in 2002, it cost Americans $194 billion to comply with the federal income tax code. Put another way, 5.8 billion hours were spent in compliance activities. Businesses, with the most complex requirements by far, shouldered 52.5 percent of that total burden. However, many small business owners file taxes as individuals, so the actual business share would be even greater if those 1040s were also included. The case for increasing complexity is supported by the data: the 2002 burden marks a 70 percent increase over the 1995 burden. Extending the analysis even further, between 1955 and 2001 the Internal Revenue Code income tax provisions grew a staggering 478 percent, from 172,000 words to 995,000 words.[6] Crain employed the Tax Foundation's burden estimates to derive the costs of tax compliance to American businesses.[7] In 2004 the average American business taxpayer spent $894 per employee on tax compliance activities, but small employers (with fewer than 20 employees) spent $1,304 per employee.

A broader concept of complexity will be used for the remainder of this paper, in part because no one has devised a genuine complexity measure; However, the paper will continue to highlight the importance of the main components of complexity from the public finance literature. A broad definition of complexity is taken from Heyndels and Smolders (1995), who discuss complexity within the framework of fiscal illusion.[8] Edmiston, Mudd, and Valev (2003) adopt

---

6 Tax Foundation, "The Cost of Complying with the Federal Income Tax," Special Report, July 2002, No.114.

7 Crain, 2005.

8 Fiscal illusion is the distortion in government budgets caused by the inability of taxpayers to monitor all aspects of taxes and expenditures. Tax complexity increases fiscal illusion by making the tax system less transparent. Wagner (1976) introduces the measurement of fiscal illusion with concentration indices from the industrial organization literature. Heyndels and Smolders (1995) find that complexity increases fiscal illusion leading to larger government budgets.

the Heyndels-Smolders framework and perform an empirical investigation in which they measure the effects of tax complexity on foreign direct investment. Their work also incorporates tax uncertainty and ascribes to it the same general negative effect as complexity. The innovation here will be the development of a simple model that shows how and why complexity and uncertainty are linked. Previous work, such as that of Edmiston, Mudd, and Valev, merely relied on the fact that both complexity and uncertainty carry costs.

In relatively unrestricted empirical models, major components of complexity show positive results in regressions testing the theoretical effects of complexity. However, they do not specify a causal relationship between complexity and its costs. The authors here specify how the concepts are related and demonstrate how increasing complexity also increases uncertainty.

Complexity and uncertainty are intertwined through the impact that complexity has on the level of uncertainty. As suggested above, complexity in and of itself is not terribly concerning; after all, it can be overcome with expert advice and even technology, and its costs diminish over time provided the level of complexity is constant, and most of the individual rules and components of the tax code remain constant.

From an empirical standpoint, complexity is a difficult quantity to establish. It is relatively trivial to list at least some of the features that make a tax code complex: multiple and ill-defined tax bases, variable and numerous rates, complex rules for deductions and exemptions, and many others. Furthermore it is only somewhat more difficult to measure these complexity components individually. It is another matter altogether to establish a single measure that signifies a level of complexity by integrating all of these component variables. No attempt is made to solve this conundrum here either; instead, a simple proposal drives the results. The level of complexity is assumed to be monotonically increasing in all of the constituent parts that one could include under the rubric of complexity if one were inclined to produce an exhaustive list. It is also assumed for simplicity that complexity is a continuous function.[9] In order to

---

9   In actuality, it is likely that any mapping of the features of the tax code called complexity components onto an integrated metric called complexity would *not* be a continuous function. In fact, it is likely to be a rather irregular step function. Nevertheless, the important factor is that it is a monotonically increasing function in all its arguments, without respect to the actual functional form.

demonstrate the connection between complexity and uncertainty it is not necessary to be able to actually measure or specify complexity, only to simply state that it is an integration of its constituent parts and possesses the quality of increasing in them.

$$X = f(B,r,Z)$$

Where X is the complexity function, B is a vector of variables describing the tax base(s), r is a vector describing the tax rate(s), and Z is a vector that describes the other relevant features of the tax code, including deductions, exemptions, and credits. Note that each argument is a vector of unspecified dimension exactly because not all of the relevant arguments are known. The simple assumptions lead to the fact that the relevant partial derivatives are positive:

$$\delta X/\delta B > 0;\ \delta X/\delta r > 0;\ \delta X/\delta Z > 0.$$

Complexity, then, can be expressed as a single value whose magnitude indicates the absolute level of complexity. Complexity in this sense is related to costs, thus bridging the gap to the literature on compliance costs. In the simple complexity function above, costs are assumed to be rising in complexity monotonically. However, this complexity function is not equal to the costs tracked by the compliance cost literature in any way. Measuring compliance costs in that way would require intimate knowledge of the functional forms of the complexity arguments, which are not speculated upon here.

Complexity can increase dramatically by adding even a few additional wrinkles to the tax code. Because tax rates, bases, deductions, exemptions, and other features of the tax code tend to vary not independently, but with one another, the complexity function is not a simple additively separable function of the arguments. Again, although no attempt is made here to specify a functional form, it is likely that the form of the complexity function is combinatorial and thus increasing rapidly with respect to its arguments as they are interdependent. The result is that even small changes in a few complexity variables, or the addition of new dimensions of complexity, can result in a combinatorial explosion where complexity increases rapidly. Because small business owners face higher compliance burdens than the average taxpayer, the complexity of their taxes may be much higher as well. If this is the case, even moderate levels of complexity can carry significant cost burdens, and can enhance uncertainty over future tax burdens and further raise costs to taxpayers.

The Effect of Complexity on Uncertainty

"While taxes may be certain, U.S. tax policy has certainly not been."[10] The natural transition to this argument is that the variability of U.S. tax policy unequivocally creates variability in the certainty of taxes.[11] The randomness inherent in elections is linked to that existing in tax rates.[12] In other words, the inability to correctly predict what fiscal regime will prevail at the next election cycle forces businesses to optimize looking backwards as opposed to forward, hence the suboptimality of their endeavors. It is worth pointing out, at this point, that this paper is not going to deal with the additional dimension of uncertainty arising from intrinsic economic risk. In sum, where the expected rate next period, t_1, $(E(\tau_{t1}))$, based on all the information known to taxpayers in the current period (I_{t0}), is the realized rate next period (τ_{t1}) plus some measure of uncertainty (u_{t1}), uncertainty is expressed in the range of possible outcomes in the next period.

$$E(\tau_{t1})|I_{t0} = \tau_{t1} + u_{t1}$$

Rearranging terms, the measure for uncertainty is:

$$u_{t1} = E(\tau_{t1})|I_{t0} - \tau_{t1}$$

As argued above, it is undeniable that the more complex the system is, the more uncertainty there is. Thus, where X is complexity, and $Var(u_t)$ is the

---

10   Bizer and Judd, 1989.

11   As more fully argued in Saade (2002), the expectation of future tax obligations is the significant variable in the decision to move forward. While the actual rate may coincide with the predicted rate, *ex ante*, what matters is the belief that the expectation will be fulfilled, i.e., no uncertainty. With uncertainty in the system, the setting of optimal plans becomes more costly and difficult.

12   *Ibid.*

variance of the uncertainty term, uncertainty is a function of complexity and can be expressed as follows:

$$\text{Var}(u_t) = f(X) \text{ and } \delta\text{Var}(u_t)/\delta X > 0$$

It is assumed that $\text{Var}(u_t)$ is symmetrical for any level of complexity. In this setup, complexity is not allowed to affect expectation formation, but is going to affect the probability of being wrong in the assessment for the next period. Basically, complexity increases the possibility frontier for policy change by increasing the number of tax policy dimensions. In a simple example, imagine the case of a flat tax where policy is defined solely by the definition of the tax base and a single rate. While either of these variables may change from one tax period to the next, taxpayers still have a fairly easy time forming expectations because the number of possible changes and combinations of changes is rather limited. Add further dimensions to the tax code and the range of possible outcomes increases exponentially because of the combinatorial possibilities from varying multiple dimensions at the same time. Uncertainty will be dealt with more analytically below, but it is helpful at this point to think of it as "noise" in the planning of business activity. Complexity thus adds to the noise in business planning, further increasing compliance costs.

The costs of uncertainty and complexity are considerable. Complexity carries the cost of increased compliance burden, a cost well discussed and documented in the economics and policy literature. Consider, however, the effect of complexity on uncertainty and the considerable costs this entails. Assuming standard von Neuman-Morgenstern utility functions prevail for taxpayers, greater uncertainty is costly even if the expected tax rate for these taxpayers remains unchanged from what would prevail under a simpler tax regime. Taxpayers will try to maximize expected utility, forming expectations about future utility similarly to the way they form expectations for tax obligations. Because greater complexity increases the variance in expected tax payments, it also increases the variance in expected future after-tax income. If taxpayers are risk-averse, then diminishing marginal utility dictates that the possible downside loss in utility from lower income is greater than any upside gain from higher income when tax burdens are lower. Consider:

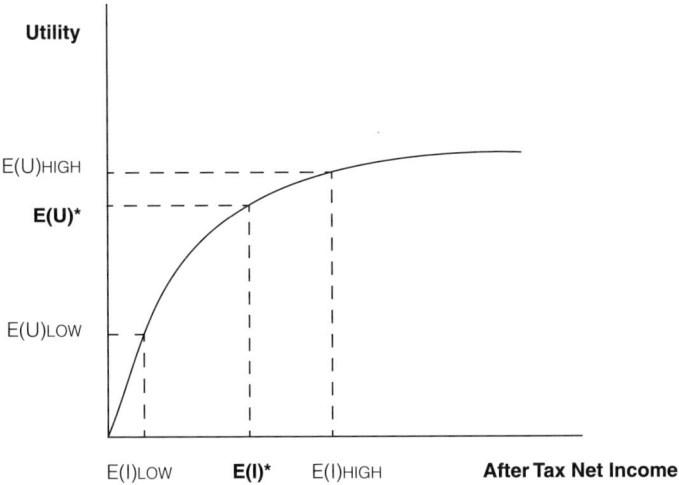

Expected utility is graphed against expected income, with utility taking the standard functional form and exhibiting diminishing returns in income. **E(I)***
is equidistant from E(I)HIGH and E(I)LOW, and each income level translates into the corresponding expected utility levels, **E(U)***, E(U)HIGH and E(U)LOW.
Now, if after-tax net expected income has variance with bounds indicated by E(I)LOW and E(I)HIGH, then the variance in expected utility is necessarily greater than the variance in income because of the shape of the standard utility curve. More to the point, taxpayers face greater potential disutility if income is low (because taxes are high) than the utility gain they would receive if income were high (because taxes were low). This is illustrated by the fact that the distance **E(U)*** to E(U)HIGH is much smaller than the distance **E(U)*** to E(U)LOW. The result is that taxpayers are forced to hedge against the potential downside risk, and therefore must incur costs from the uncertainty of the tax regime. The costs of the uncertainty are a function of its magnitude, as measured by $Var(u_t)$.

While the costs of complexity and subsequently uncertainty hit all taxpayers, they are especially burdensome to small business owners. As mentioned previously, small business owners face the most complex tax burdens of any individual taxpayers. Applying the logic of this complexity and uncertainty model, small business owners therefore also face much greater uncertainty in their tax obligations.

The implications derived here suggest that the health of the small business sector and the economy at large can be improved by well understood policies that promote and implement simplicity or ease of compliance. Such suggestion is in line with an Office of Advocacy study presented in 2002;[13] Saade presented a model that delineated the set of available policy choices, and showed that the cost function hit its minimum under the rules regime. Saade further proved that in the presence of discount rates, the rules equilibrium was only reachable through the use of explicit constraints. These general findings are relevant to the issues discussed here and applicable to the general suggestion presented above.

Conclusion

This paper is an attempt to push forward the discussion on simplicity and uncertainty. Although these concepts have been fleshed out elsewhere in the literature, this analysis identified a need to link them. An argument was developed supporting a definition of complexity having an impact on uncertainty. Further, during the process of expectation formation, complexity affects the probability of making the right guess. In line with research previously done by Advocacy economists, this study not only reinforces the conclusion that policies that promote ease of compliance while reducing uncertainty are more conducive to economic growth, but also provides support to the general notion that a well understood and predictable environment in which simple and stable rules are the norm is indeed optimal for small business success.

---

13   See *Supra* note 11.

References

Arthur D. Little, *Development of Methodology for Estimating the Taxpayer Paperwork Burden*, Final Report to the Department of the Treasury, Internal Revenue Service, Washington, D.C., June 1988.

Barro, Robert J. and David Gordon, "Rules, Discretion, and Reputation in a Model of Monetary Policy," *Journal of Monetary Economics* (12.n1) 1983a: 101–21.

Barro, Robert J. and David Gordon, "A Positive Theory of Monetary Policy in a Natural Rate Model," *Journal of Political Economy* (91.n4) 1983b: 589–610.

Bizer, David S. and Kenneth L. Judd, "Taxation and Uncertainty," *American Economic Review*, (79.n2) 1989: 331–6.

Blumenthal, Marsha and Joel Slemrod, "The Compliance Cost fo the U.S. Individual Income Tax System: A Second Look After Tax Reform," *National Tax Journal*, (45.n2) 1992: 185–202.

Crain, W. Mark, *The Impact of Regulatory Costs on Small Firms*, Office of Advocacy, U.S. Small Business Administration, 2005, available at *http://www.sba. gov/advo/research/rs264tot.pdf*.

Edminston, Kelly, Shannon Mudd, and Neven Valev, "Tax Structures and FDI: The Deterrent Effects of Complexity and Uncertainty," *Fiscal Studies*, (24.n3) 2003: 341–59.

Heyndels, Bruno, and Carine Smolders, "Tax Complexity and Fiscal Illusion," *Public Choice*, (85.n1–2) 1995: 127–141.

Saade, N. Radwan, "Rules versus Discretion in Tax Policy," working paper, Office of Advocacy, U.S. Small Business Administration, 2002, available at *http://www. sba.gov/advo/stats/wkp02rs.pdf*.

Slemrod, Joel, "Did the Tax Reform Act of 1986 Simplify Tax Matters?" *Journal of Economic Perspectives*, (6.n1) 1992: 45–57.

Slemrod, Joel, and Nikki Sorum, "The Compliance Cost of the U.S. Individual Income Tax System," *National Tax Journal*, (37.n4) 1984: 461–74.

Wagner, Richard E., "Revenue Structure, Fiscal Illusion and Budgetary Choice," *Public Choice*, (25.n1–2) 1976: 45–61.

7 *The* REGULATORY FLEXIBILITY ACT: HISTORY *and* CURRENT STATUS *of* RFA IMPLEMENTATION

Synopsis

The Regulatory Flexibility Act (RFA), enacted in 1980, requires federal agencies to determine the impact of their rules on small entities, consider alternatives that minimize small entity impacts, and make their analyses available for public comment. In August 2002, President Bush signed Executive Order 13272, providing a renewed incentive for agencies to improve their compliance with the RFA and give proper consideration to small entities in the agency rulemaking process.

Throughout 2004, the Office of Advocacy (Advocacy), charged with ensuring agency compliance with the RFA, continued its efforts to represent small entities before regulatory agencies, lawmakers, and policymakers. The office worked closely with small entities and their representatives to identify and comment on agency rules that would affect their interests.

Advocacy focused on the issues most important to small entities, significantly reducing regulatory burdens and producing substantial cost savings. In fiscal year 2004, the Office of Advocacy helped small businesses achieve more than $17 billion in regulatory cost savings and more than $2 billion in recurring annual savings.

Overview of the Regulatory Flexibility Act and Related Policy

History of the RFA

Before Congress enacted the Regulatory Flexibility Act[1] in 1980, federal agencies did not, in the rulemaking process, recognize the pivotal role of small

---

1   The Regulatory Flexibility Act, Pub. L. 96–354, 94 Stat. 1164 (codified at 5 U.S.C. § 601 et seq.), became law on September 19, 1980. The full law as amended appears as Appendix A of this report.

business in an efficient marketplace, nor did they consider the possibility that agency regulations could put small businesses at a competitive disadvantage with large businesses or even constitute a complete barrier to small business market entry. Similarly, agencies did not appreciate that small businesses were restricted in their ability to spread costs over output because of their lower production levels. As a result, when agencies implemented "one-size-fits-all" regulations, small businesses were placed at a competitive disadvantage with respect to their larger competitors.

The problem was exacerbated by the fact that small businesses were also disadvantaged by larger businesses' ability to influence final decisions on regulations. Large businesses had more resources and could afford to hire staff to monitor proposed regulations to ensure effective input in the regulatory process. As a result, consumers and competition were undercut, while larger companies were rewarded.

Over the past 25 years, U.S. presidents have taken leadership positions in standing up for small business. In 1980, when the first White House Conference on Small Business was held, small business delegates told the president and Congress that they needed relief from the unfair burdens of federal regulation. President Jimmy Carter listened when small businesses explained that the burden of federal agency regulations often fell hardest on them. They asserted that "one-size-fits-all" regulations, although easier to design and enforce, disproportionately affected small businesses. This led the federal government to recognize the different impacts of regulations on firms of different sizes and the disparity between large and small firms in the level of input in the regulatory process. In 1980, Congress and the president enacted the RFA to alter how agencies craft regulatory solutions to problems and to change the "one-size-fits-all" approach to regulatory policy.[2]

In 1993, President Bill Clinton issued Executive Order 12866, which required federal agencies to determine whether a regulatory action was "significant" and therefore subject to review by the Office of Management and Budget (OMB)

---

2   Congress agreed with small businesses when it specifically found in the preamble to the RFA that "laws and regulations designed for application to large-scale entities have been applied uniformly to small [entities,...] even though the problems that gave rise to the government action may not have been caused by those small entities." As a result, Congress found that these regulations have "imposed unnecessary and disproportionately burdensome demands" upon small businesses with limited resources, which, in turn, has "adversely affected competition." Findings and Purposes, Pub. L. No. 96–354.

and the analytical requirements of the executive order. In September 2003, OMB issued Circular A-4, which provides guidance to federal agencies for preparing regulatory analyses of economically significant regulatory actions under Executive Order 12866.[3]

In 1996, Congress and the president strengthened the RFA by enacting the Small Business Regulatory Enforcement Fairness Act (SBREFA).[4] SBREFA amended the RFA to allow a small business, appealing from an agency final action, to seek judicial review of an agency's compliance with the RFA. Not surprisingly, this change has encouraged some agencies to increase their compliance with the requirements of the RFA.

In 2002, President George W. Bush signed Executive Order 13272, titled "Proper Consideration of Small Entities in Agency Rulemaking." The E.O. requires agencies to place emphasis on the consideration of potential impacts on small entities when promulgating regulations in compliance with the RFA. Advocacy is required to provide the agencies with information and training on how to comply with the RFA and must report to OMB annually on agency compliance with the E.O. By signing this executive order, the president provided the small business community with another important tool to ensure that federal regulatory agencies comply with the RFA.

Analysis Required by the RFA

The RFA requires each federal agency to review its proposed and final rules to determine if the rules will have a "significant economic impact on a substantial number of small entities." Section 601 of the RFA defines small entities to include small businesses, small organizations, and small governmental jurisdictions. Unless the head of the agency can certify that a proposed rule is not expected to have a significant economic impact on a substantial number of small entities,[5] an initial regulatory flexibility analysis (IRFA) must be pre-

---

3   See the Advocacy website at *www.sba.gov/advo/laws/sum_eo.html* for a summary of Executive Order 12866; for more detail, visit, *http://www.whitehouse.gov/omb/circulars/a004/a-4.pdf*. The circular replaces the January 1996 "best practices" and the 2000 guidance documents on Executive Order 12866.

4   Pub. L. No.. 96–354, 94 Stat. 1164 (1980) (codified at 5 U.S.C. §§ 601–612) amended by Subtitle II of the Contract with America Advancement Act, Pub. L. 104–121, 110 Stat. 857 (1996), 5 U.S.C. § 612(a).

pared and published in the *Federal Register* for public comment.[6] This initial analysis must describe the impact of the proposed rule on small entities. It must also contain a comparative analysis of alternatives to the proposed rule that would minimize the impact on small entities and document their comparative effectiveness in achieving the regulatory purpose.

When an agency issues a final rule, it must prepare a final regulatory flexibility analysis (FRFA) unless the agency head certifies that the rule will not have a significant economic impact on a substantial number of small entities and provides a statement containing the factual basis for the certification.[7] The RFA is built on the premise that when an agency undertakes a careful analysis of its proposed regulations with sufficient small business input, the agency can and will identify the economic impact on small businesses. Once an agency identifies the impact a rule will have on small businesses, the agency is expected to analyze alternative measures to reduce or eliminate the disproportionate small business burden without compromising public policy objectives. The RFA does not require special treatment or regulatory exemptions for small business, but mandates an analytical process for determining how best to achieve public policy objectives without unduly burdening small businesses.

The Small Business Regulatory Enforcement Fairness Act of 1996

The Small Business Regulatory Enforcement Fairness Act amended the RFA in several critical respects. First, the SBREFA amendments to the RFA were specifically designed to ensure meaningful small business input during the earliest stages of the regulatory development process.

---

5 5 U.S.C. § 605 (b). If a regulation is found not to have a significant economic impact on a substantial number of small entities, the head of an agency may certify to that effect, but must provide a factual basis for this determination. This certification must be published with the proposed rule or at the time of publication of the final rule in the *Federal Register* and is subject to public comment in order to ensure that the certification is warranted.

6 5 U.S.C. § 603.

7 5 U.S.C. § 604.

Most significantly, SBREFA authorized judicial review of agency compliance with the RFA, and strengthened the authority of the chief counsel for advocacy to file *amicus curiae* briefs in regulatory appeals brought by small entities.

SBREFA also added a new provision to the RFA requiring the Environmental Protection Agency (EPA) and the Occupational Safety and Health Administration (OSHA) to convene small business advocacy review panels (SBREFA panels) to review regulatory proposals that may have a significant economic impact on a substantial number of small entities. The purpose of a SBREFA panel is to ensure small business participation in the rulemaking process, to solicit comments, and to discuss less burdensome alternatives to the regulatory proposal. Included on the SBREFA panel are representatives from the rulemaking agency, the Office of Management and Budget's Office of Information and Regulatory Affairs (OIRA), and the chief counsel for advocacy. The Office of Advocacy assists the rulemaking agency in identifying small entity representatives from affected industries, who provide advice and comments to the SBREFA panel on the potential impacts of the proposal. Finally, the panel must develop a report on its findings and submit the report to the head of the agency within 60 days.

Additionally, SBREFA amended the RFA to bring certain interpretative rulemakings of the Internal Revenue Service (IRS) within the scope of the RFA. The law now applies to those IRS rules—including those that would normally be exempt from the RFA as interpretative—published in the *Federal Register* that impose a "collection of information" requirement on small entities.[8] Congress took care to define the term "collection of information" as identical to the term used in the Paperwork Reduction Act, which means that a collection of information includes any reporting or recordkeeping requirement for more than nine people.

---

8   5 U.S.C. § 601(b)(1)(a).

Executive Order 13272

On August 13, 2002, President George W. Bush signed Executive Order 13272, titled "Proper Consideration of Small Entities in Agency Rulemaking."[9] The E.O. strengthened the Office of Advocacy by enhancing its relationship with OIRA and directing agencies to work closely with the Office of Advocacy to properly consider the impact of their regulations on small entities.

The E.O. first required federal regulatory agencies to establish written procedures and policies on how they intend to measure the impact of their regulatory proposals on small entities, and vet those policies with the Office of Advocacy before publishing them.[10] Second, the agencies must notify the Office of Advocacy of draft rules expected to have a significant economic impact on a substantial number of small entities under the RFA.[11] Third, agencies must consider the Office of Advocacy's written comments on proposed rules and publish a response to those comments with the final rule.[12] The Office of Advocacy, in turn, must provide periodic notification, as well as training, to all federal regulatory agencies on how to comply with the RFA.[13] These preliminary steps set the stage for agencies to work closely with the Office of Advocacy and properly consider the impact of their regulations on small entities.

Federal Agency Compliance and the Office of Advocacy's Role

By independently representing the views of small business, the Office of Advocacy is an effective voice for small business before Congress and federal regulatory

---

9   Exec. Order No. 13272, 67 Fed. Reg. 53461 (Aug. 16, 2002), available on the Office of Advocacy website at *http://www.sba.gov/advo/laws/eo13272.pdf*. The full executive order is reprinted in this report in Appendix B.

10   Id. at § 3(a).

11   Id. at § 3(b). Under the Regulatory Flexibility Act (RFA), an agency must determine if a rule, if promulgated, will have a "significant economic impact on a substantial number of small entities." If the head of the agency certifies the rule will not have such an impact, further analysis under the RFA is not needed. If, however, the agency cannot certify the rule, the agency must perform regulatory flexibility analysis under the RFA. (5 U.S.C. § 603–605).

12   Id. at § 3(c).

13   Id. at § 2 (a)–(b).

agencies. Since its creation in 1976, the Office of Advocacy has pursued its mission of creating research products that help lawmakers understand the contribution of small businesses to the U.S. economy. Since enactment of the RFA in 1980, Advocacy's regulatory experts have monitored federal agency compliance with the law and worked to persuade federal agencies to consider the impact of their rules on small businesses before the rules go into effect. In 2003, the Office of Advocacy added a new component: reducing regulatory burdens for small businesses at the state level. The Office of Advocacy's regional advocates promoted state model legislation based on Advocacy's experience with the federal RFA and E.O. 13272.

Executive Order 13272 Requirements

With the new E.O., some agencies are increasingly recognizing the importance of small business to the nation's economy and the benefit of considering the impacts of their rulemakings on small entities. Those agencies trying to comply with the requirements of the E.O. are coming to Advocacy earlier in the rule development process, resulting in earlier consideration of small business impacts of draft regulations.

Section 3(a) of the E.O requires agencies to issue written procedures and policies to ensure that their regulations consider the potential impact on small entities and make them publicly available.

Section 3(b) of E.O. 13272 requires agencies to notify Advocacy of any draft rules that may have a significant economic impact on a substantial number of small entities under the RFA. Such notifications are to be made (i) when the agency submits a draft rule to OIRA under Executive Order 12866, or (ii) if no submission to OIRA is required, at a reasonable time prior to publication of the rule by the agency. To make it easier for agencies to comply electronically with the notice requirements of the E.O. and the RFA, Advocacy established an email address, notify.advocacy@sba.gov.

Section 3(c) of E.O. 13272 requires agencies to give every appropriate consideration to Advocacy's comments on a proposed rule. In the final rule published in the *Federal Register*, an agency must respond to any written comments submitted by Advocacy on the proposed rule.

RFA Training under E.O. 13272

Executive Order 13272 requires Advocacy to train regulatory agencies on how to comply with the RFA and the E.O. Advocacy identified 66 departments, agencies, and independent commissions that promulgate regulations affecting small business. By training approximately 25 agencies each year, Advocacy hopes to complete training of all 66 agencies before FY 2008.

The government-wide rollout of the RFA training began in October 2003. Since that time, Advocacy has trained more than 40 federal agencies in how to comply with the RFA and the E.O. Agencies that have participated in the rigorous half-day training are more aware of their compliance responsibilities under the RFA and the E.O. Increasingly, agency staff are willing to share draft rules and other important information with Advocacy. Such pre-decisional interagency information is kept confidential. This process enables Advocacy to better assist the agencies in assessing the small business impacts of their draft rules. Moreover, a large part of the training is laying the foundation for productive relationships between Advocacy and the regulatory agencies. For those agencies willing to take advantage of Advocacy's expertise, knowing where to go for assistance on RFA issues is vital.

Advocacy is in the process of developing the next phase of its RFA training program. The office is working with an outside contractor to create an online computer-based RFA training module. The online training will be useful for both new agency employees and as a review for existing employees. It is not intended to replace the initial face-to-face training.

Advocacy remains optimistic that small businesses will begin to realize the benefits of E.O. 13272 when agencies adjust their regulatory development processes to accommodate the requirements of the RFA and the E.O. As more agencies work with the Office of Advocacy earlier in the rule development process and give small entity impacts appropriate consideration, regulations should show more sensitivity to small business considerations. The E.O. is an important tool designed to guarantee small businesses a seat at the table where regulatory decisions are made. Advocacy will continue working closely with all federal regulatory agencies to train them on the RFA and increase compliance with both the RFA and E.O. 13272.

RFA and SBREFA Implementation

Advocacy promotes agency compliance with the RFA in several ways. Advocacy staff members regularly review proposed regulations and work closely with small entities, trade associations, and federal regulatory contacts to identify areas of concern, then work to ensure that the RFA's requirements are fulfilled *(see, for example, Charts 7.1 and 7.2)*.

Early intervention by the Office of Advocacy has helped federal agencies develop a greater appreciation of the role small business plays in the economy and the rationale for ensuring that regulations do not unduly stifle entrepreneurial growth. The Office of Advocacy continues to provide economic data, whenever possible, to help agencies identify industrial sectors dominated by small firms. Statistics show regulators why rules should be written to fit the unique characteristics of small businesses if public policy objectives will not otherwise be compromised. Advocacy makes statistics available on its Internet website and maintains information on trade associations that can be helpful to federal agencies seeking input from small businesses.

The Office of Advocacy also promotes agency compliance with the RFA through its collaboration with a network of small business representatives. Advocacy staff regularly meet with small businesses and their trade associations regarding federal agency responsibilities under the RFA, factors to be addressed in agency economic analyses, and the judicial review provision enacted in the SBREFA amendments. Roundtable meetings with small businesses and trade associations focus on specific regulations and issues, such as procurement reform, environmental regulations, and industrial safety. Advocacy also plays a key role as a participant in the SBREFA panels convened to review EPA and OSHA rules.

As regulatory proposals and final rules are developed, the Office of Advocacy is involved through pre-proposal consultation, interagency review under E.O. 12866, formal comment letters and informal comments to the agency, congressional testimony and *amicus curiae* (friend of the court) briefs. In 2004, Advocacy submitted a notice of intent to file an *amicus curiae* brief in a litigation proceeding involving the FCC's memorandum opinion and order on local number portability. Ultimately, the notice of intent was withdrawn, as Advocacy and the FCC were able to reach a settlement agreement.

Chart 7.1 Advocacy Comments, by Key RFA Compliance Issue, FY 2004 (percent)

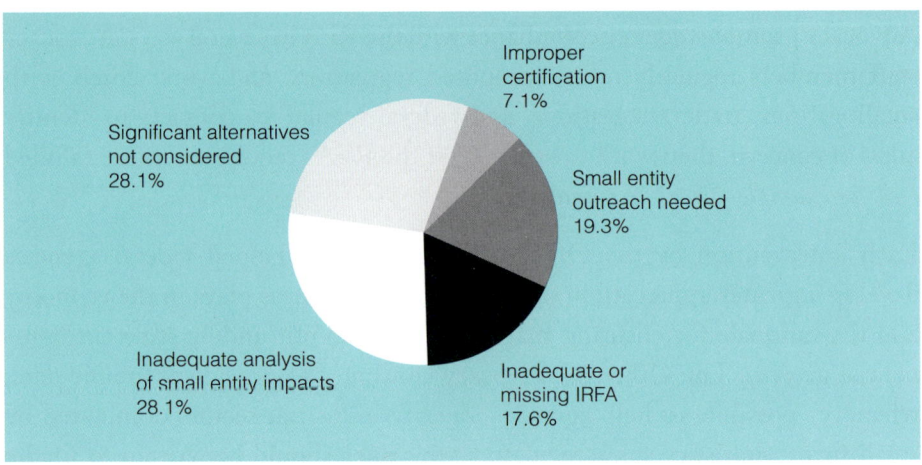

Throughout Fiscal Year 2004, the Office of Advocacy advised many agencies on how to comply with the RFA. Chart 1 illustrates the key concerns raised by Advocacy's comment letters and pre-publication review of draft rules. The chart highlights areas for improved compliance based on Advocacy's analysis of its FY 2004 comment letters and other regulatory interventions summarized in this report.

Chart 7.2 Advocacy Comments and Regulatory Interventions by Agency, FY 2004 (percent)

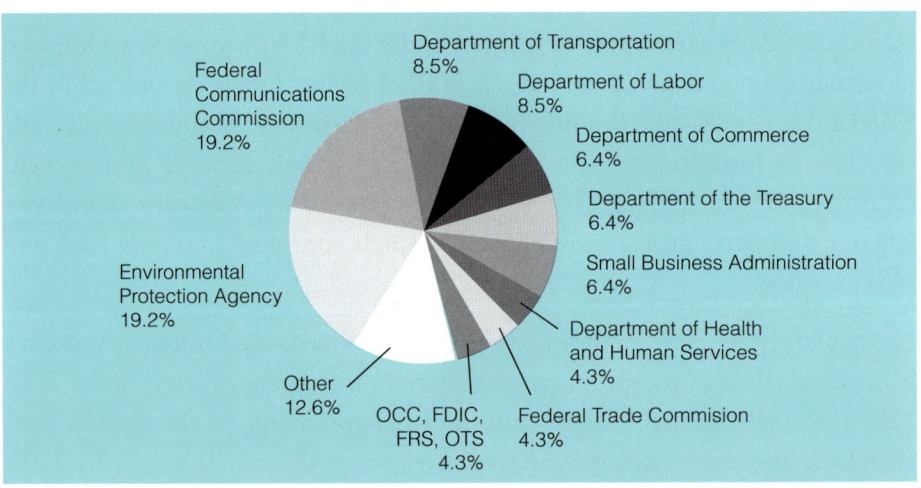

Chart 2 identifies agencies that were the focus of Advocacy's letters and regulatory interventions during Fiscal Year 2004. With the volume of rulemakings in progress each year, Advocacy cannot review every rule for RFA compliance. Instead, Advocacy takes its direction from small businesses, focusing its regulatory interventions on rulemakings identified by small businesses as a priority. This chart simply illustrates the distribution of Advocacy's comment letters and other regulatory interventions across agencies and may not reflect the agencies' overall RFA compliance records.

D.C. Circuit Court Orders FCC To Consider Small Business Regulatory Impact

On March 11, 2005, the U.S. Court of Appeals for the D.C. Circuit issued a ruling that strengthened the RFA and provided needed relief to small businesses. In *U.S. Telecom Assoc. and CenturyTel, Inc. v. FCC*, the court found that the RFA applies to a rule issued by the Federal Communications Commission (FCC) concerning wireless number portability, requiring the transfer of a telephone number from one carrier to another at a customer's request. The court sent the rule back to the agency with instructions to conduct a regulatory flexibility analysis. The court's decision delayed enforcement of the FCC rule on small businesses until the agency finished the regulatory flexibility analysis.

"This is a landmark decision for the RFA and a victory for small business. The court clearly ruled that federal agencies must follow the RFA, listen to the voice of small business, and consider alternatives that lessen the impact on small business before issuing a final rule," Chief Counsel for Advocacy Thomas M. Sullivan said. This case is significant for three reasons. First, it reaffirms the importance of the RFA in agency rulemaking. Second, the decision was made by the D.C. Circuit, which is the appellate court most likely to hear appeals from federal agency rulemakings. Third, the FCC embraced the ruling as an opportunity to accommodate small business concerns.

The FCC had adopted the rule in response to a petition by the Cellular Telecommunications and Internet Association (CTIA). CTIA asked the FCC to require wireline carriers to transfer telephone numbers to wireless carriers whose service area overlapped a wireline carrier's rate center, even when no point of interconnection between the two networks existed. On November 10, 2003, the FCC granted CTIA's petition, stating that the order "clarified" an earlier final rule, hence it was not a legislative rulemaking requiring notice and comment under the Administrative Procedure Act. The FCC did not conduct an RFA analysis of either CTIA's petition or of the resulting final rule.

Two small business organizations that represent small and rural wireline carriers—the National Telephone Cooperative Association (NTCA) and the Organization for the Promotion and Advancement of Small Telecommunications Companies (OPASTCO)—challenged the order on December 15, 2003, on the grounds that it violated the RFA. The two groups charged that the rule would cost their small business members an estimated $76,000 per telecom carrier in initial costs and $46,000 in annual recurring costs.

On February 13, 2004, the Office of Advocacy filed a notice of intent with the U.S. Court of Appeals for the D.C. Circuit that it was preparing to file an *amicus curiae* brief in support of the challenge by OPASTCO and NTCA. On June 10, 2004, Advocacy and the FCC reached a settlement. Advocacy withdrew its intent to file, and FCC Chairman Michael Powell issued a letter to state regulators, urging them to consider the burdens of the local number portability requirement on small rural carriers if they petitioned for relief.

The settlement between Advocacy and the FCC did not keep the case from going forward, and on March 11, 2005, the U.S. Court of Appeals for the D.C. Circuit issued a decision that concluded that the FCC failed to comply with the RFA's requirement to prepare a final regulatory flexibility analysis regarding the order's impact on small entities. The court remanded the order to the FCC to prepare the analysis. It also stayed the effect of the order as it applies to those carriers that qualify as small entities under the RFA. The court's ruling is online at *www.cadc.uscourts.gov/internet/internet.nsf*.

Model RFA Legislation for the States

Model Legislation for the States

A vibrant and growing small business sector is critical to creating jobs in a dynamic economy. While there are federal measures in place to reduce regulatory burdens on small businesses, the need does not stop at the federal level. More than 93 percent of businesses in every state are small businesses, which bear a disproportionate share of regulatory costs and burdens.

The U.S. Small Business Administration's Office of Advocacy recognized that, like the federal government, state and local governments can be a source of burdensome and costly regulations on small businesses. Advocacy presented state model legislation, patterned after the federal Regulatory Flexibility Act, to improve the state regulatory climate for small business. Under this legislation, agencies are required to analyze the economic impact of a proposed rule on small business and determine whether alternative regulatory approaches are available without compromising the agency's objective.[14]

In FY 2004, Advocacy's regional advocates focused on educating governors, state officials, state legislators, and small business representatives about the need to change the regulatory and enforcement culture of state agencies to make them aware of small business concerns. As a result of Advocacy's efforts and the support of state legislators and policymakers, 17 states introduced regulatory flexibility legislation and seven states signed regulatory flexibility legislation into law. These seven states include Connecticut, Kentucky, Missouri, South Carolina, South Dakota, Rhode Island and Wisconsin *(see Table 7.1 for the status of state RFA legislation as of August 2005)*.

In 2002, the Wisconsin Department of Commerce started the process of improving the regulatory climate for small entities in Wisconsin by organizing a task force on small business regulatory reform. The task force included small business owners and trade association representatives from various industries who were responsible for identifying issues, barriers, and concerns affecting Wisconsin's small entities. The group submitted a number of recommendations to reduce the negative impact of regulations on small businesses while increasing the level of regulatory compliance. Subsequently, legislators in the Wisconsin State Senate and Assembly incorporated the task force's recommendations into Senate Bill 100, which gained bipartisan support and was passed in March 2004. The law affects both state agencies and the small business community by changing the agency rulemaking and implementation process. Among other things, the law significantly strengthened Wisconsin's Regulatory Flexibility Act, appointed small business regulatory coordinators in each agency, and created a Small Business Regulatory Review Board.

Once enacted, implementing regulatory flexibility law becomes an important next step. A common misconception among policymakers and agencies is that requiring agencies to prepare a small business economic impact statement and regulatory flexibility analysis imposes an overwhelming amount of time and paperwork. However, a few states have created a simple and efficient cost analysis questionnaire for agencies. In 2004, South Dakota passed legislation

---

14 A complete copy of the model legislation can be found on Advocacy's webpage at
    www.sba.gov/advo/laws/law_modeleg.html.

Table 7.1 State Administrative Procedure and Regulatory Flexibility Statutes, August 2005

State	Citation	Small Business Definition	Economic Impact Analysis	Regulatory Flexibility Analysis	Periodic Review	Judicial Review	Exemptions	Legislation Introduced in 2005
Alabama	Ala. Code T. 41 Ch. 22	None.	41-22-23(f)[1]	42-22-23(g)[1]	None.	41-22-10[1]	41-22-2(e) 41-22-3(1)	HB 745
Alaska	Ak. Stat. T. 24, Ch. 20 T. 44, Ch. 62	44.62.218[2]	44.62.218(a) 44.62.218(c)	44.62.218(a) 44.62.218(d)	44.62.125 (b)(3)	44.62.218(h) 44.62.300[1]	44.62.218(g)	HB 33 effective 1/1/06
Arizona	Ariz. Rev. Stat. T. 41, Ch. 6	41-1001(19)	41-1055(B)	41-1035 41-1055(B)	41-1056(A)	41-1034[1] 41-1056.01	41-1005 41-1057	N/A[3]
Arkansas	Ark. Code T. 25 Ch. 15	EO Sec.1	15-204(d)[1] EO Sec.3	EO Sec.3	25-15-216	25-15-207[1]	25-15-202(2)(C)	Executive Order in effect[4]
California	Cal. Gov. Code T. 2 Div. 3 Ch. 3.5	11342.610	11346.3[1] 11346.5(a)(7)	11346.2(b)(3) 11346.5(a)(7) 11346.9(a)(4) 11346.9(a)(5)	11349.1 11349.7	11350[1]	11340.9 11346.1	None.
Colorado	Col. Rev. Stat. T. 24 Art. 4	24-4-102(18)	24-4-103(2.5)	24-4-103(2.5)	None.	24-4-106[1,5]	24-4-102(3) 24-4-103	None.
Connecticut	Conn. Gen. Stat. T. 4 Ch.54	4-168a	None.	4-168a(b)	None.	4-175[1,5] 4-183	4-166(1) 4-168(a)(d)	N/A[3]
Delaware	Del. Code T. 29 Ch. 101	10403(3)	10404	10404	10407	10141[1]	10102(1) 10161	None.

State	Code							
District of Columbia	DC Code T. 1	None.	None.	None.	None.	Sec. 110	None.	None.
Florida	Fla. Stat. T. X Ch. 120	288.703	120.54 120.541(2)(d)	120.54(3)(b)	120.74	120.68[1]	120.50 120.63 120.80 120.81	None.
Georgia	Ga. Code T. 50 Ch. 13	50-13-4(a)(3)	None.	50-13-4(a)(3) 50-13-4(a)(4)	None.	50-13-10[1]	50-13-2(1) 50-13-4(b) 15-13-42	None.
Guam	5 GCA Ch. 9	None.	9301(f)[1]	None.	None.	9309[5]	9301(i) 9302	None.
Hawaii	Haw. Rev. Stat. Ch. 201M	201M-1	201M-2	201M-2	201M-7	201M-6 91-7[1]	201M-2(c)	HB 602 SB 422
Idaho	Idaho Code T. 67, Ch. 52	None.	67-5223(2)[1]	None.	None.	67-5271[1,5]	67-5201(2)	None.
Illinois	5 Ill. Comp. Stat. 100	100/1-75	100/5-30(c)	100/5-30(a)	100/5-130	5-150[1,5]	1-5(c)	None.

Note: All section numbers in columns 3 through 8 refer to the law cited in column 2, except as noted otherwise.

1 Not small business specific.

2 Alaska passed its regulatory flexibility legislation in the summer of 2005. A small business definition, small business specific economic impact statement, and small business regulatory flexibility analysis were added to current law as a result of this bill.

3 This column is not applicable to this state because it has a regulatory flexibility statute in active use.

4 Governor Huckabee implemented regulatory flexibility through Executive Order 05-04 in February of 2005. This executive order provides a small business definition and requires agencies to prepare a small business economic impact statement and to consider alternative means for accomplishing the objectives of the proposed rule that may be less burdensome to small businesses.

5 Petitioner must first exhaust administrative remedies.

(continued, next page)

Table 7.1 (Continued)

State	Citation	Small Business Definition	Economic Impact Analysis	Regulatory Flexibility Analysis	Periodic Review	Judicial Review	Exemptions	Legislation Introduced in 2005
Indiana	Ind. Code T.4, Art. 22	4-22-2.1-4	4-22-2.1-5	4-22-2.1-5	4-22-2.5-3.1	4-22-2.1-8	4-22-2-13(b)	HB 1822,[6] in effect
Iowa	Iowa Code T. 1, Subt. 6 Ch. 17A	17A.4A	17A.4(3)[1] 17A.4A(2)(a)	17A.4A(2)(b)	17A.33	17A.19[1,5]	None.	SF 65
Kansas	Kan. Sta. Ch. 77	None.	77-416(b)[1]	77-416(b)[1]	None.	77-607[1,5] 77-612 77-621	None.	None.
Kentucky	Ky. Rev. Stat. T. 3, Ch. 13A	13A.010	13A.240[1]	13A.210	None.	13A.337[1]	None.	None.
Louisiana	La. Rev. Stat. T. 49 Ch. 13	49:965.1	49:953[1]	None.	None.	49:963[1,5] 49:964 49:965.1	49:967	None.
Maine	Me. Rev. Stat. T. 5, Pt. 18 Ch. 375	8052.5-A	8057-A.1(D)	8052.5-A	None.	8058[1]	8054	None.
Maryland	Md. Code State Govt.	None.	10-124[1]	10-124[1]	10-132.1 10-133	10-125[1]	10-102(b) 10-110(a)	None.
Massachusetts	Mass. Gen. Law T. III Ch. 30A	None.	30A-5 EO (Sec.5)[7]	30A-5 EO (Sec.5)	None.	30A-7[1]	None.	None.
Michigan	Mich. Comp. Laws Ch. 24 Act 306	24.207a 24.240(2)	24.240 24.245(3)	24.240	None.	24.264[1,5] 24.301	24.315	N/A[3]

Minnesota	Minn. Stat. Ch. 14	None.	14.131[1]	14.131[1] 14.055	14.05 (subd.5)	14.44[1]	14.03	None.
Mississippi	Miss. Code T. 25 Ch. 43	None.	25.43-3.105(2)(d)	25.43-3.105(2)(f)[1] 3.105(2)(g)[1]	25.43-3.114	25.43-3.105(3) 25.43-17	25.43-3.108 25.43-6	HB 1472 SB 2795
Missouri	Mo. Rev. Stat. T. 36 Ch. 536	536.010	536.300	536.300.2	536.325	536.328	536.025 536.300(4)	HB 576[8] effective 8/28/05
Montana	Mt. Code T. 2 Ch. 4	None.	2-4-302[1] 2-4-405[1]	2-4-405[1]	2-4-314	2-4-506[1]	2-4-102(2)	HB 630
Nebraska	Ne. Rev. St. Ch. 84	None.	84-907[1]	None.	None.	84-911[1]	84-901	None.
Nevada	Nev. Rev. Stat. T. 18 Ch. 233B	233B.0382	233B.0608 233B.0609	233B.0608 233B.0609	233B.050 (1)(e)	233B.105 233B.110[1,5]	233B.039	N/A[3]
New Hampshire	N.H. Rev. Stat. T. LV Ch. 541A	541-A:5(IV)(e)	541-A:5(IV)(e)	None.	None.	541-A:24[1]	541-A:21	None.

Note: All section numbers in columns 3 through 8 refer to the law cited in column 2, except as noted otherwise.

6 Indiana passed its regulatory flexibility legislation in the 2005 legislative session and it became effective July 1, 2005. HB 1822 added all of the key elements of Advocacy's model legislation to Indiana's current administrative procedure laws.

7 Governor Romney implemented regulatory flexibility through Executive Order No. 453 (No. 03-11) in September of 2003. This executive order requires agencies to prepare a small business economic impact statement and regulatory flexibility analysis and creates a Small Business Advocate position.

8 HB 576 added periodic review and judicial review provisions to existing Missouri administrative procedure law in the 2005 legislative session.

(continued, next page)

Table 7.1 (Continued)

State	Citation	Small Business Definition	Economic Impact Analysis	Regulatory Flexibility Analysis	Periodic Review	Judicial Review	Exemptions	Legislation Introduced in 2005
New Jersey	N.J. Stat. T. 52, Subt. 3 Ch. 14B	52:14B-17	52:14B-19	52:14B-18	None.	None.	None.	A 3973 S 2754
New Mexico	N.M. Stat. Ch. 12 Art. 8	HB 869 Sec.3.E	None.	HB 869 Sec.4.B	HB 869 Sec.6	12-8-(A)[1]	None.	HB 869[9] SB 842 in effect
New York	NY CLS St. Admin. P Act	102(8)	202-b	202-b	207	205[1,5]	202-b(3)	N/A[3]
North Carolina	N.C. Gen. Stat. Ch. 150B	None.	150B-21.4(b1)[1]	None.	None.	150B-43[1,5]	150B-1 150B-21.1A 150B-21.5	HB 757 SB 664 SB 622
North Dakota	N.D. Cent. Code T. 28 Ch. 32	28-32-08.1	28-32-08.1	28-32-08.1	28-32-08.1	28-32-08.1	28-32-08.1	N/A[3]
Ohio	Ohio Rev. Code T.1 Ch. 119	121.24	121.24(B) 127.18	None.	119.3.2 121.24(D)	119.12[1,5]	119.01 119.03(H)	SB 15
Oklahoma	Okla. Stat. T. 74	75-502	75-303 75-504	75-303(A)(4) 75-504	75-250.10 75-307.1	75-306[1] 75-505	75-250.4 75-250.5	N/A[3]
Oregon	Or. Revised Stat. Ch. 183	183.310	183.335(2)(b) HB 3238 Sec.2	183.540	HB 3238 Sec.3	183.400[1]	183.315	HB 3238[10]

State	(col 2)	(col 3)	(col 4)	(col 5)	(col 6)	(col 7)	(col 8)
Pennsylvania 71 Pa. Cons. Stat. Ch. 4A	None.	745.5(a)[1]	745.5(a)	745.8.1	None.	None.	HB 236 SB 842
Puerto Rico PR St T. 3, Ch. 79	2251(d)	2254	2254	2259	2260	2251(a)	N/A[3]
Rhode Island R.I. Gen. Laws T. 42 Ch. 35	42-35-1	42-35-3.3	42-35-3.3	42-35-3.4	42-35-7[1]	42-35-1.1 42-35-3.3(d)	None.
South Carolina S.C. Code T. 1, Ch. 23	1-23-270(B)	1-23-270(C)	1-23-270(D)	1-23-270(F)	1-23-270(E)	1-23-120(G)	N/A[3]
South Dakota S.D. Codified Laws T. 1 Ch. 26	1-26-1(8A)	1-26-2.1	None.	None.	1-26-14[1]	None.	None.
Tennessee Tenn. Code T. 4, Ch. 5	None.	4-5-226(i)[1]	None.	4-5-226(e)	4-5-225[1,5]	4-5-106 4-5-208	HB 279 SB 1276
Texas Tex. Govt. Code T. 10 Ch. 2006	2006.001	2006.002	2006.002	2001.39	2001.038[1,5]	2006.012	None.
Utah Utah Code T. 63 Ch. 46a	None.	63-46a-4[1]	63-46a-4[1]	63-46a-9	63-46a-12.1	63-46a-7	HB 209

Note: All section numbers in columns 3 through 8 refer to the law cited in column 2, except as noted otherwise.

9 New Mexico passed its regulatory flexibility legislation, titled the Small Business Regulatory Relief Act, in the 2005 legislative session. This bill added a small business definition, a small business regulatory flexibility analysis, and periodic review of existing regulations to its current administrative procedure laws.

10 Oregon passed its regulatory flexibility legislation in the 2005 legislative session. HB 3238 enhances Oregon's current regulatory flexibility laws by requiring the small business economic impact statement to include the elements outlined in Advocacy's model legislation and to conduct periodic review of existing regulations.

(continued, next page)

Table 7.1 (Continued)

State	Citation	Small Business Definition	Economic Impact Analysis	Regulatory Flexibility Analysis	Periodic Review	Judicial Review	Exemptions	Legislation Introduced in 2005
Vermont	Vt. Stat. T. 3 Ch. 25	3-801	3-838(c)	3-832a 3-838(c)(3)	834	3-807[1]	3-816 3-832	None.
Virgin Islands	None.	None.	None.	None.	None.	None.	None.	None.
Virginia	Va. Code T. 2.2 Ch. 40	2.2-4007.1(A)	2.2-4007(H)	2.2-4007.1(B)	2.2-4007.1 (D), (E), (F)	2.2-4027	2.2-4002 2.2-4006	HB 1948[11] SB 1122 in effect
Washington	Wash. Rev. Code T. 19, Ch. 85 T. 34, Ch. 5	19.85.020	19.85.030 19.85.040	19.85.030	34.05.630	34.05.570[1]	19.85.025 34.05.030	HB 1445
West Virginia	W. Va. Code Ch. 29A	None.	EO[12]	EO	EO	29A-4-2[1]	29A-1-3	None.
Wisconsin	Wis. Stat. Ch. 27	227.114(1)	227.19(3)(e)	227.114(2) 227.19(3)(e)	227.30	227.40[1]	227.24	N/A[3]
Wyoming	Wyo. Stat. T. 16, Ch. 3	None.	None.	None.	None.	16-3-114[1,5]	16-3-103(b)	None.

Note: All section numbers in columns 3 through 8 refer to the law cited in column 2, except as noted otherwise.

11 Virginia passed its regulatory flexibility bill in the 2005 legislative session and it is currently effective. The bill added all of the key components of Advocacy's model legislation to current Virginia administrative procedure laws.

12 Governor Wise signed Executive Order No. 20-03 in 2003, which included a small business specific economic impact statement, regulatory flexibility analysis, and periodic review of existing regulations.

requiring agencies promulgating rules under its Administrative Procedures Act to prepare a statement of the rule's economic impact on small business. Subsequently it has created a one-page Small Business Impact Form to assist agencies in the analysis.[15] Agencies are asked eight questions about the impact of the rule on small entities and are reminded only to use "readily available information and existing resources." This simple form assists agencies in complying with the law without requiring them to expend a burdensome amount of additional time and resources.

Also to aid agencies in developing small-business-friendly regulations, many states' regulatory flexibility laws create a small business rules review committee. Working closely with agencies, these committees encourage open communication and strengthen relationships between small businesses and state agencies. In 2004, the Kentucky legislature passed the Kentucky Small Business and Government Regulatory Fairness Act of 2004, which strengthened the authority of the Commission on Small Business Advocacy. Located within the Kentucky Commerce Cabinet, the commission consists of board members representing a variety of small business sectors and government agencies. Its purpose is to review proposed agency regulations with economic impacts on small business and to submit comments, which agencies must consider. These rule review committees have proven to be a valuable voice for small entities early in the agency rulemaking process, an important check on agency rulemaking, and a good source of advice for state agencies.

While enacting regulatory flexibility is important, the value of the law cannot be realized unless small businesses are aware of proposed rules and can become actively involved in the rulemaking process. Therefore, various state chambers of commerce and other groups that monitor legislation post proposed rules on the Internet to make small business owners aware and encourage comments. In 2004, Rhode Island passed small business regulatory flexibility legislation and subsequently the Rhode Island Economic Development Corporation created a centralized website on agency proposed rules.[16] Small business owners can search the website by agency name or by keyword and view the proposed rule as well as information about the public comment period and hearing dates.

---

15   *See* http://legis.state.sd.us/rules/index.cfm?FuseAction=Manual.

16   *See* http://www.rules.state.ri.us/rules.

The Colorado Department of Regulatory Agencies has also created a web service for small entities.[17] Through free email regulatory notices, small businesses are able to keep abreast of proposed rules and are provided an opportunity to comment on rules affecting their businesses.

Small businesses are integral to a healthy and growing economy. The Office of Advocacy continues to build on state and federal RFA successes to urge state legislators and policymakers to enact new legislation or amend current statutes. By proactively addressing regulatory concerns, small businesses will be protected from regulations that require them to bear disproportionate costs and burdens. Giving small employers a voice early in the process is a key to reducing the negative impact of regulations on small businesses, increasing the level of regulatory compliance and passing on cost savings to state economies.

Conclusion

In FY 2004, the Office of Advocacy continued to work closely with federal regulatory agencies to reduce regulatory burdens on small entities. The U.S. Court of Appeals for the Washington, D.C., Circuit reaffirmed the importance of agency compliance with the RFA, and seven states signed regulatory flexibility legislation into law. In FY 2004, more agencies approached Advocacy requesting RFA training or seeking advice early in the rulemaking process and overall, 17 states introduced regulatory flexibility legislation. Small entities are increasingly recognizing that working with Advocacy; with state advocacy commissions, boards, and task forces; and directly with federal and state agencies can help improve the regulatory environment. The progress made in FY 2004 suggests that states, small entities, and agencies are beginning to fully appreciate the value and importance of regulatory flexibility.

---

17 *See* http://legis.state.sd.us/rules/index.cfm?FuseAction=Manual.

Abbreviations

CTIA   Cellular Telecommunications and Internet Association

DOC   Department of Commerce

DOD   Department of Defense

DOL   Department of Labor

DOT   Department of Transportation

E.O.   Executive Order

EPA   Environmental Protection Agency

FCC   Federal Communications Commission

FDIC   Federal Deposit Insurance Corporation

FRS   Federal Reserve System

FTC   Federal Trade Commission

HHS   Department of Health and Human Services

IRS   Internal Revenue Service

NTCA   National Telephone Cooperative Association

OCC   Office of the Comptroller of the Currency

OIRA   Office of Information and Regulatory Affairs

OMB   Office of Management and Budget

OPASTCO   Organization for the Promotion and Advancement of Small Telecommunications Companies

OSHA   Occupational Safety and Health Administration

OTS   Office of Thrift Supervision

P.L.   Public Law

RFA   Regulatory Flexibility Act

SBA   Small Business Administration

SBREFA   Small Business Regulatory Enforcement Fairness Act

U.S.C.   United States Code

8 SMALL FIRMS: *Why* MARKET-DRIVEN INNOVATION CAN'T GET ALONG *Without* THEM

Synopsis

William Baumol[1] has provided striking evidence indicating that private innovative activity has been divided by market forces between small firms and large, with each tending to specialize in a different part of the task.[2] Even though the preponderance of private expenditure on research and development (R&D) is provided by the giant business enterprises, a critical share of the innovative breakthroughs of recent centuries has been contributed by firms of very modest size. These radical inventions then have been sold, leased or otherwise put into the hands of the giant companies, which have then proceeded to develop them—adding capacity, reliability, user friendliness and marketability more generally—to turn them into the novel consumer products that have transformed the way Americans live. Baumol has referred to this division of labor as the "David-Goliath partnership," the value of whose combined products clearly exceed the sum of the parts.

To the extent that the facts confirm this characterization, it is evident that the small enterprises have made and continue to make a critical contribution to the market economies' unprecedented growth and innovation accomplishments. Without breakthroughs such as the airplane, FM radio, and the personal computer, all introduced by small firms, life in the industrialized economies would be very different today. Moreover, without these breakthrough inventions to build upon, the big companies would be confined to a much more restricted body of ideas to which to devote their development activities.

In recounting these broadly accurate tendencies, the author was not previously able to provide a tenable explanation. This left open the possibility that the observed division of labor was merely a historical happenstance, an accidental

---

1   This chapter was prepared under contract with the Office of Advocacy by William J. Baumol, who expresses appreciation to Dr. Ying Lowrey of the U.S. Small Business Administration.

2   Baumol, 2002.

development. If that were so, it could imply that the breakthroughs were not necessarily something only the small firms could have provided. Then they would not have been indispensable players of that role and the oligopolies might just as easily have taken their place.

This paper seeks to show that the division of innovative labor is no accident. It is the market mechanism that assigns each type of firm to its differentiated job. It is the market mechanism that assigns the search for radical inventions to the small enterprises and their subsequent development to the large. The author describes how the market does so, and how it prevents either group from a massive invasion of the other's terrain. If, as the evidence indicates,[3] the free market is of critical importance for America's unparalleled flood of innovation, and if widely and rapidly adapted innovation is the primary key to that growth, then it will follow from the analysis that small firms are indeed indispensable components of the process and that rapid and sustained growth cannot get along without them.

First, Baumol reviews some of the evidence indicating that such a division is indeed a reality.

The Specializations of Large and Small Firms in Reality

Radical Invention and Incremental Improvements: The Role of Small Firms

For ease of thinking, it is convenient to divide up inventions into two polar categories: revolutionary breakthroughs and cumulative incremental improvements. Of course, many new products and processes fall into neither extreme category, but are somewhere in between. Still, it will become clear that the distinction is useful. Moreover, there are many examples that clearly fit into one of these categories or the other quite easily. For instance, the electric light, alternating electric current, the internal combustion engine, and a host of other advances must surely be deemed revolutionary, while successive models of washing machines and refrigerators—with each new model a bit longer

---

3 See Baumol, 2002b.

lasting, a bit less susceptible to breakdown, and a bit easier to use—constitute a sequence of incremental improvements.

The relevance of the distinction should be evident, given the fact that the working and organization of R&D in the large business enterprise tends characteristically to be bureaucratic, with management deciding the R&D budget, staffing, and even the projects to which the R&D division should be devoting its efforts. The inherent conservatism of the process naturally leads to the expectation that these firms will tend to specialize in the incremental improvements and tend to avoid the risks of the unknown that the revolutionary breakthrough entails. The latter, rather, is left most often to small or newly founded enterprises, guided by their enterprising entrepreneurs. Though that is to be expected, the degree of asymmetry in the apportionment of this specialized activity between large and small firms in reality is striking. The U.S. Small Business Administration Office of Advocacy has prepared a chart listing breakthrough innovations of the twentieth century for which small firms are responsible *(Table 8.1)*, and as will be seen, its menu of inventions literally spans the range from A to Z, from the airplane to the zipper. This remarkable list includes a strikingly substantial share of the technical breakthroughs of the twentieth century. Besides the airplane, it lists FM radio, the helicopter, the personal computer, and the pacemaker, among a host of others, many of enormous significance for the U.S. economy.

A more recent study, also sponsored by the U.S. Small Business Administration's Office of Advocacy, provides more systematic and powerful evidence to similar effect.[4] The report examines technical change through patenting and it defines small firms as "businesses with fewer than 500 employees." Perhaps most notably, the study finds that "…a small firm patent is more likely than a large firm patent to be among the top 1 percent of most frequently cited patents." Among other conclusions, in the words of its authors, this study reports that,

- Small firms represent one-third of the most prolific patenting companies that have 15 or more U.S. patents.

---

4 See U.S. Small Business Administration, Office of Advocacy, 2003. Quoting the press release describing the study, "A total of 1,071 firms with 15 or more patents issued between 1996 and 2000 were examined. A total of 193,976 patents were analyzed. CHI [the firm that carried out the study] created a database of these firms and their patents. This list excluded foreign-owned firms, universities, government laboratories, and nonprofit institutions."

Table 8.1 Some Important Innovations by U.S. Small Firms in the Twentieth Century

Air Conditioning	Link Trainer
Air Passenger Service	Microprocessor
Airplane	Nuclear Magnetic Resonance Scanner
Articulated Tractor Chassis	Optical Scanner
Cellophane Artificial Skin	Oral Contraceptives
Assembly Line	Outboard Engine
Audio Tape Recorder	Overnight National Delivery
Bakelite	Pacemaker
Biomagnetic Imaging	Personal Computer
Biosynthetic Insulin	Photo Typesetting
Catalytic Petroleum Cracking	Polaroid Camera
Computerized Blood Pressure Controller	Portable Computer
Continuous Casting	Prestressed Concrete
Cotton Picker	Prefabricated Housing
Defibrillator	Pressure Sensitive Tape
DNA Fingerprinting	Programmable Computer
Double-Knit Fabric	Quick-Frozen Food
Electronic Spreadsheet	Reading Machine
Freewing Aircraft	Rotary Oil Drilling Bit
FM Radio	Safety Razor
Front-End Loader	Six-Axis Robot Arm
Geodesic Dome	Soft Contact Lens
Gyrocompass	Solid Fuel Rocket Engine
Heart Valve	Stereoscopic Map Scanner
Heat Sensor	Strain Gauge
Helicopter	Strobe Lights
High Resolution CAT Scanner	Supercomputer
High Resolution Digital X-Ray	Two-Armed Mobile Robot
High Resolution X-Ray Microscope	Vacuum Tube
Human Growth Hormone	Variable Output Transformer
Hydraulic Brake	Vascular Lesion Laser
Integrated Circuit	Xerography
Kidney Stone Laser	X-Ray Telescope
Large Computer	Zipper

Source: The State of Small Business: A Report of the President, 1994, prepared by the U.S. Small Business Administration, Office of Advocacy, 1995, 114.

- Small firm innovation is twice as closely linked to scientific research as large firm innovation on average, and so is substantially more high-tech or leading edge.

- Small firms are more effective in producing high-value innovations—the citation index for small firm patents averaged 1.53 compared to 1.19 for large firms.

- Small patenting firms are roughly 13 times more innovative per employee than large patenting firms. A small firm patent is at least twice as likely to be found among the top 1 percent of highest-impact patents as a patent from a large firm.[5]

One is, then, led to the plausible conjecture that most of the revolutionary new ideas of the past two centuries have been, and are likely to continue to be, provided more heavily by independent innovators who, essentially, operate small business enterprises. Indeed, the small entrepreneurial firms have come close to monopolizing the portion of R&D activity that is engaged in the search for revolutionary breakthroughs.

But having demonstrated the vital role of the small enterprises, does it follow that there is little left for the large enterprises to do? This concern may, moreover, be exacerbated when it is recognized that the bulk of the country's R&D spending is contributed by large enterprises. According to data gathered by the National Science Foundation,[6] in 2000, 46 percent of total U.S. industrial R&D funding was spent by just 167 companies, each of which employed 25,000 or more workers; that is, nearly half the business expenditure on R&D was provided by 167 giant firms of the more than 30,000 U.S. firms that engaged in such activity. Does it then also follow that the giant companies are spending a great deal to achieve very little? These concerns are misplaced, the author maintains.

---

5 U.S. Small Business Administration, 2003, 2.

6 National Science Board, 2000, 24.

The Significance of Aggregated Incremental Improvements by Large Firms

As noted, the type of innovation in which the giant enterprises tend to specialize is primarily devoted to product improvement, increased reliability and enhanced user friendliness of products and the finding of new uses for those products. The approach tends to be conservative, seeking results whose applicability is clear and whose markets are relatively unspeculative. The bureaucratic control typical of innovative activity in the large firm serves to ensure that the resulting changes will be modest, predictable, and incremental. These firms are not predisposed to welcome the romantic flights of the imagination, the entrepreneurial leaps of faith and plunges into the unknown that often lead only to disaster, but which alone are likely to open up new worlds. Nonetheless, the incremental contributions of the large firms' routine activity at least sometimes adds even more to economic growth than do the more revolutionary prototype innovations. Though each such small improvement may be relatively unspectacular, added together they can become very significant indeed. Consider, for instance, how little computing power the first clumsy and enormously expensive computers provided, and what huge multiples of such power have been added by the many subsequent incremental improvements.

A set of extreme examples of the contributions of the small, entrepreneurial firms appeared in Table 8.1. But one can easily obtain equally startling examples of the magnitude of the innovative contributions of large companies, whose incremental contributions can add up and compound to results of enormous magnitude. One such illustration is the progress in computer chip manufacture by the Intel Corporation, the leading manufacturer of this device that has brought to market successive generations of chips and transistors, on which the performance of computers is so heavily dependent. According to a recent report,[7] over the 1971–2003 period, the clock speed of Intel's microprocessor chips—that is, the number of instructions each chip can carry out per second—has increased by some *3 million percent*, reaching about 3 billion computations per second today. During the period 1968–2003, the number of transistors embedded in a single chip has expanded more than

---

7 John Markoff, "Technology; Is There Life After Silicon Valley's Fast Lane?," *New York Times*, Business Financial Desk, Section C, April 9, 2003, p. 1.

10 million percent, and the number of transistors that can be purchased for a dollar has grown by *5 billion percent*. These are no minor contributions. Added up, they surely contribute far more computing capacity than was provided by the original revolutionary breakthrough of the invention of the electronic computer. Of course, that initial invention was an indispensable necessity for all of the later improvements. But it is only the combined work of the two together that made possible the powerful and inexpensive apparatus that is so effective today.

What Drives the Small Enterprise-Large Firm Specialization Pattern: The Role of Market Forces

The central contention here is that the division of innovative effort between small firms and large is neither accidental nor it easily terminated. On the contrary, strong market forces drive both actors toward these assigned roles and make it difficult for the entrepreneurs and firm managers to act otherwise. The distinction between the two explanations—historical happenstance versus market forces that induce or perhaps even enforce it—is important not only for research and understanding, but for policy as well, because it can help in anticipating whether this apparently efficient arrangement can be expected to continue with no deliberate intervention to preserve it, or whether some policy measures will be required for the purpose.

To begin to determine which of these two possible explanations is valid, it is necessary to provide a theoretical model, or at least a scenario with logical underpinnings that can account for the types of innovative activities in which the two classes of firms tend to specialize. Here one is driven to deal with "representative firms" in a sense even more amorphous than Marshall's,[8] because giant oligopoly firms are not all cut from the same cloth and entrepreneurial establishments are surely even less homogeneous in structure or behavior. Moreover, the explanation of the hypothesized division of labor between the two firm types will undoubtedly entail some shading at the edges, if it is to fit reality. At least some breakthrough technology has, of course, emerged from large and established corporations (such as the much-noted case of the

---

8 Alfred Marshall (1842–1924), a British economics professor at Oxford University, developed the economist's "analytical toolkit" with concepts such as price elasticity and the representative firm.

transistor, contributed by AT&T's Bell Laboratories and their special regulatory circumstances at the time), while the number of minor incremental improvements that have been contributed by new small firms is undoubtedly enormous.

It will be suggested here that there are nevertheless significant overall differences in the influences faced by the two types of enterprise, and that these differences can account for the division of innovative labor that one observes between them. Moreover, if these causal attributions are valid, it will follow that the specializations of the two types of firm are not markedly transitory but, on the contrary, can be expected to remain for a substantial period in the future.

What Drives the Pursuit of Breakthroughs by Innovative Entrepreneurial Firms?

The heterogeneity of enterprising behavior precludes any universally applicable scenario, particularly one that imposes a uniform response upon the entrepreneurial firms. In this respect, the story differs from that of the innovating oligopolists who, the author maintains, are normally driven in similar ways by powerful market forces toward their specialization in incremental improvement. For the small firm, several pertinent and important influences are also ingrained in the economic environment, but these are rather more amorphous, not stemming from a pure profit calculus or any market-imposed threat to their survival.

The focus here is on three mechanisms that characterize the relation between the market and the entrepreneurial firm. They can be suggestively referred to as: 1) the superstar reward structure; 2) the psychic rewards to innovative activity; and 3) the scarcity and cost disadvantage of large firm competition in the arena of breakthrough innovation. Each will be discussed in turn, but first an observation that relates to them all. As is to be expected, the market does provide clear incentives for entrepreneurs to undertake the hazards of radical innovation. But, paradoxically, each of the three mechanisms to be discussed entails *financial underpayment* of the average innovative entrepreneur. That is, it entails the expectation of financial returns lower than those to corporate employees with similar education and experience who provide comparable efforts.

A few preliminary words must also be said to avoid misunderstanding of just what it is that is to be explained. It is not the hypothesis here that a large percentage of entrepreneurs employ innovation in the new firms they create. On the contrary, the evidence, imperfect though it is, suggests that most new firms are virtual replicas of many firms already in existence, and there is nothing innovative about them. Second, there is no suggestion here that even among that relatively uncommon species, the innovative entrepreneur, the preponderant focus is on anything that can reasonably be deemed breakthrough innovations. Here again, casual empiricism indicates the reverse—that the bulk of the novelties they introduce are only slightly better mousetraps. So the claim is not that most entrepreneurs devote themselves to radical innovation or even to any innovation at all. Rather, the converse is proposed: that among the (rare) innovations that can be considered to be radical, a disproportionate share is provided by independent innovators and their affiliated entrepreneurs.

Thus, in what follows, it will be necessary to account, first, for the comparative paucity of breakthroughs that emerge from the sizeable labs and affiliated facilities of the large, established, and innovative firms. Second, why are a significant group of entrepreneurs and inventors, albeit a comparatively small one, willing to undertake the great uncertainties and the typically enormous personal effort that pursuit of this objective requires? The issue is not why there are so many that do so, but why there is a significant set of these adventurers at all.

Superstar Market Reward Structure, or the Multimillion Dollar Lottery

The most obvious incentive to which one can attribute the relatively frequent focus of independent inventors and their entrepreneur partners upon more radical ideas is, of course, the great wealth and enormous prestige that success in their undertaking appears to promise. Among inventor-entrepreneurs who are enduring legends are Eli Whitney, James Watt, Elias Singer, Thomas Edison, the Wright Brothers, and so on. Indeed, it is striking how familiar they are.

There is an immediate consequence: The enormous prestige and great financial rewards, *along with their rarity*, transform the innovative entrepreneur's activities into a lottery that offers just a few mega-prizes, like so many of the lotteries that now capture the headlines. An innovator's activity is like such a mega-lottery, or like the pursuit of an occupation that offers a limited number of superstar positions. But the prize is available only to those who provide *breakthrough* innovations. A technological contribution that permits humanity to fly or to send messages through the air can elicit headlines, but a minor improvement in automobile door handles is hardly likely to compete. And just as multimillion dollar lotteries have a greater attraction than a thousand-dollar lottery of the local club, even though the latter's terms are better actuarially, the pursuit of breakthrough innovations surely has a very special attraction to the independent entrepreneur.

Monetary Compensation, Psychic Compensation

A very well-recognized attribute of lotteries is their built-in unfairness, as measured in actuarial terms. The average payout is sure to be less than the per-ticket-holder take of the lottery operator—that is why he is in the business. There is a somewhat similar loss prospect for the representative entrepreneur. In part, the willingness of innovators, like the buyers of lottery tickets, to accept these biased terms may be attributable to over-optimism or to sheer miscalculation. But that is hardly the end of the story. Each of these activities—innovative entrepreneurship and the purchase of lottery tickets—also provides an important payoff of a second sort. Both activities offer distinct psychic rewards, and not only to those who have already achieved success or who even have a real and substantial likelihood of success. The *prospects* of glory, of wealth and fame, are something of value even if they never materialize. They are, indeed, the stuff that dreams are made of. And for the entrepreneur, contemplation of imagined success is only part of the psychic reward. Reading the biographies of the great inventors, one must be struck by the fascination that the process of their work elicited, by the moments of triumph, and even by the pleasure of puzzle solving and experimentation, though punctured by frustration and exhaustion.

These observations find support in some significant economic data. There is systematic evidence[9] that the average earnings of self-employed individuals are significantly lower than those of employees with similar qualifications, and the same is presumably true, in particular, of self-employed innovative entrepreneurs. At least two studies support this hypothesis for innovative entrepreneurs. Thomas Astebro reports on the basis of a sample of 1,091 inventions that,

---

9 See, for example, Freeman, 1978.

"The average IRR on a portfolio investment in these inventions is 11.4 percent. This is higher than the risk-free rate but lower than the long-run return on high-risk securities and the long-run return on early-stage venture capital funds…the distribution of return is skew; only between 7 and 9 percent reach the market. Of the 75 inventions that did, six received returns above 1400 percent, 60 percent obtained negative returns and the median was negative."[10] Perhaps even more striking is the recent work of Nordhaus, who provides evidence showing how little of the efficiency rent goes to the innovator: "Using data from the U.S. nonfarm business sector, it is estimated that innovators are able to capture about 2.2 percent of the total surplus from innovation. This number results from a low rate of initial appropriability (estimated to be around 7 percent) along with a high rate of depreciation of Schumpeterian profits (judged to be around 20 percent per year)….the rate of profit on the replacement cost of capital over the 1948–2001 period is estimated to be 0.19 percent per year."[11]

Perhaps even more striking and more extreme is the phenomenon of open sourcing and shareware in computer programming. Here, a great and growing body of complex and valuable material has been painstakingly created, and much of it is evidently of enormous value in economic and other terms. Yet it has been created and offered to others with modest, if any, restrictions, and without financial reward. Thus, a much noted and much valued activity is produced with zero financial reward, a payoff evidently far below what the work could have elicited if performed inside an established business enterprise. But the enthusiasm of those involved seems equally manifest.

An explanation is readily available and follows immediately from the attributes of the activities just noted. The representative entrepreneur may indeed be underpaid in terms of financial reward alone. But his *total* payoff may be closer to what economic theory would lead one to expect, though part of the payoff takes a form other than money. It is as though he were being paid off in two different currencies: partly in dollars, partly in euros. In equilibrium, such two-coin payment recipients could clearly expect fewer dollars than someone

---

10   Thomas Astebro, 2003, 226.

11   Nordhaus, 2004, 34. Using a cruder and more intuitive approach the present author also reached a very low figure for the returns to innovation that are not dissipated in spillovers (see Baumol 2002b, pp. 134–5).

similarly engaged whose contract calls for payment only in that one currency.[12] That this is how markets work is easily confirmed by casual observation.

The story pertains not only to the entrepreneur. It recurs throughout the economy. The fact that multimillion-dollar lotteries are carefully and openly structured to be actuarially unfair means, as already noted, that the purchasers of tickets in such a lottery will on average and as a whole receive back less than they put into it. It is arguable that the masses of purchasers who endure long and time-consuming queues to grab up the tickets are not irrational but that they receive an adequate payment in another currency: the psychic rewards. That same scenario helps to explain, in another example, why despite the rigors of their training and the difficulties of their work, the typical earnings of dancers are so miserable.[13] One can easily think of other occupations with similar attributes.

And the reason is not just sheer willingness of the recipient of psychic benefits to be exploited in financial terms. The market mechanism enforces it, as Adam Smith pointed out: Given two occupations, one very distasteful and the other a source of great pleasure, if other things including payoffs and ability requirements were equal, one must expect the work force to shun the one and flock to the other, driving wages up in the former and depressing them in the latter as a garden-variety manifestation of supply and demand.[14]

---

12 This suggests one way in which it may sometimes be possible to place a monetary value on psychological enjoyment and even esthetic pleasure. A similar situation has been noted in other arenas. For example, there are data showing that the average financial return to investment in works of art is significantly lower than the return to investment in bonds, the difference being interpreted as the financial valuation of the esthetic yield of painting ownership. See Frey and Pommerehne, 1989.

13 Other areas where some element of nonpecuniary income is likely to exist include scientific research, academic occupations, and perhaps professional work more generally (Friedman and Kuznets, 1945, pp. 130–132). It may also arise among the self-employed in their enjoyment of freedom from control by superiors (Hamilton, 2000; Frey and Benz, 2003). This phenomenon and its relation to the work of innovators has long been recognized: "The knowledge of the man of science, indispensable as it is to the development of industry, circulates with ease and rapidity from one nation to all the rest. And men of science have themselves an interest in its diffusion; for upon that diffusion they rest their hopes of fortune, and, what is more prized by them, of reputation too" (Say, 1819, 1834, p. 82).

14 "The wages of labour vary with the ease or hardship, the cleanliness or dirtiness, the honourableness or dishonourableness of the employment…. A journeyman weaver earns less than a journeyman blacksmith. His work is not always easier, but it is much cleaner…The exorbitant rewards of players, opera-singers and opera-dances, &c. are founded upon these two principles: the rarity and beauty of the talents, and the discredit of employing them in this manner. It seems absurd at first that we should despise their person, and yet reward their talents with the most profuse liberality. While we do the one, however, we must of necessity do the other" (Smith, 1776, Book I, Chapter X, Part I).

Entrepreneurs' Competitive Position and the Low Supply Cost of Psychic Benefits

Until now a critical role has not been assigned for the market mechanism in eliciting disproportionate allocation of entrepreneurial activity to breakthrough innovation. The market does play such a role. Psychic benefits are a very tangible reward to the recipient but are generally *costless to the provider*. This implies that an innovative entrepreneur who on average receives great pleasure but meager financial rewards from the activity may nevertheless be richly rewarded overall. But the low financial payment means that innovations obtained from this source are purchased cheaply in financial terms, giving this sector of the economy a marked competitive advantage. That is, the independent innovative entrepreneur will tend to be the economical supplier of breakthrough innovation to the economy. One of the virtues of markets and competition is their ability to move economic activities toward those suppliers who can provide them most economically. In the case at hand, it means that the low-cost psychic reward component of the independent innovator's compensation will make it more economical for the large firm, in considering its make-or-buy options, more generally to acquire its breakthroughs from others rather than seeking to provide them in-house. Firms are forced to do so for fear that if they do not, their rivals will. This, then, suggests one market-based reason (that is not mere happenstance) why a disproportionate share of radical innovation stems from the independent entrepreneur.

There is one more observation to be offered here. Why does this low-wage competitive advantage of the independent innovator-entrepreneur not extend also to the less radical innovations—the cumulative incremental improvements that are a giant firm specialty? At least part of the answer is the greater complexity and investment cost characteristic of the latter. A Boeing 777 is obviously far more complicated than the primitive device the Wright brothers made airborne at Kitty Hawk, and the transformation of the Boeing 747 into the Boeing 777 entailed an army of engineers and designers and an expenditure that made the outlays of the Wrights dramatically insignificant by comparison. This, too, is not accidental. By its very nature, this revolutionary invention, like so many before it, grew ever more complex as it was repeatedly modified and improved. Thus, the independent innovator was and continues to be at a marked disadvantage in the financing of incremental improvements of inventions that have reached an advanced stage of sophistication.

This completes the scenario seeking to describe how market forces drive the individual actor away from the small developments and toward the breakthroughs. Next, the other side of the story: the giant firm and its characteristic preoccupation with the small changes that are designed to provide only gradual improvement.

The Market's Enforcement of Large-Firm Caution

The tendency of large firms to be risk averse in their R&D activities is well recognized.[15] As a clear illustration of that attitude and its implication for the innovation process, the author has previously quoted the following observations by a member of management of one of the world's major high-tech enterprises:

> In established businesses, innovation is mostly shaped through small, incremental steps of additional features to augment basic functionalities. With short product lifecycles, time to recoup R&D investments is limited.... Success is relatively predictable through the execution of well-defined innovation processes and in-depth knowledge of their markets in the respective business units.[16]

One may well want to ask what drives these firms to such fear of risk, and their consequent preference for the unexciting incremental development. After all, they are apparently better established and more firmly financed than the entrepreneurial firms, and should therefore be in a better position to cope with risk. Particularly if the attempted breakthrough is just one item in a substantial portfolio of current R&D activities, should that not provide a degree of protection?

Preliminary consideration suggests that there are two features of pursuit of a breakthrough that make a difference. First, given today's state of communication and publicity activities, it is the attempted breakthrough that is apt to attract public attention, and that of investors and prospective investors in particular. Second, breakthrough efforts are unlikely to produce a modest success.

---

15 See, for example, Kaplan and Henderson, 2005, 18–29.

16 A. Huijser, PhD., executive vice president and chief technology officer, Royal Phillips Electronics, the Hague, September 2003.

The outcome is all too likely to be one extreme or the other. Embarkation on such an activity is a decision like that before the hero of *The Lady or the Tiger*: the choice between two portals, behind one the lady of his dreams, behind the other a hungry man eater. But the subject requires more extensive treatment, particularly in showing the powerful role played by the market in assigning the R&D tasks to the giant oligopoly enterprise.

The Usual Suspects

A variety of explanations from different sources are described in Kaplan and Henderson.[17] For example, they cite some well known and striking cases in which the large firms simply overlooked such opportunities, as when Xerox neglected the computer mouse or when IBM delayed its adoption of the personal computer. The observations are valid, but are hardly general. An overlooked breakthrough is indeed an avoided breakthrough. But no structural reason seems to lead one to expect errors of foresight to be more frequent in big companies and therefore to explain their avoidance of the search for breakthroughs. More convincing is the argument based on Schumpeter's creative destruction—if the prospective invention is likely to be a substitute for some of the firm's currently profitable products, those products can be rendered obsolete by a radically superior substitute. This can be threatening to the large firm that fears cannibalization of its own successful products. The entrant without such vested interests has a clear advantage here. Other possible and previously offered explanations include a propensity of large firms to consider only options not far from the range of their current experience and conservatism imposed by the demands of their larger customers. The management of large firms may meticulously seek to avoid technological changes that threaten obsolescence of their own specialized knowledge, even where those changes promise to benefit stockholders, and managerial ingrained habits of mind may make them unreceptive to novelty. Older firms organized appropriately for one generation of technology may find that the same organization handicaps their use of newer techniques. These hypotheses are all very suggestive, and given that complex phenomena discussed here never have a single and simple explanation, they must be taken seriously. But they nevertheless must be considered with at least one reservation. It does not seem plausible that any of them affects

---

17   Kaplan and Henderson, 2005

any preponderant set of large firms in the same way, and what is examined here appears to be a widespread attribute of R&D in giant enterprises as a body. The hypothesis here is that there are *systematic* forces that impel large firms in general to avoid the search for radical technological change, noteworthy exceptions though there may be.[18]

All of these ascriptions of the characteristic pattern of innovative specialization of the giant enterprises appear to have some validity. But there are also powerful market forces that more systematically drive the big firms toward marked conservatism in their innovative activities, consistently favoring the incremental improvements.

The Innovation Arms Race and the "Pauper Oligopolies"

Perhaps the most compelling force that can drive a firm to avoid risky undertakings with vigilance and determination arises when the enterprise is continually close to the edge. The lack of protective margin means that even a moderate failure can drive it over that edge. It will be argued next that this is a primary force that leads the enterprises with the largest R&D undertakings to employ those resources as conservatively as is possible.

This bald assertion is surely implausible. For it claims that some of the largest and most powerful of the enterprises in the economy are characteristically, if not actually, short of funds, and certainly are endowed with no overabundance. And this is not a matter of mismanagement or dangerous market conditions, but is the result of a critical component of their activities, indeed, of the very mechanism that ensures the vigor and magnitude of their innovative activities. It is part of what the author elsewhere describes as the free-market innovation machine.

The heart of the matter is the nature of the competitive strategy that has become standard in the high-tech sectors of the economy. It is clear that since early in

---

18 Bell Labs and the transistor is, of course, a prime example, but it is easily arguable that this was a very special case. AT&T, the parent company, was then regulated to determine prices essentially on a cost-plus basis, allowing the firm to recoup costs that could be shown to have any legitimacy, *plus a "fair rate of return"* on such outlays. Thus, the underlying pure research was virtually guaranteed to bring in something like normal profits. But the current author was there, consulting both with Bell Labs and the company headquarters, and knows that even so, top management was worried about continuation of such questionable outlays.

the 20ᵗʰ century, in these arenas, innovation has become the firm's principal weapon of competition. Continual improvement in products and processes, preferably a bit ahead of one's rivals, has become the primary instrument in the struggle for market. So much so, that successful and continuous investment in R&D is often a matter of life and death, with loss of market to the firm that falls behind in attractiveness of product or efficiency of production. Because no firm dares to be last and all strive to be first, the result must be a unceasing stream of market-attracting innovations, turned out dependably on a dedicated assembly line. This, evidently, helps to explain the explosion of innovation and the speed of its utilization and introduction into the market that is the most spectacular accomplishment of the free market economies.

But, paradoxically, rather than providing an abundance of revenues, this process also tends to impose scarcity of finances upon the firms involved. The reason is simple. While the resulting revenues can, indeed, be abundant, there is reason to be sure that the need for spending will easily keep pace. The point is that what is going on in this process is accurately described as an innovation arms race—a battle in which innovation is the principal weapon, and in which no combatant dares fall behind. And the history of arms races confirms that they can be expected to impoverish the participants. It is on these grounds that historians have described medieval monarchs as the "pauper kings." Whenever one of them raised the ante by acquiring more troops or better military equipment, his rival had no alternative but to match and even raise the outlay. And so, even Phillip II of Spain, perhaps the wealthiest monarch of Renaissance history, was eight times driven into bankruptcy.

An analogous situation is faced by the modern oligopolist in an innovating industry. In the innovation arms race, each firm must seek to be second to none. And as a result, most of them are bound to find themselves frequently under substantial financial pressure. They will, indeed, be the "pauper oligopolies." Of course, a few will beat the game, but others will be fortunate if they can receive a minimally viable financial rate of return over the long run.[19]

---

19 There is, indeed, no rarity of large firms in financial trouble. The causes do vary from case to case, but the examples, including airlines, automobile manufacturers, and telecommunications firms, are striking. An easy exercise is to make a list of the firms that were mightiest perhaps a half century ago, and confirm how many of those mighty have fallen.

And in that position, no management will willingly dare to undertake the risks that invite serious trouble. They will only devote precious resources to innovative projects for which reasonably reassuring market and technical information is available—the incremental product improvements.

The Marginal Investor

Even if the firm is in the unusual position of having an abundant financial margin and substantial reserves, the pressures it faces are not altogether different from those just described. But here those pressures emanate from the financial position of the firm's investors rather than from that of the company itself. Risky projects pose a special threat to stockholders, particularly to those whose investment is recent. The stock prices of the high-tech firms are closely tracked by the financial success of their innovative performance. A firm with a record of steady and dependable introduction of a succession of improved models of their products can expect their revenues to be enhanced by this performance. But the resulting rise in security prices will automatically bring down the rate of return to new investors to a level commensurate with competitive earnings elsewhere. That is, the working of the market ensures that recent buyers of the company's stocks would have had to pay stock prices sufficiently high to eliminate the prospect of excessive rate of return. This means that failure to perform up to the standards of its past will lead to investor disappointment, falling stock prices and rates of return to those stockholders below the current overall market lever. It is not uncommon to encounter cases in which even a delay beyond the promised date of introduction of an announced new model leads to a sharp drop in stock valuation. This can invite stockholder revolt, and it can hurt incumbent management even more directly through the effects on the employee stock options they are often granted. That is sufficient to force even very successful managements to be conservative in their choice of R&D projects. Radical inventions, by their nature, are far more likely to be failures, if not in terms of workability, then perhaps via heavy cost overruns or delays in the appearance of a viable model. Risk-averse management, whose stock offers new investors no more that the lowest rate of return currently permitted in comparable competitive markets, simply cannot afford to take such chances.

Outsourcing of Breakthroughs

A final part of the story has already been noted. Because of the comparatively low financial remuneration of the representative entrepreneurs described earlier, these entrepreneurs become a source of a low-wage, low-cost search for breakthrough innovations. This makes it more profitable for the large, established firm to buy rather than to make such service. The incentive is no different than that for the outsourcing of computer programming to India. The large firm is thereby given an incentive to outsource this activity, choosing to acquire the resulting intellectual property from the entrepreneurs in the market for inventions, rather than incurring the higher costs of doing the job of producing them itself.

There seems to be no reason to expect the market forces just described to be very transitory. If they are indeed enduring, it follows that the current division of innovative labor between small and large firms will continue. There is also no reason to believe that this will be damaging to the public interest.

The Bottom Line: What Entrepreneurs and their Small Firms Contribute

Given the enormous value of some of the revolutionary inventions that have been brought to society by entrepreneurs, the value of this group to the community hardly requires further evidence. Though they are not by themselves the entire engine of economic growth, they are an indispensable component of that mechanism. Their work underlies the incredible changes in the sources of the power that turns the wheels and drives the vehicles, as well as the more than dramatic upheavals in the means of communication and in the techniques of preservation of information—the three elements that can be said to be most responsible for the historically unprecedented growth of prosperity of much of the modern world. But this is well understood, and all that is added to this observation here is that this contribution of the entrepreneurs shows no evidence of slackening. That, indeed, is one of the central implications of the discussion of this paper.

But two other broad types of contribution, also of substantial importance, are not quite so obvious. One is directly related to the innovation process and to the discussion here, while the other is somewhat further afield but, nevertheless, can draw some illumination from the discussion. One relates to the allocation of resources among prospective R&D projects, and the other to the promise of a career in entrepreneurship as a route out of poverty.

Entrepreneurs and the Task of "Picking Winners" among Prospective Breakthroughs

All too often, the importance of growth for a nation's economy has enticed governments into providing support for particular innovative projects that they favor or even to entire arenas of innovative activity that they consider the wave of the future. The trouble is that the governments have not proven too successful in the task of picking winners, that is, in selecting projects where such government funding will have the highest payoff. They have, indeed, made a few felicitous choices, but the failures have hardly been rare. Yet this is not a shortcoming of government alone. Others have shown their ability to forecast anything except the future. Laughter is all too easily elicited by dramatic misjudgments of the future by businessmen who apparently should have known better (but only in hindsight). There is the prediction by the CEO of IBM that some day the sale of computers might reach five machines per year, the failure of Western Union to recognize the prospective market for the telephone, and some other striking examples have been cited earlier. The moral is not that the individuals in question were particularly dense, but that the future is impenetrable. This is not a matter of risk that can be dealt with via probabilistic approximations and actuarial calculations. Rather, the prospects for a contemplated breakthrough innovation are characteristically enveloped in uncertainty.

How then are choices to be made in the allocation of society's R&D resources in this critical arena? Government has little qualification for the task and big business will not do it. It is only the innovative entrepreneur who is prepared to take on the burden. The task is performed largely by trial and error, using what little information and what large doses of experience and intuition are available to the entrepreneur, because there is no other way. And the process entails a heavy cost to many of the entrepreneurs—those whose guess is wrong. But the basic point is that in undertaking this task, the allocation of so critical a portion of society's R&D resources, the entrepreneurs make an enormous contribution to the general welfare, often at their own expense. It is a job that needs to be done, no one else will do it, and imperfect though the selection turns out to have been in hindsight, no one else could have done it any better.

Entrepreneurship, Educational Requisites, and the Path from Poverty

Innovative entrepreneurship has yet another virtue. It is an avenue to escape from poverty. The prototype is perhaps the immigrants who became itinerant peddlers, including Messrs. Levi and Strauss, who observing a market need, invented blue jeans and made their fortunes. There are no ethnic or cultural prerequisites. The large body of African-American patent holders is described in a number of books and a mere listing of their patents takes up 75 pages.[20]

Three attributes of entrepreneurial activity facilitate its role as conduit from the ghettos and other enclaves of poverty. The first and most obvious is that it requires no consent of an employer. At least in the United States, where some minimal licensing requirements are all that impede the process, for all practical purposes, all entry requires is the determination to do so.[21] Second, there are opportunities that require very little sunk capital, and many an entrepreneur has, indeed, started on a shoestring. The third attribute, which seems not to receive the attention it deserves, is its education requirement: virtually zero. The successful entrepreneur obviously needs to be clever and, indeed, sometimes requires some wisdom. But the great success stories are populated by school dropouts and avoiders of advanced education. Both Edison and the Wright brothers were active entrepreneurs and not just inventors. Edison dropped out of school at age 12 and the Wrights never attended high school. Other examples abound, all illustrating that advanced education is hardly an inescapable job requirement or indispensable for good performance as an entrepreneur. This is important because education is time-consuming and expensive, at least in terms of income foregone, even when government pays the bill. Society's islands of poverty are also aggregations of uncompleted education.

---

20 See Sluby, 2004, 204–278.

21 Unfortunately, practices elsewhere can be very different, and the resulting barriers to entry may well be suspected as a handicap to growth for the entire economy. "It takes two days to start a business in Australia, but 203 days in Haiti and 215 days in the Democratic Republic of Congo.... There are no monetary costs to start a new business in Denmark, but it costs more than five times income per capita in Cambodia and over thirteen times in Sierra Leone. Hong Kong, Singapore, Thailand and more than three dozen other economies require no minimum capital from start-ups. In contrast, in Syria the capital requirement is equivalent to fifty-six times income per capita..." (study by the International Finance Corporation of the World Bank quoted in Friedman, 2005).

Lack of education is often a handicap that cannot be overcome by those who seek jobs with any degree of promise for the future in established enterprises. But it does not close the door to exercise of entrepreneurship, and that is no negligible virtue.

Concluding Comment

This paper has gone beyond the observation that breakthrough advance in technology is predominantly a small firm specialty. There is a good deal of evidence that this has been the case for over a century and that it continues to be so today. True, the giant oligopolies provide the overwhelming preponderance of R&D expenditures, but in general those outlays are carefully directed to projects with minimal risk, which are therefore apt to yield non-negligible improvements, but improvements that typically are only incremental. This paper has inquired into the influences that can account for this division of labor and has offered a number of observations that indicate that the phenomenon is hardly an accidental occurrence. More important, the analysis, if supported by the evidence, indicates that this distribution of the task of technological advance can, with a degree of confidence, be expected to continue.

This underscores the contribution of the innovative entrepreneurs to the growth of the economy and the welfare of society. Three such contributions are emphasized here. The first, the focus of the article, is the entrepreneur's provision of the radical innovations that underlie the profound changes, since the Industrial Revolution, in the way Americans live. Second, it has been noted that the innovative entrepreneurs as a group carry out the task of selection of the projects to which the resources available for the search for radical breakthroughs are allocated. This is a task critical for the future of the economy, but it is a task from which others shrink because of the great uncertainties it entails. Finally, recalling the evidence that innovative entrepreneurs have often succeeded, and succeeded spectacularly, with little formal education, it has been pointed out that this serves to reduce further the naturally low barriers to entry into the activity. That, it turn, helps to fill a need critical for society: an attractive and promising avenue toward prosperity.

References

Astebro, Thomas (2003), "The Return to Independent Invention: Evidence of Unrealistic Optimism, Risk Seeking or Skewness Loving," *The Economic Journal*, January, pp. 226–238.

Baumol, William J. (2002a), "Entrepreneurship, Innovation and Growth: The David-Goliath Symbiosis," *Journal of Entrepreneurial Finance and Business Ventures*, Vol. 7, Issue 2, Fall, pp. 1–10.

Baumol, William J. (2002b), *The Free-Market Innovation Machine: Analyzing the Growth Miracle of Capitalism*, Princeton, NJ: Princeton University Press.

Bowen, William G., Martin A. Kurzwell and Eugene M. Tobin (2005), *Equity and Excellence in American Higher Education*, Charlottesville, VA.: University of Virginia Press, pp. 56–60, Figures 3–5.

Chesborough, Henry W. (2001), "Assembling the Elephant: A Review of Empirical Studies of the Impact of Technical Change Upon Incumbent Firms," in Robert Burgelman and Henry W. Chesborough, eds., *Comparative Studies of Technological Evolution, Research on Technological Innovation, Management and Policy*, Vol. 7, Greenwich, CT: JAI Press.

Freeman, Richard B. (1978), "Job Satisfaction as an Economic Variable," *American Economic Review*, Vol. 68 (No. 2), pp. 135–141.

Friedman, Thomas L. (2005), *The World is Flat: A History of the Twenty-First Century*, New York, NY: Farrar, Straus and Giroux.

Frey, Bruno S. and Matthias Benz (2003), *Being Independent is a Great Thing: Subjective Evaluation of Self-Employment and Hierarchy*, University of Zurich, Institute for Empirical Research in Economics, Working Paper No. 135, May.

Frey, Bruno S. and Werner W. Pommerehne (1989), *Muses and Markets: Explorations in the Economics of the Arts*, Oxford, UK: Basil Blackwell.

Kaplan, Sarah and Rebecca Henderson (forthcoming in 2005), "Organizational Rigidity, Incentives and Technological Change: Insights from Organizational Economics."

Khan, B. Zorina, and Kenneth L. Sokoloff (2004), "Institutions and Technological Innovation during Early Economic Growth: Evidence from the Great Inventors of the United States, 1790–1930," CESifo Working Paper No. 1299, CESifo Venice Summer Institute, Workshop on Institutions and Growth, July.

National Science Board (2000), *Science and Engineering Indicators: 2000*, Arlington, VA: National Science Foundation.

Nordhaus, William D. (2004), "Schumpeterian Profits in the American Economy: Theory and Measurement," Working Paper 10433, Cambridge, MA: National Bureau of Economic Research.

Say, Jean B. (1834), *A Treatise on Political Economy*, Philadelphia: Claxton, Remsen and Haffelfinger (French original, 1819).

Sluby, Patricia Carter (2004), *The Inventive Spirit of African Americans: Patented Ingenuity*, Westport, CT: Praeger Publishers.

Smith, Adam (1776), *An Inquiry Into the Nature and Causes of the Wealth of Nations*, London.

U.S. Small Business Administration (1995), *The State of Small Business: A Report of the President*, 1994, Washington, DC: U.S. Government Printing Office.

U.S. Small Business Administration (2003), "Small Serial Innovators: The Small Firm Contribution to Technical Change," *Small Business Research Summary*, No. 225, by CHI Research Inc., Haddon Heights, NJ, under contract no. SBAHG-01-C0149 for Small Business Administration, Office of Advocacy, February.

APPENDIX A
Small Business Data

Table A.1 U.S. Business Measures, 1980–2004

Year	Employer firms	Nonemployers	Establishments[1]	Self-employment[2] (thousands)	Nonfarm business tax returns	Employer births	Employer terminations	Business bankruptcies
2004	e 5,683,700	e 18,290,800	NA	10,431	29,305,400	e 580,900	e 576,200	34,317
2003	e 5,679,000	e 17,980,700	NA	10,295	28,392,100	e 553,500	e 572,300	35,037
2002	5,697,759	17,646,062	7,200,770	9,926	26,347,100	569,750	586,890	38,540
2001	5,657,774	16,979,498	7,095,302	10,109	25,631,200	535,140	553,291	40,099
2000	5,652,544	16,529,955	7,070,048	10,215	25,106,900	574,300	542,831	35,472
1999	5,607,743	16,152,604	7,008,444	10,087	24,750,100	579,609	544,487	37,884
1998	5,579,177	15,708,727	6,941,822	10,303	24,285,900	589,982	540,601	44,367
1997	5,541,918	15,439,609	6,894,869	10,513	23,857,100	590,644	530,003	54,027
1996	5,478,047	NA	6,738,476	10,489	23,115,300	597,792	512,402	53,549
1995	5,369,068	NA	6,612,721	10,482	22,555,200	594,369	497,246	51,959
1994	5,276,964	NA	6,509,065	10,648	22,191,000	570,587	503,563	52,374
1993	5,193,642	NA	6,401,233	10,279	20,874,800	564,504	492,651	62,304
1992	5,095,356	14,325,000	6,319,300	9,960	20,476,800	544,596	521,606	70,643
1991	5,051,025	NA	6,200,859	10,274	20,498,900	541,141	546,518	71,549

Year							
1990	5,073,795	NA	6,175,559	10,097	20,219,400	584,892	531,400	64,853
1989	5,021,315	NA	6,106,922	10,008	19,560,700	NA	NA	62,449
1988	4,954,645	NA	6,016,367	9,917	18,619,400	NA	NA	62,845
1987	NA	NA	5,937,061	9,624	18,351,400	NA	NA	81,463
1986	NA	NA	5,806,973	9,328	17,524,600	NA	NA	79,926
1985	NA	NA	5,701,485	9,269	16,959,900	NA	NA	70,644
1984	NA	NA	5,517,715	9,338	16,077,000	NA	NA	64,211
1983	NA	NA	5,306,787	9,140	15,245,000	NA	NA	62,412
1982	NA	NA	4,633,960	8,898	14,546,000	NA	NA	69,242
1981	NA	NA	4,586,510	8,735	13,858,000	NA	NA	48,086
1980	NA	NA	4,543,167	8,642	13,021,600	NA	NA	43,252

1 Units with paid employees in the fourth quarter through 1983. 1984 on includes units active in any quarter of the year.

2 Unincorporated, primary occupation.

e = estimate

NA = Not Available

Sources: U.S. Small Business Administration, Office of Advocacy, from the following data: employer firms, births and terminations from the U.S. Census Bureau with 2003 and 2004 estimates based on U.S. Census Bureau and Department of Labor data; nonemployers from the U.S. Census Bureau with 2003 and 2004 Advocacy estimates based on IRS data; establishments from the U.S. Census Bureau; self-employment from the Bureau of Labor Statistics; nonfarm business tax returns from the Internal Revenue Service; bankruptcies from the Administrative Office of the U.S. Courts (business bankruptcy filings).

Table A.2 Macroeconomic Indicators, 1990–2004

	1990	1995	2000	2003	2004	Percent change 2003–2004
Gross domestic product (GDP) (billions of dollars)[1]						
Current dollars	5,803.1	7,397.7	9,817.0	11,004.0	11,733.5	6.6
Constant dollars (billions of 2000 dollars)	7,112.5	8,031.7	9,817.0	10,381.3	10,841.6	4.4
Sales (billions of dollars)[2]						
Manufacturing	242.7	290.0	350.7	333.3	369.1	10.8
Wholesale trade	149.5	176.2	228.6	240.4	273.6	13.8
Retail trade	153.7	189.0	255.8	283.3	305.4	7.8
Income (billions of dollars)						
Compensation of employees[3]	3,351.0	4,193.3	5,782.7	6,289.0	6,631.1	5.4
Nonfarm proprietors' income	349.9	469.5	705.7	812.3	884.3	8.9
Farm proprietors' income	31.1	22.7	22.7	21.8	18.2	-16.5
Corporate profits[4]	408.6	696.7	817.9	1,021.1	—	—
Output and productivity (business sector indexes, 1992=100)						
Output	98.6	111.4	140.5	149.0	156.7	5.2
Hours of all persons worked	102.6	109.6	121.2	115.1	116.4	1.1
Productivity (output per hour)	96.1	101.6	115.9	129.5	134.6	3.9

1 *Small Business Share of Private, Nonfarm Gross Domestic Product* by Joel Popkin and Company (study funded by the Office of Advocacy) estimates small businesses with fewer than 500 employees created 52 percent of the total nonfarm private output in 1999.

2 U.S. Census Bureau, Statistics of U.S. Business, showed that in 1997, small firms with fewer than 500 employees accounted for 24.8 percent of manufacturing, 52.6 percent of retail, and 46.8 percent of wholesale sales.

3 U.S. Census Bureau, Statistics of U.S. Business, showed that in 2001 small firms accounted for 44.3 percent of annual payroll and 49.9 percent of total nonfarm private employment.

4 With inventory valuation and capital consumption adjustments.

(continued, next page)

Table A.2 (continued)

	1990	1995	2000	2003	2004	Percent change 2003–2004
Employment and compensation						
Nonfarm private employment (millions)[3]	91.1	97.9	111.0	108.4	109.9	1.3
Unemployment rate (percent)	5.6	5.6	4.0	6.0	5.5	-8.3
Total compensation cost index (Dec.) (June 1989=100)	107.0	126.7	150.9	168.8	175.2	3.8
Wage and salary index (Dec) (June 1989=100)	106.1	123.1	147.7	162.3	166.2	2.4
Employee benefits cost index (Dec.) (June 1989=100)	109.4	135.9	158.6	185.8	198.7	6.9
Bank loans, interest rates, and yields						
Bank commercial & industrial loans (billions of dollars)	641.2	723.8	1,087.0	891.6	911.4	2.2
Prime rate (percent)	10.01	8.83	9.23	4.12	4.34	5.3
U.S. Treasury 10-year bond yields (percent)	8.55	6.57	6.03	4.01	4.27	6.5
Price indices (inflation measures)						
Consumer price index (urban) (1982–84 = 100)	130.7	152.4	172.2	184.0	188.9	2.7
Producer price index (finished goods) (1982 = 100)	119.2	127.9	138.0	143.3	148.5	3.6
GDP implicit price deflator (2000 = 100)	81.6	92.1	100.0	106.0	108.2	2.1

Sources: U.S. Small Business Administration, Office of Advocacy, from the U.S. Department of Commerce, Bureau of Economic Analysis and *Economic Indicators*, March 2000 and February 2005.

Table A.3 Number of Businesses by State, 2003–2004

	Employer firms		Self-employment (thousands)	
	2003	**2004**	**2003**	**2004**
United States	e 5,679,000	e 5,683,700	15,304	15,636
Alabama	85,768	86,651	204	194
Alaska	16,825	16,975	43	43
Arizona	109,692	110,153	293	298
Arkansas	60,416	61,778	149	162
California	1,063,230	1,077,390	1,987	2,138
Colorado	143,821	146,379	328	350
Connecticut	95,969	97,311	184	176
Delaware	25,280	25,833	36	32
District of Columbia	26,633	27,424	24	23
Florida	426,245	449,070	961	1,022
Georgia	196,921	202,979	492	457
Hawaii	29,217	29,791	62	66
Idaho	41,539	43,675	101	109
Illinois	281,869	285,208	571	588
Indiana	125,129	125,746	288	267
Iowa	68,737	69,354	190	186
Kansas	68,095	69,241	174	175
Kentucky	81,407	83,046	172	179
Louisiana	94,437	96,084	225	221
Maine	39,691	40,304	93	94
Maryland	134,447	137,338	275	271
Massachusetts	175,827	178,752	327	340
Michigan	210,803	213,104	474	468
Minnesota	133,419	134,438	357	360
Mississippi	53,641	54,117	126	129
Missouri	131,464	134,448	303	302
Montana	33,991	34,570	93	93
Nebraska	45,595	46,161	132	121

e estimate

(continued, next page)

Table A.3 (continued)

	Employer firms		Self-employment (thousands)	
	2003	2004	2003	2004
Nevada	48,929	51,424	91	116
New Hampshire	39,508	40,151	78	77
New Jersey	268,203	256,863	404	404
New Mexico	41,731	42,241	103	111
New York	478,270	481,858	933	930
North Carolina	179,580	182,598	384	420
North Dakota	18,817	19,177	52	53
Ohio	229,648	231,374	490	505
Oklahoma	75,486	77,027	215	209
Oregon	102,862	104,114	214	240
Pennsylvania	271,459	275,853	554	596
Rhode Island	32,594	33,253	53	52
South Carolina	90,998	92,940	180	182
South Dakota	23,161	23,713	62	63
Tennessee	110,427	109,853	327	289
Texas	398,928	404,683	1,180	1,200
Utah	58,507	61,118	128	135
Vermont	20,922	21,335	54	48
Virginia	167,527	172,785	362	357
Washington	206,699	198,635	350	369
West Virginia	37,144	36,830	70	59
Wisconsin	123,800	125,888	318	312
Wyoming	19,616	20,071	42	45

Notes: State totals do not add to the U.S. figure as firms can be in more than one state. U.S. 2003 and 2004 estimates are based on U.S. Census Bureau and U.S. Department of Labor, Employment and Training Administration (ETA) data. Self-employment is based on monthly averages of primary occupation for incorporated and unincorporated status. The figures cannot be added as the self-employed can have employees.

Sources: U.S. Small Business Administration, Office of Advocacy, from data provided by the U.S. Department of Labor (ETA) and U.S. Census Bureau, Current Population Survey, special tabulations.

Table A.4 Business Turnover by State, 2003–2004

	Firm births		Firm terminations		Business bankruptcies	
	2003	2004	2003	2004	2003	2004
U.S. Total	e 553,500	e 580,900	e 572,300	e 576,200	35,037	34,317
Alabama	9,014	9,413	10,927	10,104	287	325
Alaska	2,441	1,848	2,507	2,650	121	64
Arizona	13,322	12,421	15,488	17,553	701	480
Arkansas	7,253	7,852	6,918	6,481	429	376
California	113,500	117,016	140,435	143,115	4,501	3,748
Colorado	22,400	23,694	13,243	9,734	552	786
Connecticut	8,501	9,064	11,044	11,018	187	132
Delaware	3,439	3,270	3,148	3,362	505	276
District of Columbia	4,052	4,393	3,874	3,440	55	41
Florida	69,711	77,754	56,665	54,498	1,534	1,183
Georgia	24,217	29,547	25,898	27,835	1,585	2,090
Hawaii	3,658	3,698	4,010	3,754	72	47
Idaho	5,998	7,814	6,742	5,716	225	160
Illinois	28,933	28,453	41,112	33,472	991	912
Indiana	13,452	13,906	15,137	15,282	640	524
Iowa	5,534	5,954	7,378	7,391	323	360
Kansas	7,625	6,742	8,392	7,250	303	268
Kentucky	8,155	8,807	10,801	8,597	327	319
Louisiana	9,298	9,875	12,171	9,668	499	622
Maine	4,033	4,300	4,715	4,987	105	138
Maryland	20,687	21,751	21,697	20,636	523	417
Massachusetts	18,984	18,822	21,870	20,270	396	315
Michigan	22,022	24,625	24,748	24,584	684	681
Minnesota	14,652	15,167	17,928	15,209	1,379	1,374
Mississippi	6,020	6,141	7,267	7,380	282	170
Missouri	15,947	16,155	20,190	17,924	378	354
Montana	4,548	4,588	4,679	4,896	98	109

e estimate

(continued, next page)

Table A.4 (continued)

	Firm births		Firm terminations		Business bankruptcies	
	2003	2004	2003	2004	2003	2004
Nebraska	4,311	4,849	5,050	5,051	238	207
Nevada	9,749	10,483	8,939	9,012	321	257
New Hampshire	4,653	4,865	4,598	5,401	178	158
New Jersey	29,236	35,895	36,827	50,034	734	684
New Mexico	5,508	5,683	5,770	5,592	774	727
New York	60,569	62,854	61,199	64,013	1,987	4,070
North Carolina	22,465	23,387	23,234	22,055	528	486
North Dakota	1,456	1,747	2,049	2,621	105	85
Ohio	22,227	22,725	23,544	21,328	1,426	1,432
Oklahoma	8,802	9,263	8,434	8,018	612	659
Oregon	13,842	13,481	14,194	14,407	1,591	852
Pennsylvania	31,214	33,188	32,917	34,507	1,193	1,138
Rhode Island	3,465	3,932	4,103	4,250	48	74
South Carolina	10,759	11,745	10,711	10,975	142	175
South Dakota	1,338	1,691	1,899	2,251	110	108
Tennessee	17,700	17,415	16,315	16,520	597	548
Texas	52,677	54,098	55,461	55,792	3,153	3,094
Utah	10,656	11,357	10,368	11,597	519	440
Vermont	2,122	2,322	2,584	2,578	78	85
Virginia	22,069	24,134	20,539	19,919	956	750
Washington	36,136	31,955	35,345	47,141	737	665
West Virginia	4,126	3,937	5,550	5,136	290	247
Wisconsin	12,400	13,093	12,629	12,711	722	742
Wyoming	2,419	2,519	2,921	2,737	44	65

Notes: State birth and termination totals do not add to the U.S. figure as firms can be in more than one state. U.S. estimates are based on U.S. Census Bureau and Department of Labor, Employment and Administration, data. On occasion, some state terminations result in successor firms which are not listed as new firms.

Source: U.S. Small Business Administration, Office of Advocacy, from data provided by the U.S. Department of Labor (ETA), U.S. Census Bureau and Administrative Office of the U.S. Courts.

Table A.5 Private Firms, Establishments, Employment, Annual Payroll and Receipts by Firm Size, 1988–2002

Item	Year	Nonemployers	Employer totals	Employment size of firm		
				0–19	<500	500+
Employer firms	2002	17,646,062	5,697,759	5,090,331	5,680,914	16,845
	2001	16,979,498	5,657,774	5,036,845	5,640,407	17,367
	2000	16,529,955	5,652,544	5,035,029	5,635,391	17,153
	1999	16,152,604	5,607,743	5,007,808	5,591,003	16,740
	1998	15,708,727	5,579,177	4,988,367	5,562,799	16,378
	1997	15,439,609	5,541,918	4,958,641	5,525,839	16,079
	1996	NA	5,478,047	4,909,983	5,462,431	15,616
	1995	NA	5,369,068	4,807,533	5,353,624	15,444
	1994	NA	5,276,964	4,736,317	5,261,967	14,997
	1993	NA	5,193,642	4,661,601	5,179,013	14,629
	1992	14,325,000	5,095,356	4,572,994	5,081,234	14,122
	1991	NA	5,051,025	4,528,899	5,037,048	13,977
	1990	NA	5,073,795	4,535,575	5,059,772	14,023
	1989	NA	5,021,315	4,493,875	5,007,442	13,873
	1988	NA	4,954,645	4,444,473	4,941,821	12,824
Establishments	2002	17,646,062	7,200,770	5,147,526	6,172,809	1,027,961
	2001	16,979,498	7,095,302	5,093,660	6,079,993	1,015,309
	2000	16,529,955	7,070,048	5,093,832	6,080,050	989,998
	1999	16,152,604	7,008,444	5,068,096	6,048,129	960,315
	1998	15,708,727	6,941,822	5,048,528	6,030,325	911,497
	1997	15,439,609	6,894,869	5,026,425	6,017,638	877,231

1996	NA	6,738,476	4,976,014	5,892,934	845,542
1995	NA	6,612,721	4,876,327	5,798,936	813,785
1994	NA	6,509,065	4,809,575	5,724,681	784,384
1993	NA	6,401,233	4,737,778	5,654,835	746,398
1992	14,325,000	6,319,300	4,653,464	5,571,896	747,404
1991	NA	6,200,859	4,603,523	5,457,366	743,493
1990	NA	6,175,559	4,602,362	5,447,605	727,954
1989	NA	6,106,922	4,563,257	5,402,086	704,836
1988	NA	6,016,367	4,516,707	5,343,026	673,341

Employment

2002	0	112,400,654	20,583,371	56,366,292	56,034,362
2001	0	115,061,184	20,602,635	57,383,449	57,677,735
2000	0	114,064,976	20,587,385	57,124,044	56,940,932
1999	0	110,705,661	20,388,287	55,729,092	54,976,569
1998	0	108,117,731	20,275,405	55,064,409	53,053,322
1997	0	105,299,123	20,118,816	54,545,370	50,753,753
1996	0	102,187,297	19,881,502	53,174,502	49,012,795
1995	0	100,314,946	19,569,861	52,652,510	47,662,436
1994	0	96,721,594	19,195,318	51,007,688	45,713,906
1993	0	94,773,913	19,070,191	50,316,063	44,457,850
1992	0	92,825,797	18,772,644	49,200,841	43,624,956
1991	0	92,307,559	18,712,812	49,002,613	43,304,946
1990	0	93,469,275	18,911,906	50,166,797	43,302,478
1989	0	91,626,094	18,626,776	49,353,860	42,272,234

(continued, next page)

NA = Not available.

Table A.5 (continued)

Item	Year	Nonemployers	Employer totals	Employment size of firm		
				0–19	<500	500+
Annual payroll	1988	0	87,844,303	18,319,642	47,914,723	39,929,580
	2002	NA	3,943,179,606	617,583,597	1,777,049,574	2,166,130,032
	2001	NA	3,989,086,323	603,848,633	1,767,546,642	2,221,539,681
	2000	NA	3,879,430,052	591,123,880	1,727,114,941	2,152,315,111
	1999	NA	3,554,692,909	561,547,424	1,601,129,388	1,953,563,521
	1998	NA	3,309,405,533	535,184,511	1,512,769,153	1,796,636,380
	1997	NA	3,047,907,469	503,130,254	1,416,200,011	1,631,707,458
	1996	NA	2,848,623,049	481,008,640	1,330,258,327	1,518,364,722
	1995	NA	2,665,921,824	454,009,065	1,252,135,244	1,413,786,580
	1994	NA	2,487,959,727	432,791,911	1,176,418,685	1,311,541,042
	1993	NA	2,363,208,106	415,254,636	1,116,443,440	1,246,764,666
	1992	NA	2,272,392,408	399,804,694	1,066,948,306	1,205,444,102
	1991	NA	2,145,015,851	381,544,608	1,013,014,303	1,132,001,548
	1990	NA	2,103,971,179	375,313,660	1,007,156,385	1,096,814,794
	1989	NA	1,989,941,554	357,259,587	954,137,110	1,035,804,444
	1988	NA	1,858,652,147	342,168,460	902,566,839	956,085,308
Receipts	1997	586,315,756	18,242,632,687	2,786,839,570	7,468,211,700	10,774,420,987

NA = Not available.

Notes: A firm is as an aggregation of all establishments (locations with payroll in any quarter) owned by a parent company and employment is measured in March (startups, closures, and seasonal firms could have zero employment). This table does not show job growth as firms can annually change size classes. See *www.sba.gov/advo/research/data.html* for more detail.

Source: U.S. Small Business Administration, Office of Advocacy, based on data provided by the U.S. Census Bureau, Statistics of U.S. Business and Nonemployer Statistics.

Table A.6 Employer and Nonemployer Firms by Firm Size and State, 2002

State	Firms					Employment			
	Non-employers	Employer total	Employment size of firm			Employment total	Employment size of firm		
			0–19	<500	500+		0–19	<500	500+
United States	17,646,062	5,697,759	5,090,331	5,680,914	16,845	112,400,654	20,583,371	56,366,292	56,034,362
Alabama	239,614	78,710	67,186	76,554	2,156	1,581,117	289,056	786,023	795,094
Alaska	47,054	15,986	14,058	15,485	501	213,600	53,083	127,757	85,843
Arizona	289,300	95,908	81,828	93,178	2,730	1,945,472	328,593	930,225	1,015,247
Arkansas	162,535	52,094	45,069	50,601	1,493	974,969	185,192	475,672	499,297
California	2,252,375	674,635	591,088	669,132	5,503	12,856,426	2,390,154	6,810,807	6,045,619
Colorado	350,943	119,568	104,768	116,761	2,807	1,912,152	386,458	981,209	930,943
Connecticut	228,082	77,256	65,967	75,201	2,055	1,555,595	278,479	758,707	796,888
Delaware	44,489	20,208	16,290	18,779	1,429	389,304	63,707	170,732	218,572
District of Columbia	34,175	16,377	12,313	15,288	1,089	418,755	53,976	200,911	217,844
Florida	1,189,508	370,789	335,819	366,657	4,132	6,366,964	1,181,835	2,856,047	3,510,917
Georgia	523,818	164,252	141,929	160,442	3,810	3,381,244	554,812	1,493,178	1,888,066
Hawaii	76,398	24,912	21,198	24,120	792	439,934	89,486	252,859	187,075
Idaho	89,279	33,214	29,010	32,232	982	453,552	111,770	258,939	194,613
Illinois	720,812	253,720	218,492	249,419	4,301	5,224,293	885,047	2,576,677	2,647,616
Indiana	328,721	116,030	98,289	113,234	2,796	2,517,180	431,272	1,253,842	1,263,338

(continued, next page)

Table A.6 (continued)

State	Firms					Employment			
	Non-employers	Employer total	Employment size of firm			Employment total	Employment size of firm		
			0–19	<500	500+		0–19	<500	500+
Iowa	176,284	65,136	56,049	63,534	1,602	1,229,609	231,037	642,285	587,324
Kansas	162,656	60,949	51,924	59,082	1,867	1,098,894	212,578	588,098	510,796
Kentucky	236,520	71,874	60,753	69,753	2,121	1,462,517	263,146	734,027	728,490
Louisiana	253,694	81,684	69,478	79,693	1,991	1,583,308	303,318	853,102	730,206
Maine	102,648	34,421	30,311	33,553	868	486,766	115,687	292,458	194,308
Maryland	343,138	107,995	92,205	105,445	2,550	2,062,515	381,102	1,087,225	975,290
Massachusetts	424,172	146,080	125,755	143,191	2,889	3,023,126	512,737	1,481,475	1,541,651
Michigan	555,736	192,284	166,728	189,259	3,025	3,889,825	708,676	1,976,385	1,913,440
Minnesota	333,272	118,667	101,980	116,227	2,440	2,359,593	408,285	1,205,979	1,153,614
Mississippi	145,183	47,979	41,128	46,459	1,520	904,252	173,502	452,463	451,789
Missouri	329,854	119,561	102,627	116,855	2,706	2,354,230	414,708	1,172,541	1,181,689
Montana	72,988	28,812	25,738	28,171	641	300,636	95,777	209,551	91,085
Nebraska	106,385	41,487	35,655	40,177	1,310	749,098	145,975	382,822	366,276
Nevada	128,073	42,502	35,274	40,671	1,831	936,225	136,502	401,565	534,660
New Hampshire	94,232	32,279	27,376	31,209	1,070	550,725	113,312	301,661	249,064
New Jersey	513,492	203,467	179,467	200,273	3,194	3,596,919	691,165	1,795,534	1,801,385
New Mexico	103,298	35,597	30,178	34,223	1,374	554,156	124,325	319,416	234,740
New York	1,302,672	428,425	383,562	424,337	4,088	7,234,915	1,417,576	3,756,372	3,478,543

State								
North Carolina	492,802	165,020	143,332	161,776	3,244	3,322,004	596,501	1,570,513	1,751,491
North Dakota	40,636	17,151	14,634	16,565	586	253,980	59,410	160,941	93,039
Ohio	623,622	211,017	180,138	207,337	3,680	4,743,151	795,501	2,327,590	2,415,561
Oklahoma	228,077	70,334	61,012	68,536	1,798	1,200,477	246,834	644,719	555,758
Oregon	218,326	85,134	74,391	83,154	1,980	1,329,235	295,937	735,965	593,270
Pennsylvania	655,959	237,397	204,842	233,573	3,824	5,046,442	875,457	2,497,790	2,548,652
Rhode Island	63,292	25,469	21,675	24,584	885	415,970	86,096	238,038	177,932
South Carolina	221,692	78,608	67,547	76,473	2,135	1,538,750	283,703	739,268	799,482
South Dakota	49,991	20,877	17,966	20,212	665	303,646	72,562	189,371	114,275
Tennessee	364,587	100,720	85,271	97,856	2,864	2,291,504	363,328	1,032,883	1,258,621
Texas	1,388,284	373,059	324,811	368,118	4,941	7,993,559	1,355,135	3,758,770	4,234,789
Utah	144,443	49,259	42,307	47,572	1,687	900,428	162,795	430,064	470,364
Vermont	54,308	19,039	16,522	18,427	612	258,058	66,000	162,099	95,959
Virginia	398,777	142,593	122,839	139,513	3,080	2,914,804	512,595	1,402,928	1,511,876
Washington	334,912	138,256	121,568	135,692	2,564	2,185,658	474,351	1,196,397	989,261
West Virginia	84,185	32,669	28,009	31,597	1,072	561,478	118,561	302,598	258,880
Wisconsin	283,417	115,980	98,777	113,641	2,339	2,355,816	430,256	1,266,582	1,089,234
Wyoming	37,352	16,465	14,325	15,905	177,828	56,021	123,232	54,596

Notes: For state data, a firm is an aggregation of all establishments (locations with payroll in any quarter) owned by a parent company within a state (start-ups after March, closures before March, and seasonal firms could have zero employment). See www.sba.gov/advo/research/data.html for more detail.

Source: U.S. Small Business Administration, Office of Advocacy, based on data provided by the U.S. Department of Commerce, Bureau of the Census.

Table A.7 Employer Firms and Employment by Firm Size and Industry, 2002

Industry	Non-employers	Total	Employment size of firm		
			0–19	<500	500+
Firms					
Total	**17,646,062**	**5,657,774**	**5,036,845**	**5,640,407**	**17,367**
Agriculture, forestry, fishing, & hunting	220,050	25,802	24,171	25,715	87
Mining	82,709	19,340	16,334	19,015	325
Utilities	12,675	7,283	5,893	7,069	214
Construction	2,071,317	691,110	630,479	690,081	1,029
Manufacturing	290,380	305,160	222,184	300,627	4,533
Wholesale trade	363,781	346,027	293,814	342,772	3,255
Retail trade	1,838,992	735,135	662,922	732,718	2,417
Transportation & warehousing	808,999	157,197	138,209	156,083	1,114
Information	232,698	77,459	65,154	76,326	1,133
Finance & insurance	660,292	230,595	210,135	228,986	1,609
Real estate & rental & leasing	1,880,042	247,582	233,053	246,365	1,217
Professional, scientific, & technical services	2,552,880	682,278	635,250	679,853	2,425
Management of companies & enterprises	—	26,794	7,187	20,096	6,698
Admin., support, waste mngt. & remediation srv.	1,262,707	308,502	269,867	305,329	3,173
Educational services	344,538	63,690	47,844	62,701	989
Health care & social assistance	1,456,915	540,976	473,020	537,437	3,539
Arts, entertainment, & recreation	865,990	99,124	84,047	98,545	579
Accommodation & food services	241,688	416,464	332,965	414,792	1,672
Other services (except public administration)	2,459,409	658,412	611,924	657,151	1,261
Aux., exc corp, subsidiary, & regional mng. offices	—	5,401	326	3,018	2,383
Unclassified	—	78,644	78,315	78,644	0

(continued, next page)

Table A.7 (continued)

Industry	Non-employers	Total	Employment size of firm		
			0–19	<500	500+
Employment					
Total	—	**115,061,184**	**20,602,635**	**57,383,449**	**57,677,735**
Agriculture, forestry, fishing, & hunting	—	183,476	86,736	163,864	19,612
Mining	—	485,565	66,864	214,539	271,026
Utilities	—	654,484	23,015	105,970	548,514
Construction	—	6,491,994	2,445,277	5,527,298	964,696
Manufacturing	—	15,950,424	1,255,654	6,637,966	9,312,458
Wholesale trade	—	6,142,089	1,331,887	3,864,994	2,277,095
Retail trade	—	14,890,289	2,913,484	6,462,404	8,427,885
Transportation & warehousing	—	3,750,663	518,790	1,557,738	2,192,925
Information	—	3,754,698	270,180	994,997	2,759,701
Finance & insurance	—	6,248,400	701,387	1,941,013	4,307,387
Real estate & rental & leasing	—	2,013,673	694,852	1,380,907	632,766
Professional, scientific, & technical services	—	7,156,579	2,110,446	4,589,019	2,567,560
Management of companies & enterprises	—	2,879,223	18,954	325,473	2,553,750
Admin., support, waste mngt. & remediation srv.	—	9,061,987	1,011,065	3,525,685	5,536,302
Educational services	—	2,612,430	217,714	1,237,081	1,375,349
Health care & social assistance	—	14,534,726	2,279,569	6,905,825	7,628,901
Arts, entertainment, & recreation	—	1,780,362	314,007	1,193,078	587,284
Accommodation & food services	—	9,972,301	1,762,077	5,999,195	3,973,106
Other services (except public administration)	—	5,370,479	2,483,350	4,593,627	776,852
Aux., exc corp, subsidiary, & regional mng. offices	—	1,022,114	940	57,548	964,566
Unclassified	—	105,228	96,387	105,228	0

Notes: Employment is measured in March; thus some firms (start-ups after March, closures before March, and seasonal firms) will have zero employment. Firms are an aggregation of all establishments owned by a parent company within an industry. See www.sba.gov/advo/research/data.html for more detail.

Source: U.S. Small Business Administration, Office of Advocacy, based on data provided by the U.S. Census Bureau.

Table A.8 Employer Firm Births, Deaths, and Employment Changes by Employment Size of Firm, 1990–2002

Period	Type of change	Firms				Employment			
		Total	Beginning year employment size of firm			Total	Beginning year employment size of firm		
			<20	<500	500+		<20	<500	500+
2001–2002	Firm births	569,750	541,516	568,280	1,470	3,369,930	1,748,097	3,033,734	336,196
	Firm deaths	586,890	557,133	586,535	355	3,660,161	1,755,255	3,256,851	403,310
	Existing firm expansions					15,385,726	3,149,876	7,587,961	7,797,765
	Existing firm contractions					17,756,053	2,289,644	7,794,376	9,961,677
	Net change	-17,140	-15,617	-18,255	1,115	-2,660,558	853,074	-429,532	-2,231,026
2000–2001	Firm births	585,140	558,037	584,837	303	3,418,369	1,821,298	3,108,501	309,868
	Firm deaths	553,291	523,960	552,839	452	3,261,621	1,700,677	3,049,714	211,907
	Existing firm expansions					14,939,658	3,065,106	7,033,084	7,906,574
	Existing firm contractions					14,096,436	2,074,544	5,940,996	8,155,440
	Net change	31,849	34,077	31,998	-149	999,970	1,111,183	1,150,875	-150,905
1999–2000	Firm births	574,300	548,030	574,023	277	3,228,804	1,792,946	3,031,079	197,725
	Firm deaths	542,831	514,242	542,374	457	3,176,609	1,653,694	2,946,120	230,489
	Existing firm expansions					15,857,582	3,378,838	7,744,430	8,113,152
	Existing firm contractions					12,550,358	1,924,624	5,323,677	7,226,681
	Net change	31,469	33,788	31,649	-180	3,359,419	1,593,466	2,505,712	853,707

Year		Col1	Col2	Col3	Col4	Col5	Col6	Col7	Col8
1998–1999	Firm births	579,609	554,288	579,287	322	3,247,335	1,763,823	3,011,400	235,935
	Firm deaths	544,487	514,293	544,040	447	3,267,136	1,676,282	3,052,630	214,506
	Existing firm expansions					14,843,903	3,245,218	7,266,399	7,577,504
	Existing firm contractions					12,236,364	1,969,501	5,482,142	6,754,222
	Net change	35,122	39,995	35,247	-125	2,587,738	1,363,258	1,743,027	844,711
1997–1998	Firm births	589,982	564,804	589,706	276	3,205,451	1,812,103	3,002,401	203,050
	Firm deaths	540,601	511,567	540,112	489	3,233,412	1,661,544	2,991,722	241,690
	Existing firm expansions					14,885,560	3,238,047	7,471,622	7,413,938
	Existing firm contractions					12,044,422	2,002,313	5,747,725	6,296,697
	Net change	49,381	53,237	49,594	-213	2,813,177	1,386,293	1,734,576	1,078,601
1996–1997	Firm births	590,644	564,197	590,335	309	3,227,556	1,813,539	3,029,666	197,890
	Firm deaths	530,003	500,014	529,481	522	3,274,604	1,620,797	2,960,814	313,790
	Existing firm expansions					16,243,424	3,400,037	8,628,839	7,614,585
	Existing firm contractions					13,092,093	2,035,083	6,343,489	6,748,604
	Net change	60,641	64,183	60,854	-213	3,104,283	1,557,696	2,354,202	750,081

(continued, next page)

Notes: The data represent activity from March of the beginning year to March of the ending year. Establishments with no employment in the first quarter of the beginning year were excluded. Firm births are classified by their first quarter employment size. Percentages not calculated when changes include negative numbers. New firms represent new original establishments and deaths represent closed original establishments. See www.sba.gov/advo/research/data.html for more detail.

Source: U.S. Small Business Administration, Office of Advocacy, from data provided by the U.S. Bureau of the Census.

Table A.8 (continued)

Period	Type of change	Firms				Employment			
			Beginning year employment size of firm				Beginning year employment size of firm		
		Total	<20	<500	500+	Total	<20	<500	500+
1995–1996	Firm births	597,792	572,442	597,503	289	3,255,676	1,844,516	3,055,596	200,080
	Firm deaths	512,402	485,509	512,024	378	3,099,589	1,559,598	2,808,493	291,096
	Existing firm expansions					12,937,389	3,122,066	6,725,135	6,212,254
	Existing firm contractions					11,226,231	1,971,531	5,512,726	5,713,505
	Net change	85,390	86,933	85,479	-89	1,867,245	1,435,453	1,459,512	407,733
1994–1995	Firm births	594,369	568,896	594,119	250	3,322,001	1,836,153	3,049,456	272,545
	Firm deaths	497,246	472,441	496,874	372	2,822,627	1,516,552	2,633,587	189,040
	Existing firm expansions					13,034,649	3,235,940	7,197,705	5,836,944
	Existing firm contractions					9,942,456	1,877,758	5,000,269	4,942,187
	Net change	97,123	96,455	97,245	-122	3,591,567	1,677,783	2,613,305	978,262
1993–1994	Firm births	570,587	546,437	570,337	250	3,105,753	1,760,322	2,889,507	216,246
	Firm deaths	503,563	476,667	503,125	438	3,077,307	1,549,072	2,800,933	276,374
	Existing firm expansions					12,366,436	3,139,825	6,905,182	5,461,254
	Existing firm contractions					10,450,422	2,039,535	5,400,406	5,050,016
	Net change	67,024	69,770	67,212	-188	1,944,460	1,311,540	1,593,350	351,110

Period									
1992–1993	Firm births	564,504	539,601	564,093	411	3,438,106	1,750,662	3,053,765	384,341
	Firm deaths	492,651	466,550	492,266	385	2,906,260	1,515,896	2,697,656	208,604
	Existing firm expansions					12,157,943	3,206,101	6,817,835	5,340,108
	Existing firm contractions					10,741,536	1,965,039	5,386,708	5,354,828
	Net change	71,853	73,051	71,827	26	1,948,253	1,475,828	1,787,236	161,017
1991–1992	Firm births	544,596	519,014	544,278	318	3,200,969	1,703,491	2,863,799	337,170
	Firm deaths	521,606	492,746	521,176	430	3,126,463	1,602,579	2,894,127	232,336
	Existing firm expansions					12,894,780	3,197,959	7,510,392	5,384,388
	Existing firm contractions					12,446,175	2,156,402	6,635,366	5,810,809
	Net change	22,990	26,268	23,102	-112	523,111	1,142,469	844,698	(321,587)
1990–1991	Firm births	541,141	515,870	540,889	252	3,105,363	1,712,856	2,907,351	198,012
	Firm deaths	546,518	516,964	546,149	369	3,208,099	1,723,159	3,044,470	163,629
	Existing firm expansions					11,174,786	2,855,498	6,323,224	4,851,562
	Existing firm contractions					12,233,766	2,294,270	6,893,623	5,340,143
	Net change	-5,377	-1,094	-5,260	-117	-1,161,716	550,925	-707,518-	-454,198

Notes: The data represent activity from March of the beginning year to March of the ending year. Establishments with no employment in the first quarter of the beginning year were excluded. Firm births are classified by their first quarter employment size. Percentages not calculated when changes include negative numbers. New firms represent new original establishments and deaths represent closed original establishments. See www.sba.gov/advo/research/data.html for more detail.

Source: U.S. Small Business Administration, Office of Advocacy, from data provided by the U.S. Bureau of the Census.

Table A.9 Opening and Closing Establishments, 1992–2004 (thousands, seasonally adjusted)

Year	Quarter	Opening establishments		Closing establishments		Net	
		Number	Employment	Number	Employment	Number	Employment
2004	3	354	1,666	345	1,645	9	21
	2	343	1,565	330	1,537	13	28
	1	349	1,514	328	1,439	21	75
2003	4	348	1,583	322	1,486	26	97
	3	328	1,499	318	1,431	10	68
	2	331	1,527	328	1,564	3	-37
	1	332	1,540	334	1,555	-2	-15
2002	4	349	1,643	329	1,610	20	33
	3	341	1,680	325	1,629	16	51
	2	348	1,804	334	1,719	14	85
	1	338	1,804	331	1,729	7	75
2001	4	352	1,838	335	1,769	17	69
	3	335	1,759	367	1,955	-32	-196
	2	339	1,815	333	1,876	6	-61
	1	343	1,787	337	1,900	6	-113
2000	4	353	1,828	336	1,772	17	56
	3	355	1,890	348	1,859	7	31
	2	354	1,789	325	1,714	29	75
	1	357	1,918	328	1,727	29	191
1999	4	365	2,032	326	1,775	39	257
	3	346	1,946	339	1,872	7	74
	2	338	2,012	337	1,812	1	200
	1	335	2,011	318	1,898	17	113
1998	4	320	1,798	318	1,757	2	41
	3	336	1,965	316	1,719	20	246
	2	353	2,153	296	1,838	57	315
	1	347	2,155	323	1,934	24	221

(continued, next page)

Table A.9 (continued)

Year	Quarter	Opening establishments		Closing establishments		Net	
		Number	Employment	Number	Employment	Number	Employment
1997	4	335	2,004	328	1,961	7	43
	3	328	1,913	308	1,758	20	155
	2	321	1,756	304	1,579	17	177
	1	331	1,844	299	1,593	32	251
1996	4	327	1,869	300	1,528	27	341
	3	328	1,863	293	1,559	35	304
	2	318	1,778	299	1,544	19	234
	1	321	1,753	298	1,526	23	227
1995	4	311	1,724	294	1,536	17	188
	3	306	1,679	291	1,519	15	160
	2	306	1,697	286	1,473	20	224
	1	306	1,653	274	1,376	32	277
1994	4	295	1,632	284	1,476	11	156
	3	314	1,745	268	1,304	46	441
	2	309	1,747	285	1,491	24	256
	1	290	1,593	278	1,448	12	145
1993	4	286	1,596	263	1,375	23	221
	3	302	1,642	255	1,333	47	309
	2	293	1,536	272	1,408	21	128
	1	308	1,899	273	1,642	35	257
1992	4	289	1,636	271	1,398	18	238
	3	295	1,745	273	1,571	22	174

Note: Establishments could be new ventures or new affiliates of existing ventures.

Source: U.S. Small Business Administration, Office of Advocacy, from data provided by the U.S. Department of Labor, Bureau of Labor Statistics, Business Employment Dynamics.

Table A.10 Characteristics Self-Employed Individuals, 1995–2003 (thousands, except as noted otherwise)

Characteristic	1995		2000			2003			1995–2003
	Number	Percent	Number	Percent		Number	Percent	Rate	Percent change
Total	13,921.9	100.0	13,832.4	100.0		15,059.3	100.0	9.9	8.2
Gender									
Female	4,614.7	33.1	4,819.6	34.8		5,144.6	34.2	7.2	11.5
Male	9,307.2	66.9	9,012.8	65.2		9,914.7	65.8	12.3	6.5
Race									
Asian / American Indian	547.5	3.9	759.8	5.5		757.9	5.0	9.7	38.4
Black	612.1	4.4	679.3	4.9		736.0	4.9	4.4	20.3
White	12,762.4	91.7	12,393.3	89.6		13,377.3	88.8	10.7	4.8
Multiple	NA		NA			188.0	1.2	9.1	NA
Origin or descent									
Hispanic	698.9	5.0	775.6	5.6		1,158.8	7.7	6.1	65.8
Age									
<25	501.0	3.6	375.8	2.7		471.5	3.1	2.0	-5.9
25–34	2,181.8	15.7	1,824.3	13.2		1,925.1	2.8	5.9	-11.8
35–44	4,132.6	29.7	3,941.1	28.5		3,922.5	26.0	10.7	-5.1
45–54	3,576.0	25.7	3,995.0	28.9		4,369.5	29.0	12.8	22.2
55–64	2,214.3	15.9	2,274.6	16.4		2,945.7	19.6	15.6	33.0
65+	1,316.2	9.5	1,421.6	10.3		1,425.0	9.5	23.5	8.3

Educational level								
High school or less	6,055.0	43.5	5,485.1	39.7	5,666.5	37.6	8.8	-6.4
Some college	3,575.2	25.7	3,822.5	27.6	4,091.8	27.2	9.3	14.4
Bachelors	2,643.4	19.0	2,838.9	20.5	3,222.7	21.4	11.2	21.9
Masters or above	1,648.3	11.8	1,685.9	12.2	2,078.3	13.8	14.2	26.1
Veteran status	2,492.5	17.9	2,029.3	14.7	1,997.7	13.3	14.9	-19.9
Disability	628.6	4.5	592.5	4.3	680.0	4.5	14.7	8.2
Born in the United States	12,411.0	89.1	12,078.8	87.3	12,962.6	86.1	10.1	4.4
Location								
Central city	2,650.1	19.0	2,506.2	18.1	2,898.8	19.2	8.2	9.4
Suburban	5,988.6	43.0	6,095.6	44.1	6,742.7	44.8	9.9	12.6
Rural	3,382.9	24.3	3,321.5	24.0	3,371.9	22.4	12.5	-0.3
Not identified	1,900.3	13.6	1,909.1	13.8	2,045.8	13.6	9.6	7.7

Notes: Self-employment (incorporated and unincorporated) as used here refers to an individual's primary occupation during the year. Self-employment figures presented here differ from the more standard figures, which focus on monthly averages during a year. Asian / American Indian = Asian, Pacific, American Indian and Aleut Eskimo. Disability consists of disabilities or health problems that restrict or prevent the amount or kind of work. The rate is self-employment divided by the number of individuals that had any job during the year.

Source: U.S. Small Business Administration, Office of Advocacy, from data provided by the U.S. Department of Commerce, Bureau of the Census, March Current Population Surveys.

Table A.11 Bank Lending Information by Size of Firm, 1991–2004 (Change in percentage of senior loan officer responses on bank lending practices)

Year	Quarter	Tightening loan standards		Stronger demand for loans	
		Large and medium	Small	Large and medium	Small
2004	4	-21	-18	26	26
	3	-20	-4	31	39
	2	-23	-20	29	38
	1	-18	-11	11	22
2003	4	0	-2	-12	-4
	3	4	4	-23	-12
	2	9	13	-39	-22
	1	22	14	-32	-21
2002	4	20	18	-53	-48
	3	21	6	-45	-36
	2	25	15	-36	-29
	1	45	42	-55	-45
2001	4	51	40	-70	-50
	3	40	32	-53	-42
	2	51	36	-40	-35
	1	60	45	-50	-30
2000	4	44	27	-23	-13
	3	34	24	-5	-4
	2	25	21	-9	5
	1	11	9	9	-2
1999	4	9	2	-2	-4
	3	5	2	0	0
	2	10	8	0	10
	1	7	4	20	11
1998	4	36	15	28	8
	3	0	-5	-9	0
	2	-7	-2	29	21
	1	2	2	26	15
1997	4	-7	-4	19	19
	3	-6	-2	13	20
	2	-7	-4	5	11
	1	-5	-5	5	15

(continued, next page)

Table A.11 (continued))

Year	Quarter	Tightening loan standards		Stronger demand for loans	
		Large and medium	**Small**	**Large and medium**	**Small**
1996	4	-8	-12	1	4
	3	-4	-2	12	18
	2	-1	2	10	24
	1	7	4	-3	14
1995	4	-3	-2	3	7
	3	-6	-2	4	25
	2	-6	-7	29	17
	1	-7	-5	35	18
1994	4	-17	-18	31	32
	3	-7	-7	31	19
	2	-12	-9	38	38
	1	-13	-12	26	26
1993	4	-18	-9	9	17
	3	-19	-12	18	14
	2	-8	-2	-0	12
	1	3	-2	20	32
1992	4	4	-5	6	-2
	3	-2	-2	-9	7
	2	1	-7	6	25
	1	5	0	-27	-12
1991	4	9	5	-30	-25
	3	12	9	NA	NA
	2	16	7	NA	NA
	1	36	32	NA	NA

Notes: NA = not available. Figures should be used with caution because the sample size of the survey is relatively small—about 80 respondents—but they do represent a sizable portion of the market. Small firms are defined as having sales of less than $50 million. The survey asks the following question to gauge lending standards, "Over the past three months, how have your bank's credit standards for approving applications for C&I loans or credit lines—other than those to be used to finance mergers and acquisitions—to large and middle-market firms and to small firms changed?" The survey asks the following question to gauge lending demand, "Apart from normal seasonal variation, how has demand for C&I loans changed over the past three months?"

Source: U.S. Small Business Administration, Office of Advocacy, from data provided by the Federal Reserve Board.

APPENDIX B
The Regulatory Flexibility Act and Executive Order 13272

The following text of the Regulatory Flexibility Act of 1980, as amended, is taken from Title 5 of the United States Code, Sections 601–612. The Regulatory Flexibility Act was originally passed in 1980 (P.L. 96–354). The act was amended by the Small Business Regulatory Enforcement Fairness Act of 1996 (P.L. 104–121).

The Regulatory Flexibility Act of 1980 as amended

Congressional Findings and Declaration of Purpose

(a) The Congress finds and declares that—

(1) when adopting regulations to protect the health, safety and economic welfare of the Nation, Federal agencies should seek to achieve statutory goals as effectively and efficiently as possible without imposing unnecessary burdens on the public;

(2) laws and regulations designed for application to large scale entities have been applied uniformly to small businesses, small organizations, and small governmental jurisdictions even though the problems that gave rise to government action may not have been caused by those smaller entities;

(3) uniform Federal regulatory and reporting requirements have in numerous instances imposed unnecessary and disproportionately burdensome demands including legal, accounting and consulting costs upon small businesses, small organizations, and small governmental jurisdictions with limited resources;

(4) the failure to recognize differences in the scale and resources of regulated entities has in numerous instances adversely affected competition in the marketplace, discouraged innovation and restricted improvements in productivity;

(5) unnecessary regulations create entry barriers in many industries and discourage potential entrepreneurs from introducing beneficial products and processes;

(6) the practice of treating all regulated businesses, organizations, and governmental jurisdictions as equivalent may lead to inefficient use of regulatory agency resources, enforcement problems and, in some cases, to actions inconsistent with the legislative intent of health, safety, environmental and economic welfare legislation;

(7) alternative regulatory approaches which do not conflict with the stated objectives of applicable statutes may be available which minimize the significant economic impact of rules on small businesses, small organizations, and small governmental jurisdictions;

(8) the process by which Federal regulations are developed and adopted should be reformed to require agencies to solicit the ideas and comments of small businesses, small organizations, and small governmental jurisdictions to examine the impact of proposed and existing rules on such entities, and to review the continued need for existing rules.

(b) It is the purpose of this Act [enacting this chapter and provisions set out as notes under this section] to establish as a principle of regulatory issuance that agencies shall endeavor, consistent with the objectives of the rule and of applicable statutes, to fit regulatory and informational requirements to the scale of the businesses, organizations, and governmental jurisdictions subject to regulation. To achieve this principle, agencies are required to solicit and consider flexible regulatory proposals and to explain the rationale for their actions to assure that such proposals are given serious consideration.

Regulatory Flexibility Act

§ 601   Definitions
§ 602   Regulatory agenda
§ 603   Initial regulatory flexibility analysis
§ 604   Final regulatory flexibility analysis
§ 605   Avoidance of duplicative or unnecessary analyses
§ 606   Effect on other law

§ 601 Definitions

For purposes of this chapter—

(1) the term "agency" means an agency as defined in section 551(1) of this title;

(2) the term "rule" means any rule for which the agency publishes a general notice of proposed rulemaking pursuant to section 553(b) of this title, or any other law, including any rule of general applicability governing Federal grants to State and local governments for which the agency provides an opportunity for notice and public comment, except that the term "rule" does not include a rule of particular applicability relating to rates, wages, corporate or financial structures or reorganizations thereof, prices, facilities, appliances, services, or allowances therefor or to valuations, costs or accounting, or practices relating to such rates, wages, structures, prices, appliances, services, or allowances;

(3) the term "small business" has the same meaning as the term "small business concern" under section 3 of the Small Business Act, unless an agency, after consultation with the Office of Advocacy of the Small Business Administration and after opportunity for public comment, establishes one or more definitions of such term which are appropriate to the activities of the agency and publishes such definition(s) in the *Federal Register*;

(4) the term "small organization" means any not-for-profit enterprise which is independently owned and operated and is not dominant in its field, unless an agency establishes, after opportunity for public comment, one or more definitions of such term which are appropriate to the activities of the agency and publishes such definition(s) in the *Federal Register*;

(5) the term "small governmental jurisdiction" means governments of cities, counties, towns, townships, villages, school districts, or special districts, with a population of less than fifty thousand, unless an agency establishes, after

opportunity for public comment, one or more definitions of such term which are appropriate to the activities of the agency and which are based on such factors as location in rural or sparsely populated areas or limited revenues due to the population of such jurisdiction, and publishes such definition(s) in the *Federal Register*;

(6) the term "small entity" shall have the same meaning as the terms "small business," "small organization" and "small governmental jurisdiction" defined in paragraphs (3), (4) and (5) of this section; and

(7) the term "collection of information"—

> (A) means the obtaining, causing to be obtained, soliciting, or requiring the disclosure to third parties or the public, of facts or opinions by or for an agency, regardless of form or format, calling for either—
>
>> (i) answers to identical questions posed to, or identical reporting or recordkeeping requirements imposed on, 10 or more persons, other than agencies, instrumentalities, or employees of the United States; or
>>
>> (ii) answers to questions posed to agencies, instrumentalities, or employees of the United States which are to be used for general statistical purposes; and
>
> (B) shall not include a collection of information described under section 3518(c)(1) of title 44, United States Code.

(8) Recordkeeping requirement—The term "recordkeeping requirement" means a requirement imposed by an agency on persons to maintain specified records.

§ 602. Regulatory agenda

(a) During the months of October and April of each year, each agency shall publish in the *Federal Register* a regulatory flexibility agenda which shall contain—

> (1) a brief description of the subject area of any rule which the agency expects to propose or promulgate which is likely to have a significant economic impact on a substantial number of small entities;

(2) a summary of the nature of any such rule under consideration for each subject area listed in the agenda pursuant to paragraph (1), the objectives and legal basis for the issuance of the rule, and an approximate schedule for completing action on any rule for which the agency has issued a general notice of proposed rulemaking, and

(3) the name and telephone number of an agency official knowledgeable concerning the items listed in paragraph (1).

(b) Each regulatory flexibility agenda shall be transmitted to the Chief Counsel for Advocacy of the Small Business Administration for comment, if any.

(c) Each agency shall endeavor to provide notice of each regulatory flexibility agenda to small entities or their representatives through direct notification or publication of the agenda in publications likely to be obtained by such small entities and shall invite comments upon each subject area on the agenda.

(d) Nothing in this section precludes an agency from considering or acting on any matter not included in a regulatory flexibility agenda, or requires an agency to consider or act on any matter listed in such agenda.

§ 603. Initial regulatory flexibility analysis

(a) Whenever an agency is required by section 553 of this title, or any other law, to publish general notice of proposed rulemaking for any proposed rule, or publishes a notice of proposed rulemaking for an interpretative rule involving the internal revenue laws of the United States, the agency shall prepare and make available for public comment an initial regulatory flexibility analysis. Such analysis shall describe the impact of the proposed rule on small entities. The initial regulatory flexibility analysis or a summary shall be published in the *Federal Register* at the time of the publication of general notice of proposed rulemaking for the rule. The agency shall transmit a copy of the initial regulatory flexibility analysis to the Chief Counsel for Advocacy of the Small Business Administration. In the case of an interpretative rule involving the internal revenue laws of the United States, this chapter applies to interpretative rules published in the *Federal Register* for codification in the Code of Federal Regulations, but only to the extent that such interpretative rules impose on small entities a collection of information requirement.

(b) Each initial regulatory flexibility analysis required under this section shall contain—

(1) a description of the reasons why action by the agency is being considered;

(2) a succinct statement of the objectives of, and legal basis for, the proposed rule;

(3) a description of and, where feasible, an estimate of the number of small entities to which the proposed rule will apply;

(4) a description of the projected reporting, recordkeeping and other compliance requirements of the proposed rule, including an estimate of the classes of small entities which will be subject to the requirement and the type of professional skills necessary for preparation of the report or record;

(5) an identification, to the extent practicable, of all relevant Federal rules which may duplicate, overlap or conflict with the proposed rule.

(c) Each initial regulatory flexibility analysis shall also contain a description of any significant alternatives to the proposed rule which accomplish the stated objectives of applicable statutes and which minimize any significant economic impact of the proposed rule on small entities. Consistent with the stated objectives of applicable statutes, the analysis shall discuss significant alternatives such as—

(1) the establishment of differing compliance or reporting requirements or timetables that take into account the resources available to small entities;

(2) the clarification, consolidation, or simplification of compliance and reporting requirements under the rule for such small entities;

(3) the use of performance rather than design standards; and

(4) an exemption from coverage of the rule, or any part thereof, for such small entities.

§ 604. Final regulatory flexibility analysis

(a) When an agency promulgates a final rule under section 553 of this title, after being required by that section or any other law to publish a general notice of proposed rulemaking, or promulgates a final interpretative rule involving the internal revenue laws of the United States as described in section 603(a), the agency shall prepare a final regulatory flexibility analysis. Each final regulatory flexibility analysis shall contain—

(1) a succinct statement of the need for, and objectives of, the rule;

(2) a summary of the significant issues raised by the public comments in response to the initial regulatory flexibility analysis, a summary of the assessment of the agency of such issues, and a statement of any changes made in the proposed rule as a result of such comments;

(3) a description of and an estimate of the number of small entities to which the rule will apply or an explanation of why no such estimate is available;

(4) a description of the projected reporting, recordkeeping and other compliance requirements of the rule, including an estimate of the classes of small entities which will be subject to the requirement and the type of professional skills necessary for preparation of the report or record; and

(5) a description of the steps the agency has taken to minimize the significant economic impact on small entities consistent with the stated objectives of applicable statutes, including a statement of the factual, policy, and legal reasons for selecting the alternative adopted in the final rule and why each one of the other significant alternatives to the rule considered by the agency which affect the impact on small entities was rejected.

(b) The agency shall make copies of the final regulatory flexibility analysis available to members of the public and shall publish in the *Federal Register* such analysis or a summary thereof..

§ 605. Avoidance of duplicative or unnecessary analyses

(a) Any Federal agency may perform the analyses required by sections 602, 603, and 604 of this title in conjunction with or as a part of any other agenda or analysis required by any other law if such other analysis satisfies the provisions of such sections.

(b) Sections 603 and 604 of this title shall not apply to any proposed or final rule if the head of the agency certifies that the rule will not, if promulgated, have a significant economic impact on a substantial number of small entities. If the head of the agency makes a certification under the preceding sentence, the agency shall publish such certification in the *Federal Register* at the time of publication of general notice of proposed rulemaking for the rule or at the time of publication of the final rule, along with a statement providing the factual basis for such certification. The agency shall provide such certification and statement to the Chief Counsel for Advocacy of the Small Business Administration.

(c) In order to avoid duplicative action, an agency may consider a series of closely related rules as one rule for the purposes of sections 602, 603, 604 and 610 of this title.

§ 606. Effect on other law

The requirements of sections 603 and 604 of this title do not alter in any manner standards otherwise applicable by law to agency action.

§ 607. Preparation of analyses

In complying with the provisions of sections 603 and 604 of this title, an agency may provide either a quantifiable or numerical description of the effects of a proposed rule or alternatives to the proposed rule, or more general descriptive statements if quantification is not practicable or reliable.

§ 608. Procedure for waiver or delay of completion

(a) An agency head may waive or delay the completion of some or all of the requirements of section 603 of this title by publishing in the *Federal Register*, not later than the date of publication of the final rule, a written finding, with reasons therefor, that the final rule is being promulgated in response to an emergency that makes compliance or timely compliance with the provisions of section 603 of this title impracticable.

(b) Except as provided in section 605(b), an agency head may not waive the requirements of section 604 of this title. An agency head may delay the completion of the requirements of section 604 of this title for a period of not more than one hundred and eighty days after the date of publication in the *Federal Register* of a final rule by publishing in the *Federal Register*, not later than such date of publication, a written finding, with reasons therefor, that the final rule is being promulgated in response to an emergency that makes timely compliance with the provisions of section 604 of this title impracticable. If the agency has not prepared a final regulatory analysis pursuant to section 604 of this title within one hundred and eighty days from the date of publication of the final rule, such rule shall lapse and have no effect. Such rule shall not be repromulgated until a final regulatory flexibility analysis has been completed by the agency.

§ 609. Procedures for gathering comments

(a) When any rule is promulgated which will have a significant economic impact on a substantial number of small entities, the head of the agency promulgating the rule or the official of the agency with statutory responsibility for the promulgation of the rule shall assure that small entities have been given an opportunity to participate in the rulemaking for the rule through the reasonable use of techniques such as—

> (1) the inclusion in an advance notice of proposed rulemaking, if issued, of a statement that the proposed rule may have a significant economic effect on a substantial number of small entities;

> (2) the publication of general notice of proposed rulemaking in publications likely to be obtained by small entities;

> (3) the direct notification of interested small entities;

> (4) the conduct of open conferences or public hearings concerning the rule for small entities including soliciting and receiving comments over computer networks; and

> (5) the adoption or modification of agency procedural rules to reduce the cost or complexity of participation in the rulemaking by small entities.

(b) Prior to publication of an initial regulatory flexibility analysis which a covered agency is required to conduct by this chapter—

> (1) a covered agency shall notify the Chief Counsel for Advocacy of the Small Business Administration and provide the Chief Counsel with information on the potential impacts of the proposed rule on small entities and the type of small entities that might be affected;

(2) not later than 15 days after the date of receipt of the materials described in paragraph (1), the Chief Counsel shall identify individuals representative of affected small entities for the purpose of obtaining advice and recommendations from those individuals about the potential impacts of the proposed rule;

(3) the agency shall convene a review panel for such rule consisting wholly of full time Federal employees of the office within the agency responsible for carrying out the proposed rule, the Office of Information and Regulatory Affairs within the Office of Management and Budget, and the Chief Counsel;

(4) the panel shall review any material the agency has prepared in connection with this chapter, including any draft proposed rule, collect advice and recommendations of each individual small entity representative identified by the agency after consultation with the Chief Counsel, on issues related to subsections 603(b), paragraphs (3), (4) and (5) and 603(c);

(5) not later than 60 days after the date a covered agency convenes a review panel pursuant to paragraph (3), the review panel shall report on the comments of the small entity representatives and its findings as to issues related to subsections 603(b), paragraphs (3), (4) and (5) and 603(c), provided that such report shall be made public as part of the rulemaking record; and

(6) where appropriate, the agency shall modify the proposed rule, the initial regulatory flexibility analysis or the decision on whether an initial regulatory flexibility analysis is required.

(c) An agency may in its discretion apply subsection (b) to rules that the agency intends to certify under subsection 605(b), but the agency believes may have a greater than de minimis impact on a substantial number of small entities.

(d) For purposes of this section, the term "covered agency" means the Environmental Protection Agency and the Occupational Safety and Health Administration of the Department of Labor.

(e) The Chief Counsel for Advocacy, in consultation with the individuals identified in subsection (b)(2), and with the Administrator of the Office of Information and Regulatory Affairs within the Office of Management and Budget, may waive the requirements of subsections (b)(3), (b)(4), and (b)(5) by including in the rulemaking record a written finding, with reasons therefor, that those requirements would not advance the effective participation of small entities in the rulemaking process. For purposes of this subsection, the factors to be considered in making such a finding are as follows:

> (1) In developing a proposed rule, the extent to which the covered agency consulted with individuals representative of affected small entities with respect to the potential impacts of the rule and took such concerns into consideration.

> (2) Special circumstances requiring prompt issuance of the rule.

> (3) Whether the requirements of subsection (b) would provide the individuals identified in subsection (b)(2) with a competitive advantage relative to other small entities.

§ 610. Periodic review of rules

(a) Within one hundred and eighty days after the effective date of this chapter, each agency shall publish in the *Federal Register* a plan for the periodic review of the rules issued by the agency which have or will have a significant economic impact upon a substantial number of small entities. Such plan may be amended by the agency at any time by publishing the revision in the *Federal Register*. The purpose of the review shall be to determine whether such rules should be continued without change, or should be amended or rescinded, consistent with the stated objectives of applicable statutes, to minimize any significant economic impact of the rules upon a substantial number of such small entities. The plan shall provide for the review of all such agency rules existing on the effective date of this chapter within ten years of that date and for the review of such rules adopted after the effective date of this chapter within ten years of the publication of such rules as the final rule. If the head of the agency determines that completion of the review of existing rules is not feasible by the established date, he shall so certify in a statement published in the *Federal Register* and may extend the completion date by one year at a time for a total of not more than five years.

(b) In reviewing rules to minimize any significant economic impact of the rule on a substantial number of small entities in a manner consistent with the stated objectives of applicable statutes, the agency shall consider the following factors—

> (1) the continued need for the rule;

> (2) the nature of complaints or comments received concerning the rule from the public;

> (3) the complexity of the rule;

> (4) the extent to which the rule overlaps, duplicates or conflicts with other Federal rules, and, to the extent feasible, with State and local governmental rules; and

> (5) the length of time since the rule has been evaluated or the degree to which technology, economic conditions, or other factors have changed in the area affected by the rule.

(c) Each year, each agency shall publish in the *Federal Register* a list of the rules which have a significant economic impact on a substantial number of small entities, which are to be reviewed pursuant to this section during the succeeding twelve months. The list shall include a brief description of each rule and the need for and legal basis of such rule and shall invite public comment upon the rule.

§ 611. Judicial review

(a) (1) For any rule subject to this chapter, a small entity that is adversely affected or aggrieved by final agency action is entitled to judicial review of agency compliance with the requirements of sections 601, 604, 605(b), 608(b), and 610 in accordance with chapter 7. Agency compliance with sections 607 and 609(a) shall be judicially reviewable in connection with judicial review of section 604.

(2) Each court having jurisdiction to review such rule for compliance with section 553, or under any other provision of law, shall have jurisdiction to review any claims of noncompliance with sections 601, 604, 605(b), 608(b), and 610 in accordance with chapter 7. Agency compliance with sections 607 and 609(a) shall be judicially reviewable in connection with judicial review of section 604.

(3)   (A) A small entity may seek such review during the period beginning on the date of final agency action and ending one year later, except that where a provision of law requires that an action challenging a final agency action be commenced before the expiration of one year, such lesser period shall apply to an action for judicial review under this section.

(B) In the case where an agency delays the issuance of a final regulatory flexibility analysis pursuant to section 608(b) of this chapter, an action for judicial review under this section shall be filed not later than—

(i) one year after the date the analysis is made available to the public, or

(ii) where a provision of law requires that an action challenging a final agency regulation be commenced before the expiration of the 1-year period, the number of days specified in such provision of law that is after the date the analysis is made available to the public.

(4) In granting any relief in an action under this section, the court shall order the agency to take corrective action consistent with this chapter and chapter 7, including, but not limited to—

(A) remanding the rule to the agency, and

(B) deferring the enforcement of the rule against small entities unless the court finds that continued enforcement of the rule is in the public interest.

(5) Nothing in this subsection shall be construed to limit the authority of any court to stay the effective date of any rule or provision thereof under any other provision of law or to grant any other relief in addition to the requirements of this section.

(b) In an action for the judicial review of a rule, the regulatory flexibility analysis for such rule, including an analysis prepared or corrected pursuant to paragraph (a)(4), shall constitute part of the entire record of agency action in connection with such review.

(c) Compliance or noncompliance by an agency with the provisions of this chapter shall be subject to judicial review only in accordance with this section.

(d) Nothing in this section bars judicial review of any other impact statement or similar analysis required by any other law if judicial review of such statement or analysis is otherwise permitted by law.

§ 612. Reports and intervention rights

(a) The Chief Counsel for Advocacy of the Small Business Administration shall monitor agency compliance with this chapter and shall report at least annually thereon to the President and to the Committees on the Judiciary and Small Business of the Senate and House of Representatives.

(b) The Chief Counsel for Advocacy of the Small Business Administration is authorized to appear as *amicus curiae* in any action brought in a court of the United States to review a rule. In any such action, the Chief Counsel is authorized to present his or her views with respect to compliance with this chapter, the adequacy of the rulemaking record with respect to small entities and the effect of the rule on small entities.

(c) A court of the United States shall grant the application of the Chief Counsel for Advocacy of the Small Business Administration to appear in any such action for the purposes described in subsection (b).

Executive Order 13272

Federal Register

Vol. 67, No. 159

Friday, August 16, 2002

Presidential Documents

Title 3—

The President

Executive Order 13272 of August 13, 2002

Proper Consideration of Small Entities in Agency Rulemaking

By the authority vested in me as President by the Constitution and the laws of the United States of America, it is hereby ordered as follows:

Section 1. *General Requirements.* Each agency shall establish procedures and policies to promote compliance with the Regulatory Flexibility Act, as amended (5 U.S.C. 601 *et seq.*) (the "Act"). Agencies shall thoroughly review draft rules to assess and take appropriate account of the potential impact on small businesses, small governmental jurisdictions, and small organizations, as provided by the Act. The Chief Counsel for Advocacy of the Small Business Administration (Advocacy) shall remain available to advise agencies in performing that review consistent with the provisions of the Act.

Sec. 2. *Responsibilities of Advocacy.* Consistent with the requirements of the Act, other applicable law, and Executive Order 12866 of September 30, 1993, as amended, Advocacy:

(a) shall notify agency heads from time to time of the requirements of the Act, including by issuing notifications with respect to the basic requirements of the Act within 90 days of the date of this order;

(b) shall provide training to agencies on compliance with the Act; and

(c) may provide comment on draft rules to the agency that has proposed or intends to propose the rules and to the Office of Information and Regulatory Affairs of the Office of Management and Budget (OIRA).

Sec. 3. *Responsibilities of Federal Agencies.* Consistent with the requirements of the Act and applicable law, agencies shall:

(a) Within 180 days of the date of this order, issue written procedures and policies, consistent with the Act, to ensure that the potential impacts of agencies' draft rules on small businesses, small governmental jurisdictions, and small organizations are properly considered during the rulemaking process. Agency heads shall submit, no later than 90 days from the date of this order, their written procedures and policies to Advocacy for comment. Prior to issuing final procedures and policies, agencies shall consider any such comments received within 60 days from the date of the submission of the agencies' procedures and policies to Advocacy. Except to the extent otherwise specifically provided by statute or Executive Order, agencies shall make the final procedures and policies available to the public through the Internet or other easily accessible means;

(b) Notify Advocacy of any draft rules that may have a significant economic impact on a substantial number of small entities under the Act. Such notifications shall be made (i) when the agency submits a draft rule to OIRA under Executive Order 12866 if that order requires such submission, or (ii) if no submission to OIRA is so required, at a reasonable time prior to publication of the rule by the agency; and

(c) Give every appropriate consideration to any comments provided by Advocacy regarding a draft rule. Consistent with applicable law and appropriate protection of executive deliberations and legal privileges, an agency shall include, in any explanation or discussion accompanying publication in the **Federal Register** of a final rule, the agency's response to any written comments submitted by Advocacy on the proposed rule that preceded the final rule; provided, however, that such inclusion is not required if the head of the agency certifies that the public interest is not served thereby.

Agencies and Advocacy may, to the extent permitted by law, engage in an exchange of data and research, as appropriate, to foster the purposes of the Act.

Sec. 4. *Definitions.* Terms defined in section 601 of title 5, United States Code, including the term "agency," shall have the same meaning in this order.

Sec. 5. *Preservation of Authority.* Nothing in this order shall be construed to impair or affect the authority of the Administrator of the Small Business Administration to supervise the Small Business Administration as provided in the first sentence of section 2(b)(1) of Public Law 85–09536 (15 U.S.C. 633(b)(1)).

Sec. 6. *Reporting.* For the purpose of promoting compliance with this order, Advocacy shall submit a report not less than annually to the Director of the Office of Management and Budget on the extent of compliance with this order by agencies.

Sec. 7. *Confidentiality.* Consistent with existing law, Advocacy may publicly disclose information that it receives from the agencies in the course of carrying out this order only to the extent that such information already has been lawfully and publicly disclosed by OIRA or the relevant rulemaking agency.

Sec. 8. *Judicial Review.* This order is intended only to improve the internal management of the Federal Government. This order is not intended to, and does not, create any right or benefit, substantive or procedural, enforceable at law or equity, against the United States, its departments, agencies, or other entities, its officers or employees, or any other person.

THE WHITE HOUSE,
August 13, 2002.

Index

Census Bureau
   minority business data of, 71, 73
Chan, Tsze, on New Jersey's set-aside
      program, 94
Characteristics of Business Owners, 96, 98
   on African Africans and business, 90
   on education levels, 84
   on minority-owned businesses, 75
Chatterji, Ronnie, on set-aside
      programs, 96
Chay, Kenneth Y., on set-aside
      programs, 96
Children, *See* Dependents
Cities
   number of business owners in,
      230 *(table)*
Clinton, President William Jefferson, 160
Coate, Stephen, on labor market
      discrimination, 89
Colorado
   business turnover in, 214 *(table)*
   employers and nonemployers by size in,
      219 *(table)*
   number of businesses in, 212 *(table)*
   RFA legislation in, 172 *(table)*, 180
Colorado Department of Regulatory
      Agencies, 180
Commerce, U.S. Department of
   regulatory comments to, 168 *(chart)*
   procurement by, 48 *(table)*, 52 *(table)*
   SBIR contracting by, 53
Commercial and industrial loans,
      211 *(table)*
Commission on National
      and Community Service
   procurement by, 48 *(table)*
Commodity Futures Trading Commission
   procurement by, 48 *(table)*

Community Reinvestment Act, 23
Compensation cost index, 211 *(table)*
Competition and innovation, 198
Complexity of tax code, 145
Compliance costs as measure of tax
      complexity, 149
Computers
   and business success, 111
   innovations in, 193
   and minority business outcomes, 93
   and RFA training, 166
Connecticut
   business turnover in, 214 *(table)*
   employers and nonemployers by size in,
      219 *(table)*
   number of businesses in, 212 *(table)*
   RFA legislation in, 171, 172 *(table)*
Construction industry
   businesses by firm size in, 222 *(table)*
   and discrimination, 89
   minority business networks in, 87
Consumer discrimination, 90
Consumer price index, 211 *(table)*
Consumer Product Safety Commission
   procurement by, 48 *(table)*
Contract bundling, 43
Contract novation, 43
Contracting, *See* Procurement
Contractions of businesses, 224 *(table)*
Corporations
   borrowing by, 20, 24
   profits of, 210 *(table)*
Crain, W. Mark
   on tax compliance burden, 145, 150
Credit cards, 17, 27
Credit markets and discrimination, 90
Cuban Americans and ethnic enclaves, 88
Current Population Survey
      data on minority self-employment, 61

number of businesses in, 212 *(table)*

RFA legislation in, 171, 175 *(table)*

Monetary policy, 15, 16

Montana

business turnover in, 214 *(table)*

employers and nonemployers by size in, 219 *(table)*

number of businesses in, 212 *(table)*

RFA legislation in, 175 *(table)*

Mortgages as source of funds, 22 *(table)*

Mudd, Shannon, on measuring tax complexity, 150

Myers, Samuel, on New Jersey's set-aside program, 94

Myrdal, Gunnar, on business traditions and African Americans, 86

NASDAQ, 6

National Aeronautics and Space Administration

procurement by, 47 *(table)*, 49 *(table)*, 52 *(table)*

SBIR contracting by, 53

and set-aside programs, 94

National Archives and Records Administration

procurement by, 50 *(table)*, 52 *(table)*

National Federation of Independent Business

Small Business Problems and Priorities, 112

small business survey by, 14

National Foundation on the Arts and the Humanities

procurement by, 50 *(table)*

National Labor Relations Board

procurement by, 50 *(table)*

National Mediation Board

procurement by, 50 *(table)*

National Science Foundation

data on R&D funding, 187

procurement by, 50 *(table)*

SBIR contracting by, 53

National Survey of Veterans, 111

National Telephone Cooperative Association, 169

National Transportation Safety Board

procurement by, 50 *(table)*

Native-born business owners, 230 *(table)*

Nebraska

business turnover in, 214 *(table)*

employers and nonemployers by size in, 219 *(table)*

number of businesses in, 212 *(table)*

RFA legislation in, 175 *(table)*

Networks and minority businesses, 87

Nevada

business turnover in, 214 *(table)*

employers and nonemployers by size in, 219 *(table)*

number of businesses in, 212 *(table)*

RFA legislation in, 175 *(table)*

New Hampshire

business turnover in, 214 *(table)*

employers and nonemployers by size in, 219 *(table)*

number of businesses in, 212 *(table)*

RFA legislation in, 175 *(table)*

New Jersey

business turnover in, 214 *(table)*

employers and nonemployers by size in, 219 *(table)*

minority set-aside program of, 94

number of businesses in, 212 *(table)*

RFA legislation in, 176 *(table)*

New Mexico

business turnover in, 214 *(table)*

employers and nonemployers by size in, 219 *(table)*

number of businesses in, 212 *(table)*

RFA legislation in, 176 *(table)*

Transportation, U.S. Department of
procurement by, 49 *(table)*, 52 *(table)*
regulatory comments to, 168 *(chart)*
SBIR contracting by, 53
Treasury bond yields, 211 *(table)*
Treasury, U.S. Department of
procurement by, 49 *(table)*, 52 *(table)*
regulatory comments to, 168 *(chart)*
Turnover by type of business change,
224 *(table)*
See also Business turnover, Business
closures

U.S. Information Agency
procurement by, 51 *(table)*
U.S. Soldiers and Airmen's Home
procurement by, 51 *(table)*
U.S. Telecom Assoc. and CenturyTel,
Inc. v. FCC, 169
Uncertainty of tax code, 145
Unemployment, 6, 7 *(table)*, 211 *(table)*
Unincorporated businesses, 10
See also Microenterprise, Nonemployers,
Sole proprietorships
United Kingdom
and minority business ownership, 73
United States
minority business ownership compared
with other countries, 73, 74 *(table)*
Urban areas
number of business owners in, 230 *(table)*
Urban Institute on set-aside programs, 95
Utah
business turnover in, 214 *(table)*
employers and nonemployers by size in,
219 *(table)*
number of businesses in, 212 *(table)*
RFA legislation in, 177 *(table)*
Utilities industry, 222 *(table)*

Valev, Neven, on measuring tax
complexity, 150
Vehicle loans, 32
Venture capital, 36, 37 *(table)*
Vermont
business turnover in, 214 *(table)*
employers and nonemployers by size in,
219 *(table)*
number of businesses in, 212 *(table)*
RFA legislation in, 178 *(table)*
Veteran Entrepreneurship and Small
Business Development Act
of 1999, 110
Veterans Affairs, U.S. Department of,
procurement by, 49 *(table)*, 52 *(table)*
Veterans
active duty experience of, 117, 133
age of, 114 *(table)*, 115, 116 *(table)*,
118 *(table)*, 121 *(table)*, 122 *(table)*,
123 *(table)*, 124 *(table)*, 127,
128 *(table)*, 129 *(table)*, 131 *(table)*,
133 *(table)*, 135 *(table)*, 136 *(table)*,
137 *(table)*, 140 140 *(table)*,
141 *(table)*
age of businesses, 130, 141 *(table)*
and apprenticeship programs, 122,
123 *(table)*, 137 *(table)*
business experience of, 120, 122 *(table)*,
135, 135 *(table)*, 136 *(table)*
business ownership of, 109
business problems of, 119 *(table)*, 136,
138 *(table)*, 139 140 *(table)*,
141 *(table)*
demographics of, 114 *(table)*, 128 *(table)*
dependents of, 114 *(table)*, 115,
116 *(table)*, 128 *(table)*, 129 *(table)*,
130 *(table)*, 132 *(table)*
disability status of, 114 *(table)*,
116 *(table)*, 118 *(table)*, 119 *(table)*,
121 *(table)*, 122 *(table)*, 123 *(table)*,
124 *(table)*, 128 *(table)*, 129 *(table)*,